Working with Science 9

Living things, the earth
and its environment

SERIES EDITOR

Steuart Kellington

WRITING TEAM

Frances Cavannah · John Hill
Robert Lee · Ian McFarlane · Alison Mitchell · Tim Mitchell

Nelson

Thomas Nelson and Sons Ltd
Nelson House   Mayfield Road
Walton-on-Thames   Surrey
KT12 5PL   UK

51 York Place
Edinburgh
EH1 3JD   UK

Thomas Nelson (Hong Kong) Ltd
Toppan Building 10/F
22A Westlands Road
Quarry Bay   Hong Kong

Distributed in Australia by

Thomas Nelson Australia
480 La Trobe Street
Melbourne   Victoria 3000
and in Sydney, Brisbane, Adelaide and Perth

© Frances Cavannah, John Hill, Steuart Kellington, Robert Lee, Ian McFarlane, Alison Mitchell, Tim Mitchell 1989
First published by Thomas Nelson and Sons Ltd 1989

ISBN 0-17-438403-3

NPN 987654321

Printed and bound in Great Britain by
Ebenezer Baylis & Son Ltd, Worcester, and London

All Rights Reserved. This publication is protected in the United Kingdom by the Copyright Act 1956 and in other countries by comparable legislation. No part of it may be reproduced or recorded by any means without the permission of the publisher. This prohibition extends (with certain very limited exceptions) to photocopying and similar processes, and written permission to make a copy or copies must therefore be obtained from the publisher in advance. It is advisable to consult the publisher if there is any doubt regarding the legality of any proposed copying.

Acknowledgement is due to the following for permission to use photographs:
Anders L. Björklund (p. 76) Ardea Photo Library (p. 31) Barnaby's Photo Library (p. 7) British Gas (p. 75) Bruce Coleman Ltd (pp. 3, 8, 9, 16 *left*, 18, 19, 38) Daily Telegraph Photo Library (p. 46) Heather Angel Photo Library (p. 6) Holborn Publishing Group (pp. 84 *right*, 85) Holt Studios Ltd (pp. 32 *both*, 34, 39) Imperial War Museum (p. 36 *left*) Jodrell Bank Publicity (p. 88 *top right*) John Walmsley (pp. 10, 11, 12, 22–26 *left*, 35, 36 *right*, 42, 44, 45, 48, 50, 51 *right*, 53 *right*, 60, 82, 83, 88 *bottom right*) Mary Evans Picture Library (p. 86) National Film Archive (p. 28 *left*) National Medical Slide Bank (p. 51) Nature Photographers Ltd (p. 21) Oxford Scientific Films (p. 80 *right*) Robert Harding Picture Library (p. 71) Sally & Richard Greenhill (p. 26 *right*, 62) Science Photo Library (pp. 15 *right*, 28 *right*, 54, 57, 58, 79, 84 *left*) South American Pictures (p. 16) Stuart Powles (p. 72) The Graves Medical Audio Visual Library (pp. 52, 53 *left*) Zefa Photo Library (pp. 3, 15 *left*, 64, 66, 80 *left*, 90, 91)

The publishers are grateful to the following for permission to reproduce copyright material:
Age Concern (p. 11) Cadbury Schweppes (p. 41) Central Electricity Generating Board (p. 79) Department of Health (p. 50) Esso (p. 72) Friends of the Earth (p. 17 *right*, 83) Health Education Authority (p. 53) Jan Rocha (Mrs) (p. 17 *left*) Jodrell Bank (p. 88) John Hammond, St John's Ambulance (pp. 46, 47) Prima Magazine Ltd (pp. 42, 43) Safeway Ltd (p. 41) Tesco Foodstores Ltd (p. 23) The Body Shop (pp. 24, 83) The Daily Telegraph (pp. 70, 85) The Guardian (pp. 3, 11, 44, 53, 65, 79, 83) The New Scientist (p. 24) The Observer (p. 61) The Times Newspapers Ltd (pp. 63, 91) Van den Berge and Jurgens (p. 23).

The publishers would also like to acknowledge the assistance of:
John Hammond (St John's Ambulance).

Illustrations
Design Revolution

Cover illustration
Simon Fell

CONTENTS

Introduction		1
Chapter 1	Diversity—variety is the spice of life	2
Chapter 2	Biomass—the stuff of life	4
Chapter 3	Biomass energy—nature's joules	6
Chapter 4	Population change—cause and effect	8
Chapter 5	World population	10
Chapter 6	Sampling	12
Chapter 7	Life in the Sea	14
Chapter 8	Sharing with nature	16
Chapter 9	Red and grey squirrels	18
Chapter 10	Badgers—enemies or friends	20
Chapter 11	Weighing up food	22
Chapter 12	Enzymes	24
Chapter 13	Using enzymes	26
Chapter 14	Photosynthesis	28
Chapter 15	Improving greenhouses	30
Chapter 16	Fertilizers and nitrogen	32
Chapter 17	Fertilizers and the 'green revolution'	34
Chapter 18	Growing your own!	36
Chapter 19	Sugar from the ground	38
Chapter 20	Additives: are they in or out?	40
Chapter 21	Vitamins: are they in or out?	42
Chapter 22	Warning: food can damage your health	44
Chapter 23	Saving a life	46
Chapter 24	Lungs and breathing	48
Chapter 25	Hypothermia	50
Chapter 26	The liver	52
Chapter 27	Spectacles and contact lenses	54
Chapter 28	Hay fever—a case of mistaken identity	56
Chapter 29	Sun beds	58
Chapter 30	Cloning	60
Chapter 31	Test-tube babies	62
Chapter 32	Animal breeding	64
Chapter 33	The sea—our biggest solution	66
Chapter 34	Common salt	68
Chapter 35	Carbon dioxide and the 'greenhouse effect'	70
Chapter 36	Lead in petrol	72
Chapter 37	Gas from Morecambe Bay	74
Chapter 38	Where did oil really come from?	76
Chapter 39	Nuclear power	78
Chapter 40	The atmosphere of the Earth	80
Chapter 41	Ozone and aerosols	82
Chapter 42	Space travel	84
Chapter 43	Talking round the world	86
Chapter 44	Listening to space	88
Chapter 45	What are stars made of?	90
Index		92

INTRODUCTION

To the teacher

Working with Science is a two-book series containing resource material for broad-and-balanced GCSE (or equivalent) science courses—single or double award. The material is presented as 90 separate chapters, 45 in each book. Each chapter covers one particular topic, relating science to today's world and discussing relevant social and environmental issues.

Activities are provided throughout, to test understanding of the text and to develop the process skills essential to GCSE science. The material is designed for students of a wide range of ability, and each activity is carefully graded for its level of difficulty.

Teachers Notes for *Working with Science* are available, on request, from the publishers. These contain an analysis of the skills tested, and answers to all the questions.

To the student

Working with Science is a two-book series. It contains a total of 90 chapters, each on a different topic, showing science in the real world. Each chapter is full of activity questions, and these will help you to practise the skills you need for your science course. As you work through a chapter, try to keep a record of your answers in a notebook—this will be useful when you are revising.

You will notice that each question number has a symbol around it—this shows roughly how difficult the question is. The more lines next to the circle, the harder the question!

–○ =○ ≡○
easiest ————————————→ hardest

The authors hope you enjoy the books and enjoy *Working with Science*.

DIVERSITY— Variety is the spice of life

Have you ever wondered how many different kinds of plants and animals there are? Scientists estimate that there are about 5–10 million species living on this planet. Forty-five thousand are *vertebrates* (animals with backbones), 350 000 are plants and the rest are *invertebrates*, of which an amazing 80% are insects. All these different forms of life have evolved over a very long period of time since life first emerged 3.6 billion years ago. The word '**diversity**' is used to describe all the different kinds of animals and plants. Diversity means 'different kinds' or 'variety'.

Plants and animals live together in habitats. Tropical jungles, forests, the sea and farmland are different habitats. Change is always occurring in habitats. Change may be slow, over a long period of time, or rapid, due to disasters such as flooding or drought or through people's actions.

In this chapter, you can learn about diversity.

— ① There are four different habitats listed in the above paragraph. Make up a table and list two animals or plants found in each of them.

Making use of diversity

Animals and plants are very useful to us for food, medicines and industries. We use very few at the moment. We must help as many as possible of these different species to survive because we might need their help in the future.

Our food

Most of the world depends on only a few plant and animal species for most of its food. Twenty-four crops produce 2.5 billion tonnes. Wheat, rice, maize and potato make up the bulk of this. Ninety-

five per cent of our nutritional needs come from only 30 kinds of plant. But we know of at least 80 000 that are edible. The same story applies to our farm animals. All the milk and beef cattle in Europe come from one ancestor, the Auroch, a wild ox. Only three kinds of animals—pigs, cows and poultry—make up most of the meat in our diet.

Our medicines

Many modern medicines come from plants. The chemical substances in Aspirin were found in the bark of the White Willow and a plant called Meadowsweet. Quinine, which is used to treat malaria, was developed from the bark of the Cinchona tree in the Andes. The Mayapple plant, well known to local Indians in North America, is the basis for some cancer treatments.

Today, scientists are trying to discover drugs to help with many diseases, including AIDS, and are looking at some trees in Australia. Who knows whether the species which could have provided a cure has already died out?

Our industry

Plants are a major raw material in many of the 'goods' which we trade around the world. Plant fibres are used for ropes, paper and threads. From plants we get energy, clothing, housing, and craft products. Oils, gums and resins are used in medical drugs, cosmetics, confectionery, printing ink, varnishes and polishes. Rubber for tyres comes from trees in the Amazon. Many pesticides come from plants.

= ② Copy and complete table 1. In each column give examples of animals and plants, stating their uses.

= ③ Explain why we should try to keep as many species alive as possible.

Conserving diversity

Here are four ways of conserving diversity.

Conserving habitats

Many habitats are being destroyed around the world. For example, tropical forests are being cut down in Brazil. Some governments are now setting aside areas of land as special reserves to protect plants and animals. The Nature Conservancy Council, the National Trust, the Royal Society for the Protection of Birds and the Woodland Trust in Great Britain do some of this work.

Table 1 Using plants and animals

Food		Medicines		Industry	
Plant/animal	Uses	Plant/animal	Uses	Plant/animal	Uses
Wheat	Bread				

Many habitats are being threatened by the actions of humans. In the need for fuel and land for farming, tropical forests in Brazil are being destroyed

Using wild life productively

In some countries, people are using 'new' animals for farming. For example, in Africa the Oryx is replacing cattle. Deer and salmon are being farmed in Scotland.

New laws

Collectors, hunters and poachers of wildlife are being prosecuted under new laws. Only limited numbers of herring and whales can now be caught each year.

Zoos

Many species of animals are kept in zoos. It is possible to preserve species in zoos and then return animals to the wild.

=④ The government of Zambia is trying to protect elephants from poachers in the Luanga Valley. Use this data to explain whether you think that Zambia's efforts are helping the elephant. (Hint: Calculate the loss in each year and find the percentage. For example, the loss between 1973 and 1974 was 4000 so the percentage loss is

$$\frac{4000}{56\,000} \times 100\% = 7.2\%.)$$

1973	56 000	1981	31 000
1974	52 000	1982	30 000
1975	47 000	1983	28 000
1976	44 000	1984	26 000
1977	41 000	1985	24 000
1978	36 000	1986	23 000
1979	33 000	1987	22 000
1980	32 000		

Read the article 'The captive costs' and answer these questions.

—⑤ What percentage of all bird species have been bred in zoos?

—⑥ What percentage of all mammal species have been bred in zoos?

—⑦ What does it cost to look after one Siberian tiger and one gorilla per year?

=⑧ The writer of the article makes these two points:

(A) Zoos should not breed animals which are plentiful in the wild.

(B) Zoos should breed rare carnivores (meat eaters).

Make a list of good reasons for keeping animals in zoos. Then give some reasons why animals should *not* be kept in zoos.

≡⑨ Write a letter which you could send to the zoo keeper explaining how he should plan the way he spends his money.

The captive costs

THE GUARDIAN
Friday February 5 1988

How best do we preserve the interests of endangered species? Norman Myers on the nightmare choices before the zookeeper of tomorrow

NOAH built his Ark of wood, and it did the job. Today we build our zoos of sturdier stuff. But will they do their latter-day job of helping multitudes of threatened species?

According to Dr William Conway, director of the New York Zoo and chairman of the American Association of Zoological Parks and Aquariums, modern zoos can do a great deal to serve as a backup strategy to support the primary conservation goal of safeguarding species in their wild habitats. No less and no more.

Zoos are severely limited in terms of sheer space, let alone animal-care capacity. All the animal space in the world's zoos would comfortably fit inside the Inner London Circular. They now contain rather more than half a million individual mammals, birds, reptiles and amphibians. During the past few years they have bred about 9 per cent of all 8,700 bird species, and 19 per cent of all 4,500 mammal species.

Not all of these are yet threatened or rare creatures: this is the case for only 12 per cent of the birds and 48 per cent of the mammals. But the number of endangered forms is expanding rapidly.

It is an expensive business to care for threatened animals. To look after one Siberian tiger costs almost £2,000 a year, which means that to care for an expected total of 500 Siberian tigers in the world's zoos over a period of 20 years will cost almost £20 million.

Gorillas are even more costly: the 500 in zoos cost £2,850 each per year, making a total of £28 million over 20 years. Unless we can keep them alive in captivity, we shall probably witness, within the coming decades, the demise of around 100 large carnivore species, some 160 species of primates, and perhaps 215 herbivores other than primates, plus about 300 species from other mammalian orders, making a total of about 800 species.

Something similar will hold for birds. In addition we shall have to depend on zoos for the survival of several hundred species of reptiles and amphibians. All in all, then, we need to think in terms of zoo care for at least 2,000 large terrestrial vertebrates.

Changes in habitat may lead to the threat of extinction. Because of this endangered species are often kept in zoos and nature parks. The photo shows a caged Jaguar

2 BIOMASS—THE STUFF OF LIFE

The Earth's surface is covered with many hundreds of different plants and animals. At first, it seems that they all live together in some haphazard way. In fact most plants and animals live together in highly organised living systems called *ecosystems*, such as ponds, woodlands, fields and estuaries. One organism's survival depends on another's. Plants, for example, provide food and shelter for many animals.

Producers and consumers

Plants alone trap the energy from the sun to make 'living' energy. They are called the *producers*. Animals can only eat plants or other animals. They are called *consumers*. Finally, all living things die. Then bacteria and fungi break down the dead plants and animals and return chemicals to the soil. They are called *decomposers*.

① Look at the food chain and fill in a table like this in your notebook with names from the food chain.

Producer	Consumer

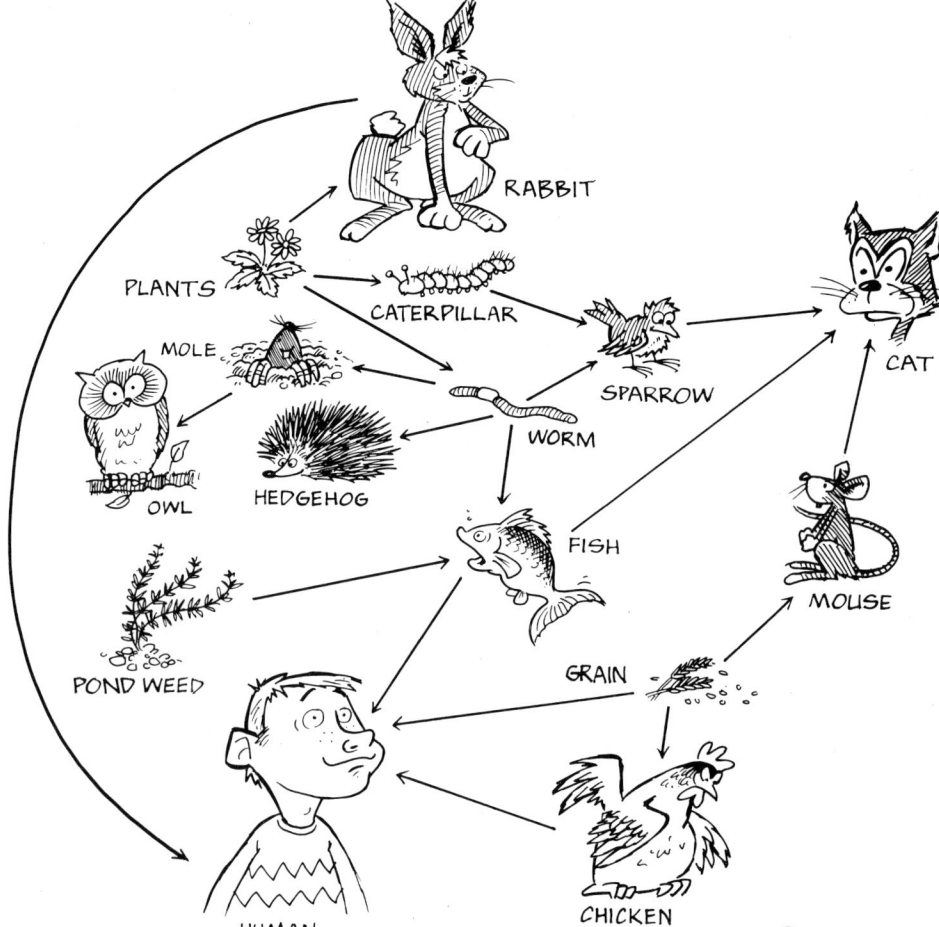

Figure 1

What is biomass?

Biomass is a measure of the amount of different kinds of living things. It can be measured as living mass or dry mass. It gives a better idea of the amount of living things than simply counting the number of organisms. This is because organisms vary so much in size. Just think how many rabbits are equivalent to an elephant!

When we think of different parts of the world, we often imagine only the animals. However 99% of all biomass is actually made up of plant material! Plant biomass is often called the 'green mantle'. Most of life depends on this 'green mantle' which covers the Earth's surface. You will find that plant material supports almost all food chains.

There's no place like biomes!

Biomass can be divided into *biomes*; a strange word which describes distinct plant and animal communities. Some examples of biomes are shown in table 1. The table also shows how much biomass is contained in different biomes.
Compared to these figures for natural biomes, mankind's crops throughout the world account for only 0.53% of all biomass. This is less than deserts! We farm a very small amount of biomass but our influence on other biomes is great. Our pollutants and our land-based activities often disturb their balance and biomass.

② Use the information in table 1 to draw a bar chart to show the percentage of total biomass contained in each biome.

Table 1 Biomes and their biomass

Biomes	Percentage of world total biomass (%)
Tundra (mossy & marshy plains near polar ice caps)	2
Northern forest (northern forest, usually coniferous)	16
Temperate grassland (pasture land)	2
Temperate forest (deciduous and coniferous woodland)	19
Desert (unproductive ground or rock, sand)	1
Tropical scrub & woodland (bushes and small trees)	7
Tropical savannah & grassland (pasture & grazing land)	5
Tropical forest	43

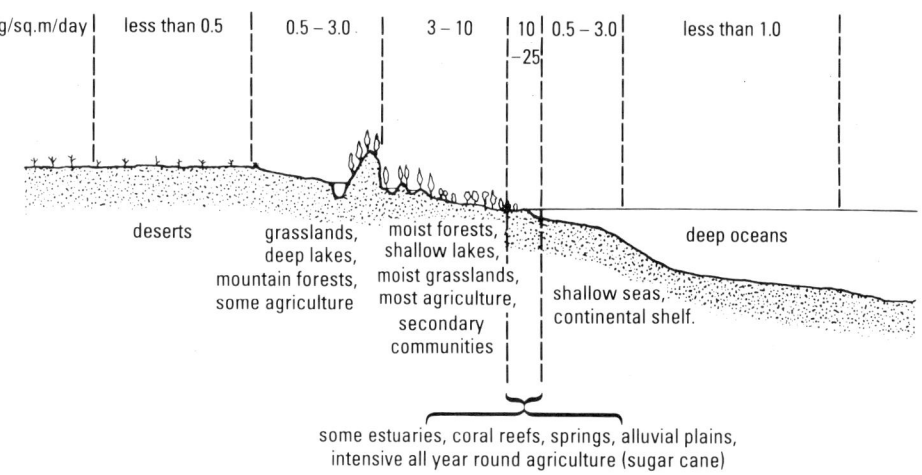

Figure 2 Productivity in plant communities

Biological productivity

All living things grow and die. A field of corn takes several months to grow, ripen and die. Small plants in the sea may live for only a few hours, or days. Biomass measures weight at any one time.

The *rate of production* of new material in a certain time gives a more accurate measure for comparing parts of different ecosystems. This is called *biological productivity*. It is measured as mass per unit area per year. Table 2 shows the differences in biological productivity in different plant communites. Figure 2 is a diagram, to illustrate the table.

Table 2 Biological productivity

Plant community	Productivity (Tonnes of wet mass/hectare/year)
Irrigated sugar cane	120–160
Papyrus swamp	50–125
Tropical rainforest	90
Well watered lawn	70
White potatoes	30
Good corn crop (USA)	15–20
Desert	3

Mankind can affect the level of productivity. For example, mowing the lawn twice a week will keep grass growing faster than if it is left uncut. So if grass is cut regularly you can increase its productivity. Unfortunately it takes more of your Saturdays and more of your energy to keep it under control! Managing crops like this is an aspect of farming.

= ③ Why do you think that sugar cane has a higher productivity than a tropical rainforest?
= ④ Mankind can increase the productivity of different plant communities. Two examples are provided of sugar cane and a grass lawn. Here are some ways in which we manage other plants and animals for our own benefit:

  application of fertilizers
  selective breeding
  irrigation
  growing in greenhouses
  addition of hormones to feed
  growing in special light or special cages
  killing animals which compete for our food supply
  thinning out weak ones.

For each of these see if you can name a plant or animal which is managed in this way.

Biomass cannot be taken for granted

The activities of mankind spread far and wide. The biomass of this planet is a vast store of living energy and contains a huge variety of plants and animals. Within biomes there are delicate relationships between producers, consumers and decomposers, which have taken millions of years to evolve. Scientists know that there is a real danger that mankind can upset the balance and reduce the productivity of biomass.

= ⑤ Look at figure 2 which shows the productivity of different plant communities. Put the communities into a list, starting with the most productive.
≡ ⑥ DDT is a poison which has been used by farmers to kill insect pests which attack crops. Think of a way DDT might have reached penguins in the Antarctic (near the South Pole). (Hint: Penguins eat fish.) You will have to think about what happens to rainfall, food chains and ocean currents.

3 BIOMASS ENERGY— NATURE'S JOULES

What is biomass energy?

Much of our energy comes from fossil fuels such as coal, oil and gas. We are using energy stored in dead material which lived millions of years ago. Our supplies of 'dead' energy are running out. One alternative is to use 'living' energy or the energy from plants and animals which are alive now. This is 'biomass energy'.

Energy can be taken from plant or animal material in different ways:

- By burning it directly, e.g. wood, dung, straw,
- By fermenting it to produce fuel such as methane or ethanol (alcohol),
- By pressing out oils which can themselves be burnt. There is an oil, for example, that can be put into diesel engines directly.

Of all the sources of biomass energy, wood provides the greatest quantity. Some 50% of the world's population rely on wood as their main energy source. Now that world supplies of coal, oil and gas are beginning to run out, everyone is looking at biomass energy for the future.

Did you know..........?

- *The largest forest in the world is in the northern USSR covering more than 1100 million hectares?*
- *England has Kielder Forest in Northumberland covering about 30 000 hectares?*
- *Wales has the forest of Glamorgan (Coad Morgannwg) covering about 17 000 hectares?*
- *About 7% of the United Kingdom is covered in forests compared with 34% of the USSR.*

Lessons from the past

In Europe, harvesting trees for fuel is a very old tradition called **coppicing**. Coppicing means cutting trees back down to ground level at regular intervals. This makes them grow lots of new stems from the cut 'stumps' (see figure 1). A tree cut like this can live for many hundreds of years, much longer than if it was left to grow by itself. A cut stump has to be left for between 10–15 years before it can be cut for firewood again. Coppicing greatly increases the productivity of trees. If you want to know more about productivity read chapter 2 (Book 2).

Coppicing declined during the Industrial Revolution as other energy sources, such as coal, replaced wood. Between the 1920s and 1950s, woodland management almost stopped because of changes in agricultural methods and increases in the costs of labour. Today, there is a return to woodland management and wood is once again becoming an economic fuel.

— ① Burning wood as a fuel is one way in which we use trees. Make a list of other ways in which we and other animals make use of trees?

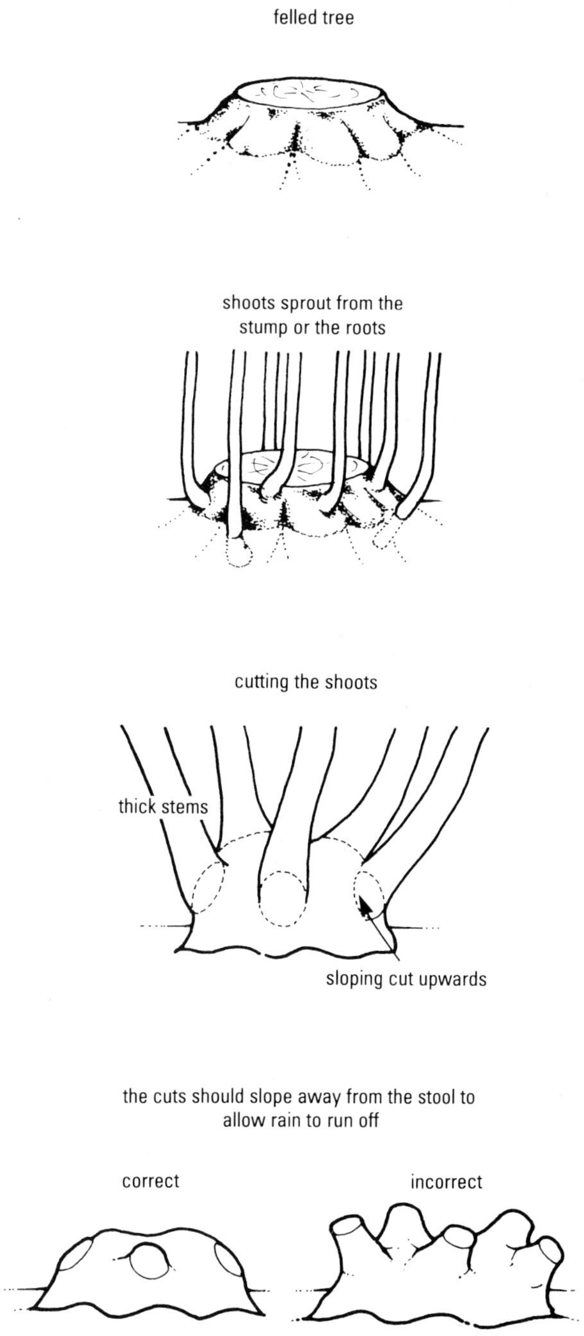

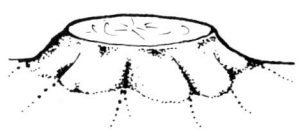
felled tree

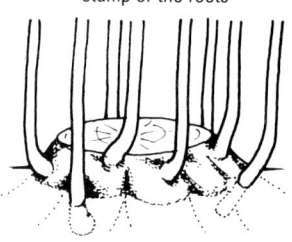
shoots sprout from the stump or the roots

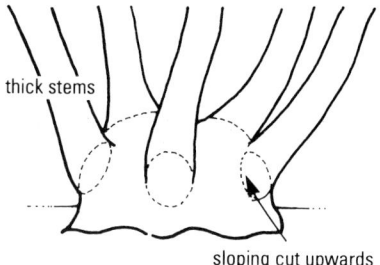
cutting the shoots
thick stems
sloping cut upwards

the cuts should slope away from the stool to allow rain to run off

correct   incorrect

Figure 1 The effects of coppicing

A future for wood as a fuel

A modern example of using biomass energy from wood is to be found in Leeds in Northern England. They are thinking of using woodlands to reduce both the costs of energy and the costs of parks. Leeds City Council plans to use a huge wood boiler to heat a plant nursery. The nursery boiler will be fuelled by woodchips from waste timber, brushwood and coppiced trees in parks and woodlands.

Here is some information about the project.

Leeds timber burning project
Energy as heat from wood = 1000 MJ per m^3
(1 MJ = 1 000 000 joules)

Timber available for burning each year = 10 000 m^3
Energy to heat 1 m^3 of water to its boiling point = 350 MJ

= ② If an average tree yields 0.5 m^3 of timber for burning, how many trees per year will the boiler use?

= ③ How much energy as heat will the boiler produce each year? (Count the zeros very carefully.)

= ④ How many m^3 of water can be boiled each year (assuming that no energy is lost)?

= ⑤ The energy given by 1 m^3 of gas is about 40 MJ. The energy from wood used in the boiler is the answer to question 3. How many m^3 of gas will be saved each year by the boiler?

= ⑥ 1 m^3 of gas costs about 15p. Calculate the money saved by burning timber instead of gas (assuming that the wood is free).

The fuel wood crisis in South Korea

In Austria and Sweden people are planting spare land with trees to provide fuel. But in developing countries, 2 billion people rely on wood for heating and cooking. On average, they collect 3 kg of wood each day. But trees need time to grow and many families have difficulty in collecting enough wood. Some families spend 40% of their income on buying wood or up to 3 hours per day collecting it.

In South Korea, 40 000 hectares of land have been planted with trees since 1976 to provide fuel for its growing population (1 hectare is about the area of a football pitch). Now about 70% of the country is covered in trees. Even so, demand for the timber will be greater than supply by 2010.

= ⑦ Why may there not be enough wood produced to supply demand in South Korea by 2010?

Burning dung

When fuel wood is not available, people burn other kinds of biomass such as animal dung and waste material after harvesting. This is a real problem for people in parts of Africa, China, South Korea and the Philippines. Burning dung stops it being used as a natural fertilizer to enrich poor soils. It is thought that 400 million tonnes of dung are burned every year. If this dung had been used as a fertilizer it would have helped to produce an extra 20 million tonnes of grain. This grain would have fed over 10 million people.

Other biomass fuels

In China, waste from vegetables, garden waste and dung is being *fermented* to produce *biogas*. This is similar to the natural gas used in Great Britain. Biogas is used for heating and can be supplied to homes.

In Brazil, cars are run on ethanol (alcohol) fermented from sugar cane.

= ⑧ Copy and complete this table:

Fuel	Good points	Bad points
Wood		
Dung		
Biogas		

= ⑨ Why are many countries seeking biomass fuels instead of using fossil fuels such as coal, oil and natural gas?

In some countries cow dung is used as a source of fuel. Here you can see a woman shaping the manure into fuel bricks for burning

4 POPULATION CHANGE—CAUSE AND EFFECT

A group of living things in an area forms a *population*. A large population in a small area can cause problems. The animals have to solve these problems if they are to survive. Movement of part or all of the population to another area is one solution. But there are other solutions as you can find out in this chapter.

Increase and survival

Here are two important terms.

- *mortality* in a population means *loss by death*.
- *natality* is the adding to a population *by birth*.

These two quantities are linked for any population. For example, a population is constant if the number of adults dying in one year equals the number of young animals born in the same year. And a population decreases if the number of young animals born is less than the number of adults dying in the same year.

=① In a population of rabbits in a large field, the number of young rabbits born in one year was greater than the number of adults dying. What happened to the population? Explain your answer using the words *mortality*, *natality* and *population*.

Did you know.........?

- The fulmar ranges over the N. Atlantic and N. Pacific and belongs to the bird family 'tubenoses'. Fulmars are **pelagic** (i.e. deep sea) species and are able to fly well, even in stormy weather. The bird defends itself by vomiting oil at its attacker, which stains and has a terrible smell.

A fulmar

The fulmar, the blue tit and the blackbird

Different kinds (species) of animals live for different periods of time. The term *life expectancy* is used to describe the expected life of an animal.

The fulmar is a sea bird spending most of its life on the ocean. It can live up to about 20 years. The blue tit lives in woods and is common in parks and gardens. It usually lives for only 2 years. The common blackbird lives about 3.5 years. Data on these three species of bird is given in table 1. Look at the data for the fulmar. Only one egg is laid per year by each pair but the life expectancy is 20 years. Out of 20 eggs laid in any year 19 birds survive for one year. It takes 8 years for a bird to reach maturity and breed.

Compare the data for the fulmar and blue tit. Many eggs are laid by blue tits in a year. Some pairs may even produce 24 eggs. But the life expectancy is only 2 years and only 6 birds are expected to survive after one year from hatching. Notice how blue tits mature and breed after one year.

Compared with the fulmar, the blue tit produces many more eggs but far fewer survive. But both species are able to keep their populations fairly steady.

=② The life expectancies of fulmars and blue tits are very different. Use table 1 to explain how both birds are able to keep their populations fairly steady.

≡③ Look at the data for blackbirds in table 1. Three figures are missing from the table. Predict each of these missing figures and explain how you came to your answers.

Table 1

	Fulmars	Blue tits	Blackbirds
Eggs in one year	1	12+	5+
Life expectancy	20 years	2 years	3.5 years
Survival rate—per year	95%	30%	
Birds surviving one year out of 20 eggs laid	19 survive	6 survive	survive
Years to mature	8	1	

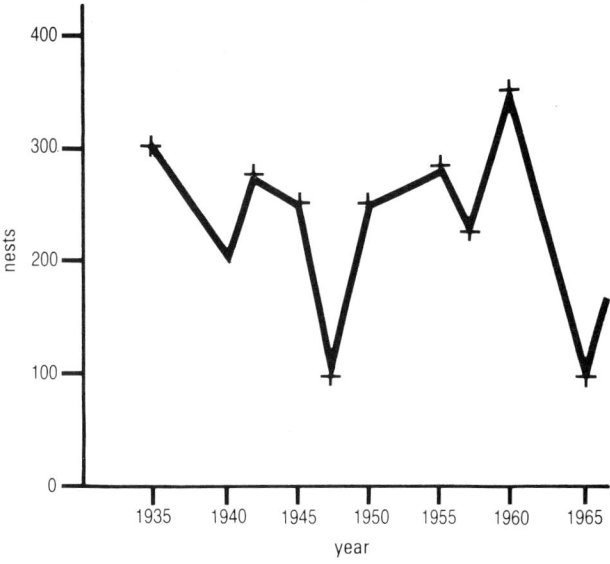

Figure 1 Heron population in Northern England

Table 2 Rabbit/Fox Predation

Stage 1	300 rabbits + 4 foxes The foxes find plenty of rabbits and kill for food.
Stage 2	100 rabbits + 8 foxes (4 babies) + 2 foxes (from another area) Plenty of rabbits for more than 8 foxes so 2 foxes come from another area.
Stage 3	20 rabbits + 10 foxes The foxes are now getting hungry!
Stage 4	50 rabbits (30 babies) + 2 foxes 8 foxes have left to find rabbits in another area.

The population from area B drops due to emigration. Animals are leaving B to find more food. Area A has more food so animals leave B for A. The population of A increases by immigration.

Carrying capacity

The heron is one of the biggest birds in Great Britain. Look at the photograph. It catches fish from lakes and rivers and swallows them whole. In very cold winters the breeding population of herons falls badly. But the numbers increase again in mild winters. It is strange, but the number of herons in an area does not go on increasing. The population reaches a maximum called the *carrying capacity* for the area. The carrying capacity depends on how much food is in the area, the number of nesting sites and other factors.

4. Look at figure 1 showing the heron population in Northern England over 30 years. List years when you think that there was a very cold winter. Explain how you chose the years.

5. Explain what the carrying capacity of an area means. Use the blue tit as an example.

Territories and predation

We all need territory—if you were sitting on a bus, alone, and the only other person to get on for the journey sat next to you, how would you feel?

Animals need an area to call their own, and they claim it by patrolling, displaying and even fighting. The size of a territory depends on how much food is available and how active the animal is. An animal who does not have any territory will not be able to feed properly, have enough shelter or even mate. A very active bird such as the wren needs a large territory, without other wrens. But the fulmar can nest on cliffs quite happily amongst hundreds of other fulmars, as she has the ocean to fish from.

If a population increases, then more individuals will be open to predation. This word comes from 'predator' meaning an animal that catches and kills another. As you can see from table 2 when more rabbits become food for foxes, the population levels out. Take the balance too far and foxes will become hungry and look elsewhere for food.

6. Look at stages 1–4 in table 2 and write down what stage 5 and 6 might contain.

7. What do you think is the carrying capacity for the foxes of the area? Explain your answer.

Immigration and emigration

All animals need enough space to find food and shelter. If the space is small, there is overcrowding and competition for food and shelter. Things get much worse when there are young to feed. Some animals may leave the area to find more food and better shelter. This is called *emigration*. When food is plentiful in an area, the population may increase due to animals moving in from poorer areas. This is called *immigration*. Look at this diagram.

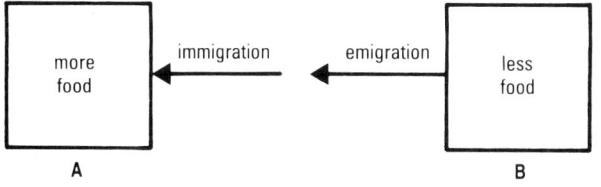

It is not only animals who emigrate, humans also move countries in search of a better standard of living. Emigration was especially popular in the 1950s

5 WORLD POPULATION

The population of human beings in the world is increasing but the *spread* of people is not even. Less developed countries, such as India and China, have huge increasing populations. But the populations of North America, Europe and Australia are becoming steady.

As the world population increases, more food will be needed. Will there be enough food? If not, what can we do about it? Can we *control* human population? If we can, should we try?

Before trying to answer these questions, we first need to think about some statistics for populations.

Counting people

Wherever you were born, you will have a 'Birth Certificate' showing the date and place of your birth and other data. In Great Britain, every birth and death has to be *registered* at a Register Office.

People called demographers add together all these figures and show them as birth rate and death rate.

People leaving a country (emigrating) and entering a country (immigrating) must also be included in the population statistics.

Every ten years in Great Britain, every citizen has to complete a *census form*. A census was carried out in 1961, 1971, 1981 and so on. The census allows the population to be compared every ten years.

Birth rate

The number of babies born each year for every 1000 people is called the *birth rate*.

= ① Copy and complete this table for the birth rate in five towns (A–E)

Town	Population	Births	Birth rate
A	48 023	25	
B	26 900	16	
C	47 223	18	
D	10 522	22	
E	19 287	29	

Look at figure 1 for the birth rate in Great Britain since 1900. There has been a large fall over the last 90 years. There are many reasons for this fall.

Many people now choose to use birth control to limit the size of their families. In the early 1900s, families of 10 children were quite common. The cost of bringing up children today is very high. So people choose to have smaller families and to use their money for other things like cars and entertainment. Many more women now have full-time jobs and do not wish to spend many years looking after many children.

= ② Use figure 1 to describe how the *birth rate* in Great Britain has changed since 1900. (Use actual numbers in your answer and note that birth rate on the graph does not begin at zero).

= ③ Predict the birth rate for Great Britain in the year 2000.

≡ ④ Make a list of reasons why the birth rate has fallen in Great Britain.

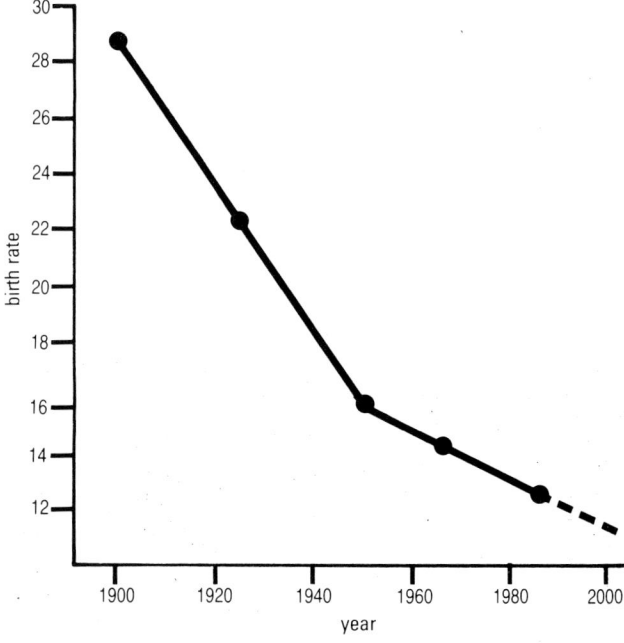

Figure 1 The changes in birth rate since 1900

Death rate

The number of deaths each year for every 1000 people is called the *death rate*. The death rate for Great Britain has dropped rapidly since the last century. It is now 11.7 for males and 11.2 for females.

A big fall has occurred in the death rate of infants under 1 year of age. In 1921 the infant death rate was 72, in 1961 it was 22 and in 1984 it was only 9.

= ⑤ Draw a graph of infant death rate against time using figure 1 to help you.
Take *x* as the year from 1900–2000 (1 cm = 10 years) and *y* as death rate from 0–100 (1 cm = a rate of 10).

= ⑥ Use your graph from question 5 to help you describe how the infant death rate has changed since 1921.

= ⑦ Predict the infant death rate for the year 2000 using your graph for question 5.

≡ (8) In Great Britain, the population is ageing. Explain what 'ageing' means and list some of the problems it brings to old people and to younger people.

≡ (9) Describe *two* ways in which changes in the birth rate and death rate of a population can make the population become *younger*.

Birth rate and death rate

In Great Britain, the birth rate and death rate are both falling. This means that fewer people are dying each year but fewer babies are being born. So the population is *ageing*. There are more older people around needing help and drawing their pensions. There are also fewer people available to earn money to help the older people.

When the birth rate and death rate are equal, a population becomes steady. In Great Britain the population is now fairly steady.

Probably most people know that between 1981 and the year 2001 the number of people aged 85 and over in Great Britain is expected to double, from 552,000 to over one million.

THE GUARDIAN Tuesday
November 22 1988

Population changes around the world

Look at table 1 showing three statistics for several countries. The first three rows are for the whole world, for develoed countries and for the less developed countries. The third column gives the age to which a baby, on average, will survive.

Use table 1 for questions 10–12.

= (10) List the countries with

(a) the highest death rate.
(b) the highest expectation of life at birth.
(c) the highest infant death rate.

Is any country in all three of your lists? Explain your answer.

= (11) Compare the data for the USA and Afghanistan and give reasons for the large differences.

≡ (12) China is a 'less developed' country. The government in China only allows couples to have *one child* by law. Explain the changes in population statistics which may now happen for China.

≡ (13) Look at figure 2. The world population in 1950 was 3500 million. Predict when this figure will double. When was the world population 500 million? Why do you think that the term 'world population explosion' is used to describe the change in the population of the world?

Between 1985 and 2001, the total number of people of pensionable age will have increased overall by 4.2%, but by 2025 it will have increased by 31.1%.

By 2001 the proportion aged 75 and over will have increased by 22% and those aged 85 and over by 71.3%.

By 2025 the proportion aged 75 and over will have increased by 46.4% and those aged 85 and over by 99.2%.

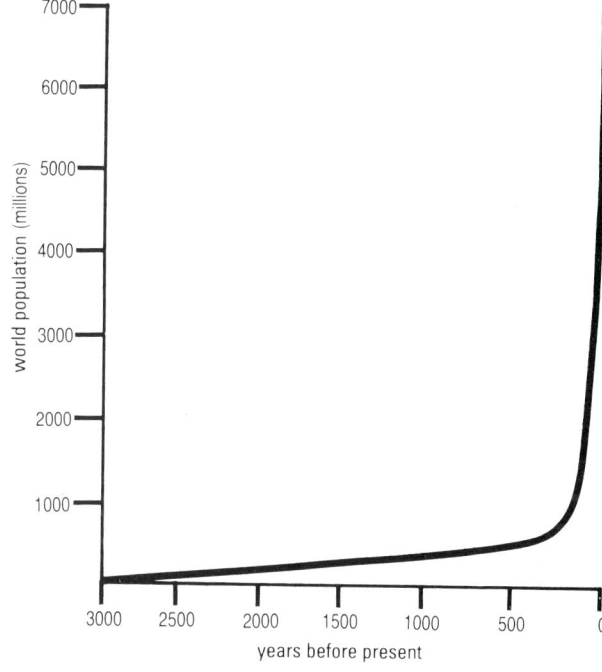

Figure 2 The changes in world population over 3000 years

Table 1 Measures of mortality for the period 1970–1977

	Death rate per 1000 of population	Expectation of life at birth (years)	Infant death rate (age 1 year and under)
World	13	56	120
Developed	9	71	27
Less developed	14	54	140
UK	11	73	14
Greece	11	73	23
USA	9	73	15
Afghanistan	22	42	220
Brazil	9	62	90
Colombia	8	62	98
Hong Kong	6	72	14
Mexico	8	65	71
Niger	22	42	over 200
Sri Lanka	6	69	41

Source: UN, USA Bureau of Census.

6 SAMPLING

Many groups and schools organize trips into woodlands to help students understand the theory behind sampling

If you have ever walked though a wood, you will have seen a large number of plants and animals living there. Think of the different kinds of trees and shrubs, birds and insects.

In this chapter, you can practise some methods of describing the living things in a wood.

Taking samples

The best way to find out how many plants or animals are in a wood is to study some sample areas. You would never have the time to study a **whole** wood. And studying just one small area would not give a true overall picture. We say that studying one or two areas would not give a **representative** sample of the wood.

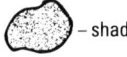

- 1 violet plant

- 1 bluebell plant

V/\ll/ - moss is present

- shade

7·2 - ph of soil (average)

Figure 1 A model wood

A model wood

In figure 1 there is a 'model' wood for you to practise some of the skills of sampling. The wood is divided into squares on a grid so that you can choose which areas to study. The shaded areas show the shadows from trees at midday.

In the bottom right-hand corner of each square is the pH value of the soil.

A pH of 7 shows that the soil is **neutral**. A pH **greater** than 7 shows that the soil is **alkaline**. A pH **less** than 7 shows that the soil is **acidic**.

The pH value of soil can be measured using a soil testing kit.

Look carefully at the key to the model wood for violet and bluebell plants and for the presence of moss.

Preparing your results table

Use a full page of your notebook to draw a table with the headings seen in table 1. You will need 20 rows in the table for the data from 20 samples.

Choosing your areas for study

You need to choose a **representative** sample to give an overall picture of the wood. It would be of little use to choose all your areas at one corner of the wood. You can choose your 20 areas using the **random number square** in figure 2. In this square there is an equal chance of finding all the numbers from 0 to 9. Follow these steps to find your 20 sample areas:

1 Choose any row of the random number square and find the first two numbers from the left-hand side. For example, in the fourth row you have 5 and 4. Now choose your own row.

2 The first number you find is x for your sample area, so write this number in the column for x in table 1. ($x = 5$ for the fourth row).

3 The second number you find is y for your sample area, so write this number in the column for y in table 1. ($y = 4$ for the fourth row).

4 Go along your row and fill in x and y for all your 20 sample areas. At the end of your row, go to the next row down and so on. After the last row in the square go to the top row of the square.

5 Using x and y for each of your sample areas, find each area in the model wood and fill in the data in table 1.

Analysing your results

— (1) Add up the total number of violets in your 20 sample areas. Then multiply by 5 to find the total number of violets in the 100 areas of the wood. Write down your answers.

— (2) Repeat question 1 for bluebells.

= (3) Using your answers to questions 1 and 2, compare the number of violets and bluebells in the wood.

= (4) Estimate the average pH of the soil in the wood by finding the average pH for your 20 sample areas.

Copy table 2 and use it for questions 5–10.

= (5) Find the average pH for the light and shady areas. Describe the difference between the two kinds of area using the terms acidic and alkaline.

Table 1 Results

Sample number	x	y	Tick if mainly in shade	pH	Tick if moss present	Number of violet plants	Number of bluebell plants
1							
2							
3							
4							
.							
.							
20							

Table 2 Light and shade

	Number of areas	Average pH	Average number of violets	Average number of bluebells	% with moss
Areas in light					
Areas mainly in shade					

= (6) Find the average number of violets and bluebells in each kind of area. Put your results in table 2. Comment on these results.

= (7) Find the number of light areas with moss from table 1 and the number of shady areas with moss. Calculate the percentage for each kind of area and put your answers in table 2.

≡ (8) Write a hypothesis about what you would expect to find in light and shady areas in the model wood. Include in your hypothesis the number of violets and bluebells you would expect, the pH you would expect and whether you would expect moss to be present.

≡ (9) Count the actual number of shady and light areas in the whole wood and calculate the percentage of dark areas. Calculate the percentage of dark areas in your sample of 20 areas. Comment on the two percentages and say whether you think that your sample was representative of the whole wood for light and shade.

5	8	8	7	8	4	4	6	3	1
0	8	0	7	7	8	0	2	6	8
3	2	0	3	3	6	2	6	2	1
5	4	5	5	3	8	5	7	9	4
8	4	1	6	0	5	8	1	0	6
4	1	3	4	5	0	5	3	4	5
0	7	7	9	0	9	1	6	0	9
2	0	7	1	9	4	0	2	1	2
2	4	0	7	3	0	5	5	0	9
8	3	0	7	9	4	7	9	6	9

Figure 2 Random number square

7 LIFE IN THE SEA

Life in the sea begins with plants. Only plants can take energy from the Sun to grow and provide food for animals. There would be no fish in the sea if there were no plants.

The simplest of all plants in the sea are the *phytoplankton*. They are minute plants which drift near the surface and grow by *photosynthesis*. (You can read about photosynthesis in chapter 14 (Book 2).)

What do phytoplankton need to grow?

(1) *Light*
Photosynthesis needs sunlight for energy to change water and carbon dioxide gas into living matter. In clear seas, light can reach down to about 110 m from the surface. In the North Sea, it can only reach 40 m but near the shore it may only reach 15 m or less.

(2) *Carbon dioxide gas*
Photosynthesis needs carbon dioxide. Air contains about 0.3% of carbon dioxide but the gas is very soluble in water. Water in contact with the air dissolves carbon dioxide.

(3) *Nutrients*
Crops on land need fertilizer to grow if the land is sown year after year. In the same way, phytoplankton need nutrients such as compounds of phosphorus, nitrogen and iron. Nutrients tend to settle on the sea bed. The water must be stirred up by currents or by wind to bring nutrients to the surface for the phytoplankton.

(4) *Warm water*
Phytoplankton tend to multiply more quickly in warm water. This is because chemical reactions go faster as the temperature rises. (See chapter 2 (Book 1).)

= (1) Phytoplankton live near the *surface* of the sea. Write about *two* important reasons for them being near the surface.

= (2) Why is it important for phytoplankton that the sea is stirred up?

Life in the North Sea

The North Sea is between the east coast of Great Britain and the mainland of Europe. Plants and fish grow well in the North Sea. Look at figure 1 as you read about changes in the surface water of the North Sea during the year.

Light and temperature
Graph A in figure 1 shows how the amount of light each day changes during the year. (Remember the dark nights of winter?). Graph B shows how the surface temperature of the water changes.

= (3) From graphs A and B, during which months would you expect phytoplankton to multiply quickly?

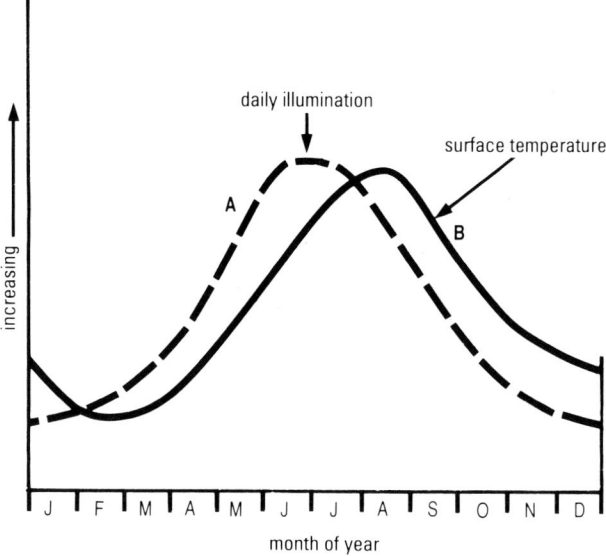

Figure 1 Variation in daily illumination and surface temperature of the North Sea

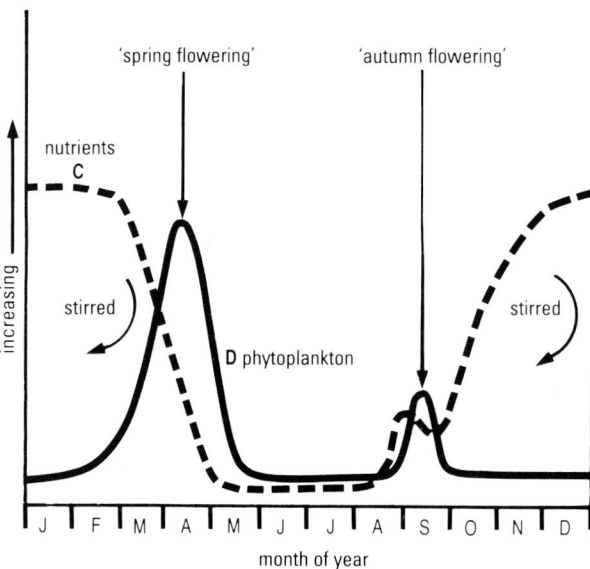

Figure 2 Variation in nutrient concentration and phytoplankton in the North Sea

Nutrients

Graph C in figure 2 shows how the concentration of nutrients near the surface changes during the year. In winter the nutrient concentration is high because the winds are often strong in winter and stir up the water. In summer, the nutrient concentration is low because the water is much calmer. The small increase in nutrient concentration around September is because of the gales which occur in September.

Many people spend their lives studying, filming and writing about the huge number of creatures living in the sea

Phytoplankton

Graph D in figure 2 shows the change in phytoplankton during the year. See how quickly it grows in March and April. In one week it may multiply by a hundred and in two weeks by a thousand! In May it decreases quickly because of the lack of nutrients and because it is eaten by tiny animals called zooplankton.

(4) Phytoplankton multiplies very quickly in the North Sea during March and April. This is called the 'spring flowering'. Explain in your own words why this happens in the spring. Write about light, temperature and nutrients in your answer.

(5) Why are there so few phytoplankton in the summer?

(6) At the end of summer, there is an 'autumn flowering' when phytoplankton multiply again but not so much as in the spring. Give some reasons for the autumn flowering.

(7) Sewage from London reaches the North Sea off the Thames Estuary. The sewage carries 2 900 tonnes of phosphorus in chemical compounds into this area each year. Explain why more fish are caught here than in the rest of the North Sea.

Did you know.........?

- The words 'phytoplankton' and 'photosynthesis' come from the Greek language.

phytoplankton 'phyto' from 'phuton' meaning **plant**.
'plankton' from 'plagktos' meaning **wandering**.

So phytoplankton are 'wandering plants'. This is a good name because phytoplankton 'wander' about the seas driven by currents and wind.

photosynthesis 'photo' from 'photos' meaning light (remember photography?)
'synthesis' from 'sunthesis' meaning 'putting together'

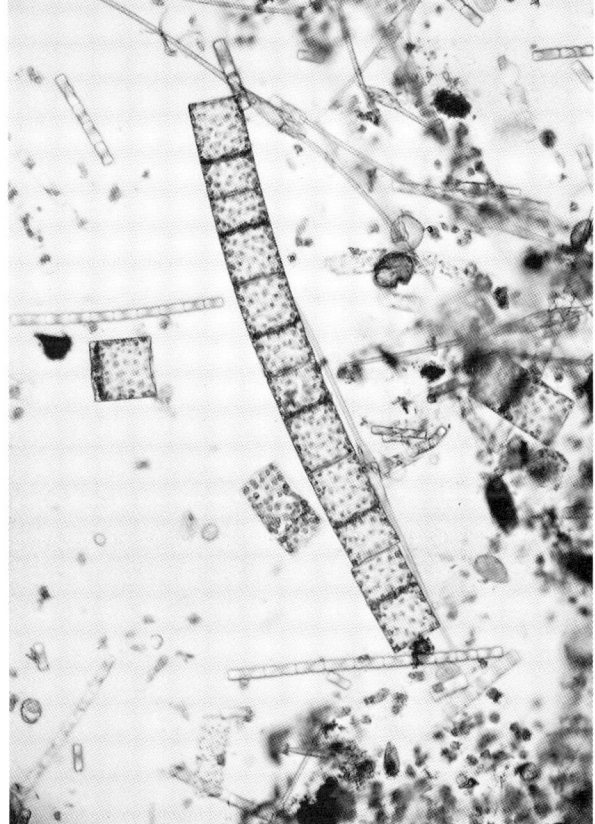

Photomicrograph of phytoplankton

Phytoplankton and the colour of the sea

It is calculated that about 110 000 000 000 tonnes of phytoplankton are produced in the seas of the world every year! This is about the same mass which is produced by plants on the land.

In some parts of the seas, there is so much phytoplankton that the sea is coloured. Sometimes the sea looks milky due to a species of phytoplankton which herring eat. The Red Sea gets its name from the red colour of the water. The red comes from a species of phytoplankton.

8 SHARING WITH NATURE

Most plants and animals in their natural surroundings live in 'balance'. Animals and plants do not take out of their environment more than they need for survival.

Sadly, human beings have disturbed the environment and threaten many kinds of animals and plants. In time, the damage caused to these living things will affect humans too. We must learn to live in 'balance' with nature.

In this chapter you can read about two problems caused by humans.

The Guanay Cormorant

Living in balance

Left alone, a wood can theoretically survive for ever. Plants 'collect' energy from the sun and produce food by photosynthesis. Animals eat this food and produce dung. Droppings from animals, and in time their decayed bodies, provide nutrients for plants.

A problem in Peru

Off the coast of Peru, in South America, lives the *guanay* bird. It is a kind of cormorant. The guanay eats *anchovetas*. These are small fish like the anchovy which is a member of the herring family. When these have been caught, anchovetas are not eaten by humans but are fed to cattle and chickens and used in pet food.

Guanay birds live on the rocks and islands along the coastline of Peru. About 20% of their droppings are left on the rocks. These droppings form a fertilizer called *guano* which is rich in nitrates. Sales of guano once provided more than half of Peru's national income.

The rest of the guano drops into the sea and is taken in by *plankton*. Anchovetas eat plankton. But anchovetas are also food for bigger fish such as *sea bass* and *tuna*. These bigger fish were caught by local fishermen and were valuable food for many Peruvians.

= (1) Draw a food web including these items:

anchovetas, cattle, chickens, guanay, guano, humans, plankton, sea bass, tuna.

Use your food web to explain how guanays help to provide food for humans.

The people of Peru were 'sharing food with nature' and the food web worked well. But a big change has occurred.

About 30 years ago, artificial fertilizers became cheaper than guano. (You can read about these fertilizers in chapter 16 (Book 2) and chapter 17 (Book 2).) The price of guano fell. Peruvians switched from selling guano to catching anchovetas. In one year, 14 million tonnes were hauled out of the Pacific! In a few years, anchovetas had almost disappeared.

Due to the sudden increase in the numbers of anchovetas caught around Peru thousands of guanay birds starved and there are now very few sea bass and tuna off the coast

With few anchovetas, guanays starved to death in their thousands. With few guanays, very little guano reached the sea. With little guano, plankton could not thrive. With fewer plankton, anchovetas could not find as much food.

The people of Peru destroyed a food web. By catching so many anchovetas they destroyed food for guanays and for themselves. There are now very few tuna and sea bass off their coast.

= (2) Why did guanays starve to death in their thousands?

= (3) Why were there fewer plankton?

= (4) Mark on your food web for question 1 the breaks caused by the Peruvians.

= (5) Give *two* reasons why catching so many anchovetas reduced the number of tuna and sea bass caught.

Burning the Amazon Forest

The article on the Amazon Forest is from The Guardian newspaper. It explains the problems of trying to stop the forest being destroyed.

In the article you can read that 200 000 km² of forest was destroyed in 1987 out of the 5.5 million km². You can also read *why* the forest is being destroyed.

At the end of the article, you can find out the damage being caused to the Earth's atmosphere by burning the forest. The 'greenhouse effect' and its link with carbon dioxide is explained in chapter 35 (Book 2).

= (6) Calculate the percentage of the Amazon forest destroyed in 1987. Comment on what the President of the Forest Service said about the percentage of forest destroyed. Calculate how many years it will take for *all* the forest to be destroyed if the same area is destroyed every year.

= (7) Write down *two* reasons why the forest is being destroyed.

= (8) Describe the changes being caused to the atmosphere by burning the forest. How may these changes affect the Earth?

World conservation

What can we do to help in the conservation of nature? The first thing is to learn much more about the lives of animals and plants and how *we link to them*. The second is to take action ourselves to help conservation. The third is to try and persuade others to conserve nature, including those in industry and the government.

A catch phrase in conservation is

'Think globally, act locally'.

Another way of giving the message is
'We must learn again that we belong to the Earth and that the Earth does not belong to us.'

= (9) Make a list of four things that you and your family do which have an effect on nature. Say whether the effect is helpful or harmful.

= (10) Design a poster or a leaflet to persuade people not to destroy nature by 'taking out more than they need'. You could warn about over-fishing or cutting down too many trees.

Amazon forest burning is 'beyond control'

Jan Rocha in Sao Paulo

A TOP official of Brazil's Forest Defence Service has admitted for the first time that they have no means of stopping the deliberate burning down of the Amazon rain forest caused by thousands of man-made fires which are devastating thousands of square miles of forest, scrub, and bush to clear the land for farming.

Projections made by Brazil's Space Research Institute, which last year began monitoring forest fires for the first time with the help of a Nasa satellite, indicate that there could be a 30 per cent increase in the Amazon area burnt down this year.

In 1987, just over 200,000 square kilometres was burnt, about half of it virgin forest.

The general secretary of the Forest Defence Service, Mr José Carlos Carvalho, in an unusually outspoken interview, said: "The situation is most serious. We don't have the money, equipment or men to stop the Amazon fires."

The service has only 300 forest guards and inspectors deployed in the Amazon basin region, which covers an area of 5½ million square kilometres.

"The practice of burning the forest is a direct result of the government's wrong policy of occupation in the 1970s," said Mr Carvalho. "It's the land sharks and the big companies from the south of Brazil who profit from the burning.

"Volkswagen, for example, had a ranch covering an area the size of one of Brazil's north-eastern states, and transformed the forest there into cattle pasture, using fire. The fires don't bring any benefit to the local people, the poorer population. They only transform wealth, that is trees, into ashes.

"It's the same as throwing money away. Only if we change our policies will there be a chance of improving the situation."

Officials also put the blame for some of the more recent fires on the government's policy of land reform.

As any so-called "productive" land is excluded from confiscation, landowners burn down forest cover and install a few cows to demonstrate productivity.

Until recently, forest service officials refused to admit there was an immediate danger to the Amazon rain forest. Last year the forest service president said that only 2 per cent of the forest had been destroyed.

Now, thanks to the precise data being provided by Space Institute researchers, awareness of the size of the destruction is at last growing.

Researchers also estimate that up to 44 million tonnes of carbon monoxide and 10 per cent of global carbon dioxide emanations come from the Amazon, contributing considerably to the heating of the earth's atmosphere and the greenhouse effect.

Unfortunately, this awareness comes at a time when the government is trying to make drastic cuts in public spending, and the forest service has little chance of getting the extra money it needs to stop the fires.

THE GUARDIAN Thursday September 1 1988

9 RED AND GREY SQUIRRELS

Squirrels are very attractive mammals. The red squirrel is the favourite with many people, especially when sitting on a branch with its bushy tail curled up its back.

Sadly, the red squirrel is rare in most areas of Great Britain. Our grandparents may have seen many red squirrels but we usually only see grey ones.

Why should this be? Has the grey squirrel 'taken over'? In this chapter you can find out some of the problems of the red squirrel.

The grey squirrel now outnumbers the red many times

The red squirrel

From its nose to the tip of its tail, the red squirrel measures about 39 cm. Its mass is between 230 and 350 g. The red squirrel is a member of the rodent family, along with beavers and rats, but spends most of its life in trees.

The nest of the squirrel is called a *drey* and a squirrel usually has three young in the spring or summer. The red squirrel does not hibernate in winter and eats buried roots and nuts.

The red squirrel is a native of Great Britain and it has lived in the whole of England and Wales with 'pockets' in Scotland and Ireland. It is found in woods and particularly likes conifers. It is quite a destructive animal because it eats pine seedlings and strips bark. Trees can be damaged by squirrels and grow crooked. This makes trees of little value for building.

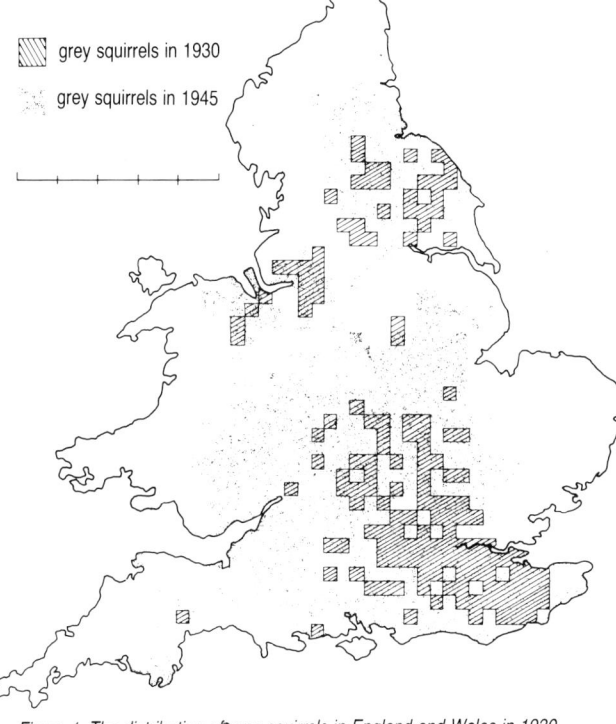

Figure 1 The distribution of grey squirrels in England and Wales in 1930 and 1945

The grey squirrel

The grey squirrel is bigger than the red squirrel. It has a mass between 450 and 600 g and is about 50 cm long. Its tail is less bushy than in the red squirrel and it has no ear tufts. The grey squirrel eats acorns, nuts and bark as does the red squirrel. But the grey squirrel also eats toadstools, puff balls and young buds of trees. Beach trees are very popular with grey squirrels and whole woods have been badly damaged.

The grey squirrel is a native of North America and was first brought to Great Britain in the early 19th Century. Sailors may have brought them into the country as pets.

1. Copy table 1 and complete it to show the differences between red and grey squirrels.

Table 1 Comparison between the red and grey squirrel

	Red squirrel	Grey squirrel
Length (cm) Mass (g) Food Habitat Country of origin		

The advance of the grey squirrel

The grey squirrel was first recorded in the wild in Wales in 1828. Red squirrels have always been in Great Britain. For some reason, several greys were set free at various points around the country. A very large group soon formed at Woburn Park, Bedfordshire. By 1914 this group had spread from Buckinghamshire to Hertfordshire, then to Kent, Dorset, Cornwall and northwards to the Scottish border.

The grey squirrel is absent from the Isles of Man and Wight, Norfolk and Northumberland. The grey squirrel seems to prefer woodland and parkland rather than coniferous forests. It also does not live at a high altitude, unlike the red squirrel.

The red squirrel, made famous by Beatrix Potter's character Squirrel Nutkin. At the time she wrote the red squirrel was the most prominent species

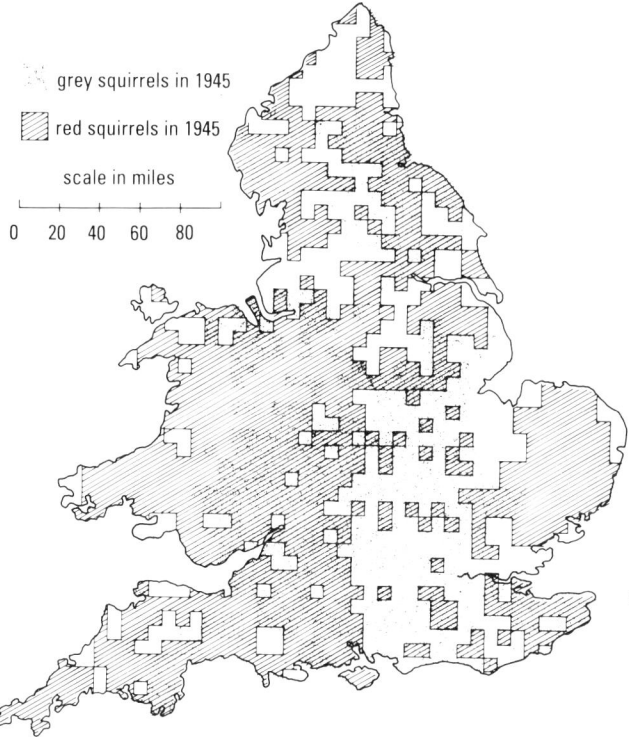

Figure 2 The distribution of red and grey squirrels in England and Wales in 1945

Grey versus red?

It is often said that the grey squirrel has taken the place of the red squirrel. But it is now known that the red squirrel had a fatal disease when the grey squirrel was brought into the country. Many red squirrels died, leaving space and food for the grey squirrels.

The grey squirrel is bigger and stronger than the red and can easily defend an area against attack by red squirrels.

The grey breeds more quickly than the red. The red can only rear young once each year unless conditions are very good. They must have enough food and protection from grey squirrels to rear more than one brood per year.

Distribution of squirrels in England and Wales

Look at figure 1. The dots show areas with grey squirrels in 1945. Diagonal lines show areas with grey squirrels in 1930.

Look at figure 2 showing the distribution of red and grey squirrels in 1945. The diagonal lines show that red squirrels are present.

(2) Compare the diagonal lines with the dots in figure 1 and describe the spread of grey squirrels between 1930 and 1945.

(3) Write down which of these areas had *red* squirrels in 1945. Anglesey, Cornwall, Devon, Isle of Wight, Lincolnshire, Norfolk, South Wales, Suffolk.

(4) Write down which of the areas listed in question 3 had grey squirrels in 1945.

(5) Compare your answers to questions 3 and 4. State a hypothesis (give a theory) to 'explain' this comparison.

(6) Look at the large area of Southern England between the Isle of Wight and the Wash. Comment on the presence of red and grey squirrels. Does this support your hypothesis for question 5? (**Hint:** Grey squirrels formed a large group in Bedfordshire in the 19th Century).

(7) List the counties or areas where red squirrels were present but grey squirrels were absent in 1945.

The red squirrel now

A survey covering 202 forests in Scotland was made in 1957. No red squirrels were found in 77 forests, very few in 109 and only three forests had a lot. But there were more grey squirrels in Scotland at the time. The fall in the red squirrel population of Scotland was not due to grey squirrels.

Sadly for the red squirrel, the vast conifer forests planted in Scotland are not the kind needed by the red squirrel. The red squirrel likes the Scots Pine which does not grow in dense, dark forests. Around Scots Pine trees, dense undergrowth survives. This protects younger trees and allows the Scots Pine forest to grow naturally. Red squirrels thrive in this habitat unless attacked by the grey squirrel.

(8) Explain what we should do if we want red squirrels to become common again in England and Wales.

10 BADGERS—ENEMIES OR FRIENDS?

The badger is protected by law in Great Britain. It is our largest wild omnivore (eating both plants and meat). The badger has no natural enemies except man, so its population stays fairly steady.

Some people think that badgers infect cattle with tuberculosis (TB) and that all wild badgers should be killed. In this chapter you can read some evidence about badgers and make up your own mind.

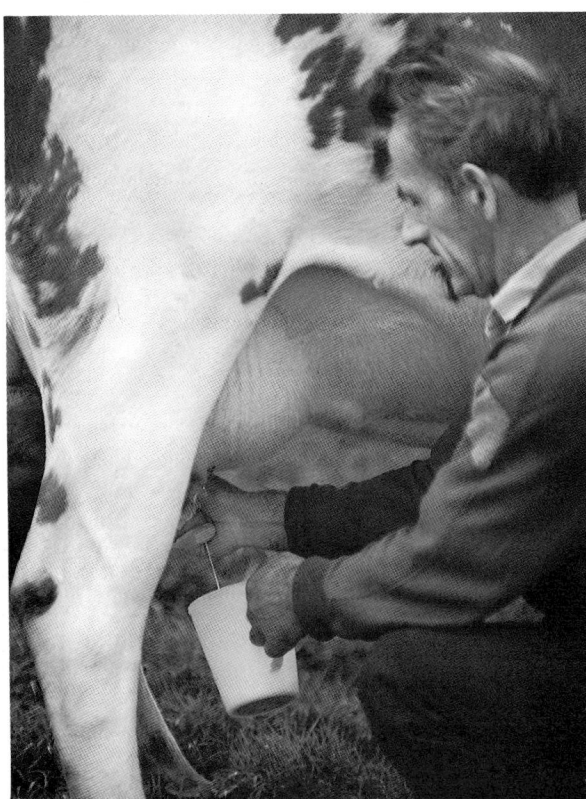

Figure 1 Because of the threat to humans, all dairy cattle are checked for 'TB' before their milk is sold

'TB' and 'TT'

Some people think that the badger spreads TB in cattle. Tuberculosis is a disease caused by bacteria. The disease affects the lungs and breathing in humans. If TB is not treated it can cause death.

In the 1930's, over 20 000 cattle were infected. The disease was passed from one animal to another. A national system of checking cattle for TB began. All infected cattle were killed. Nowadays, all herds of cattle are checked from time to time. This checking is called *tuberculin testing* or 'TT'. You may have seen milk labelled 'TT'. This tells you that the cattle producing the milk have been checked for TB.

Look at table 1 showing the fall in numbers of infected cattle since 1935. Nowadays, only a few cases of TB in cattle arise. Most cases are in South-West England. Killing infected cattle does not stop the disease. Some people blame badgers for carrying and spreading TB.

— (1) What does the label 'TT' on a bottle of milk mean? Why is it a good idea to buy milk carrying this label?

= (2) When a herd of cattle is tested for TB, only some animals are checked. Why is it not necessary to check *all* the animals (**Hint:** Read paragraph 2 again in 'TB' and 'TT').

= (3) Look at table 1. Comment on the time taken from 1935 to reduce the number of cattle infected with TB.

Table 1 Numbers of TB infected cattle (England and Wales)

Year	Infected cattle
1935	20 000
1955	1500
1965	20
1970	occasional cases only

Figure 2

The badger and TB

Scientists have proved that badgers are easily infected with TB. They can catch the disease from cattle. Badgers can spread the disease through urine on grassland eaten by cattle.

Areas most at risk from badgers spreading TB are Cornwall, Devon and Dorset (see figure 2). In these counties there are about 40 setts per 100 km^2. But some local areas have 10 times this number. The three counties are similar in climate and vegetation. The average number of setts in Great Britain is about 20 setts per 100 km^2. Look at the data in table 2.

Unfortunately for the badger, TB still affects cattle in the three counties. But it is difficult to *prove* that the badger is the *cause* of the disease.

Table 2 Badgers in three counties

County	Surface area/km^2	Number of badger setts	Setts per 100 km^2
Cornwall	3548	1420	40
Devon	6711	2680	40
Dorset	2654	1060	40

The case for the defence ... many scientists no longer believe that the badger is solely responsible for the spread of tuberculosis in cattle

Saving the badger

The law protecting badgers was passed to stop people catching them and making them fight with dogs. Now the badger is being killed because it has caught a disease from cattle!

Many scientists do not believe that the badger is solely to blame for the spread of TB.

Fortunately for the badger, its population is fairly steady in Great Britain. The population is about 150 000 breeding pairs.

= (8) Suppose that a local farmer called Mr Weston, wants to gas a family of badgers near your home. Write a letter to Mr Weston explaining why he should change his mind. Try to persuade him that he will not stop TB spreading in his cattle by killing the badgers.

= (4) Why do you think that there are the same numbers of badgers per 100 km² in all three counties? (You may find a clue to the answer in 'Carrying Capacity' in chapter 4 (Book 2)).

= (5) Why is it 'unfortunate' for the badger that TB still affects cattle in Cornwall, Devon and Dorset?

Killing the badger

The badger is protected by law in Great Britain. But the animal may be killed by people holding a special badger licence. Badgers are killed by pumping deadly *cyanide* gas into the sett. *All* badgers in the sett are killed whether they carry TB or not.

Some people argue that all the infected badger's family is killed and so the disease is controlled. But badgers look for food up to 10 km from the sett. So they could spread TB to other badgers within this distance of their sett. To prevent the spread of TB, *all* badgers inside a circle of radius 10 km around the infected sett must be gassed. Even so, bacteria carrying TB can stay alive in the soil for months. And other animals such as foxes, rats and moles can carry and spread TB.

= (6) Write out the argument used by people who want to kill badgers to prevent TB spreading.

= (7) Explain why it is impossible to stop TB spreading even if *all* the badgers in an area are killed. Try to give four reasons.

Did you know..........?

- Chief features of the European badger are its short, strong legs, long flat feet and pointed muzzle. The head markings of the badger distinguish it from any other animal and are thought to be a form of camouflage. (the badger is a nocturnal animal). It is about 70 cm long and stands about 30 cm high, with a mass of about 10 kg. The badger's food includes roots, insects, frogs and small mammals.

- Eight species of badgers exist around the world (seven in Europe and Asia and one in North America).

11 WEIGHING UP FOOD

'You are what you eat!'

This seems a strange saying but there is a lot of truth in it. All your cells need energy and food to survive and to carry out their special functions. All energy and food in the body comes from what we eat. It is important that we eat *enough* of the *kinds* of food the cells in our body need.

This chapter is about the energy in the different kinds of food we eat.

Energy to lie in bed!

We need a lot of energy from food just to lie in bed all day! A lot of energy is needed to keep the body temperature at 37 °C. Heat is lost all the time to the surroundings which are usually below 20 °C. Heat lost has to be replaced from food. We also need energy to keep the heart, lungs and other organs working.

The energy needed by a person weighing 70 kg is about *7 million joules per day*. This quantity of energy is usually written as 7000 kJ. (1 kJ = 1000 joules.) When active, an adult needs between about 10 000 kJ and 20 000 kJ per day. So how much food has to be eaten to produce this quantity of energy?

Energy in food

The energy in 1 g of some fresh foods is given in table 1. Foods containing mostly water have the lowest energy. Foods containing fats, such as butter and chocolate, have the highest energy. (About 25% of the energy in food is changed by the cells of the body into energy of movement with the rest being changed into heat.)

= ① Irene Kellet works in an electronics design office and has two children. She needs about 14 000 kJ of energy per day from food. Copy this table in your notebook and fill in all the foods in table 1. Then calculate the cost per day, to the nearest penny, for Irene's food if she just ate *one* of these kinds of food. The first is calculated for you.

Food	J/g	Cost (p/g)	Mass needed per day in g for 14 000 kJ	Cost per day
Lager Milk	2200	0.15	6364 g	£9.55

Which food is the cheapest to give her the 14 000 J she needs per day? And which is the most expensive?

In question 1 you work out the cost per day of eating just one kind of food to obtain the energy needed by the body. Not only would it be boring

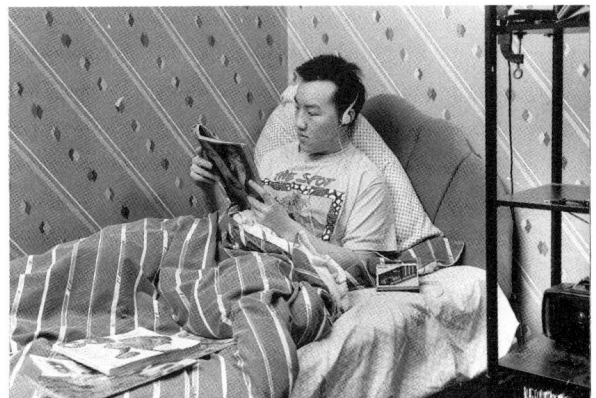

to eat one kind of food all day, even chocolate, but you would eventually become ill and die. You would not be eating the *different kinds* of food needed by the body. The next paragraphs are about the *different foods* we need to eat.

Carbohydrates
These foods contain molecules with carbon, hydrogen and oxygen atoms. (Carbohydrates have a formula $C_n(H_2O)_n$). Examples of food containing carbohydrates are sugar, bread, carrots and potatoes. Cane sugar is almost 100% carbohydrate. The body can change sugar into energy in about an hour.

You can read about some of the problems of eating sugar in chapter 22 (Book 2).

Fats
Fats also contain molecules with carbon, hydrogen and oxygen atoms. But they take about 5–6 hours in the body before they can be used. So we do not feel hungry as quickly after eating fats as we do if we eat sugars. Butter, margarine and many meats contain fats.

Proteins
Proteins are very important foodstuffs. But no food we eat is pure protein. The white of an egg with 40% protein and breast of chicken with 25% protein are amongst the foods with the highest protein content.

Proteins are needed to build up the body. Most of the flesh and muscles in the body are made from proteins. So without proteins we could not replace parts of our bodies which are wearing away! You know that your hair continues to grow, but did you know that a lot of skin rubs off and that your teeth and other organs gradually wear away? We need about 80 g of protein per day to help replace cells in our body.

Protein in our food comes from meat, milk, cheese, eggs, which are all from animals. We also obtain protein from bread, cereals, nuts, fruit and vegetables. Proteins from animals are fairly rich in proteins. Proteins from vegetables contain a smaller percentage of protein but are less expensive.

22

Look at table 2 showing data on proteins in food eaten by Kirsty Kellet in one particular day. Kirsty is 15 years old, 1.45 m in height and weighs 50 kg. On this day she ate the following:

Breakfast —bacon & eggs, toast, tea
Lunch —tuna sandwiches, crisps, crunchy cereal bar
Afternoon snack —piece of cheese
Dinner —chicken curry, spiced potato & peas, rice

In question 2 you are asked to analyse these data to find the cost of the protein and to check that she is eating enough of it.

= ② Copy this table in your notebook and complete it using the data in table 2 'Proteins in food' eaten by Kirsty Kellet
  (a) You can find the data for column (1) in table 2.
  (b) Data in column (3) is the mass in column (2) multiplied by the % protein content from table 2.
  (c) Data in column (4) is column (3) divided by column (2).

(1) Food eaten	(2) Mass of protein/g	(3) Cost of food /p	(4) Cost of protein (p/g)
Peanuts	2.0	5.25	
Cheese			
Totals			XXXXXX

Use your data to copy and complete the following sentences in your notebook.

There are many leaflets available advising people on healthy eating

= ③ Total cost of Kirsty's food for the day = _____ p.
− ④ The food eaten which costs the most is _____.
= ⑤ The food giving the *cheapest* protein per g is _____ at a cost of _____ p/g.
= ⑥ The food giving the most *expensive* protein per g is _____ at a cost of _____ p/g.
≡ ⑦ The *total* mass of protein eaten by Kirsty in the day is _____ g. Do you think that this is enough protein for her? We all need about 80 g of protein per day. If not, suggest the extra foods she might eat and give the mass required for each kind of food suggested.

Do we need to eat anything else?

We need
- energy from carbohydrates and fats
- proteins to build and repair our cells
- water and minerals (e.g. salt)
- roughage (e.g. husks in wholemeal bread).

But we also need minute quantities of *vitamins*. Without even 1 mg of some of these vitamins each day we could become ill.

You can read more about vitamins in chapter 21 (Book 2).

Table 1 Energy in some common foods

Food (fresh)	Joules per gram/ (J/g)	Cost per gram/ (p/g)
Lager	2200	0.15
Milk	2900	0.01
Potatoes	3800	0.02
Beef	7100	0.45
Bread	9700	0.12
Sugar	17 000	0.04
Chocolate	23 000	0.40
Butter	34 000	0.20

Table 2 Proteins in food eaten by Kirsty Kellet

Food	Protein content /%	Mass of food /g	Mass of protein /g	Cost of food/ (p/g)
Peanuts	28	7	2.0	0.75
Cheese	25	20	5.0	0.22
Chicken	25	20	5.0	0.20
Bacon	21	25	5.3	0.25
Fish	18	40	7.2	0.28
Oatmeal	12	10	1.2	0.15
Eggs	12	30	3.4	0.25
Bread	9	80	7.2	0.12
Crisps	6	25	1.5	0.60
Milk	3	25	0.8	0.01
Potatoes	2	50	1.0	0.02
Peas	2	10	0.2	0.04
Cereals	2	10	0.2	0.16

12 ENZYMES

Enzymes are proteins, but proteins with a difference! Enzymes are catalysts. They work with *organic* substances. There are many enzymes in our bodies.

Enzymes and change

All kinds of chemical reactions in living things are helped by enzymes. About 2000 enzymes have been found. In humans, enzymes work in muscles, in releasing energy for the body to move, and in moving chemicals to cells.

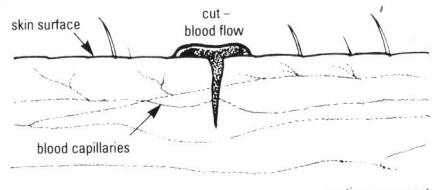
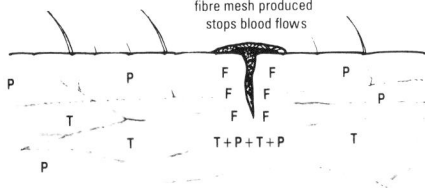
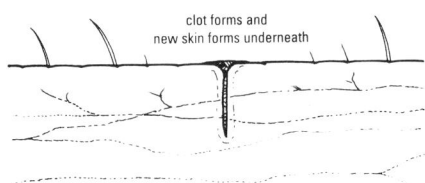

Figure 1 Clotting of blood

Clotting of blood

If we cut ourselves, blood flows out of the cut. The blood flows quickly at first, then slows down and forms a clot. Look at figure 1 on the 'Clotting of blood'. See how two enzymes 'P' and 'T' help the blood to clot.

= ① Using figure 1, explain how enzymes help blood to clot over a cut in the skin. What do you think would happen without enzymes when we had a cut?

Enzymes in digestion

We have a body temperature of 37 °C. This is quite a low temperature for chemical reactions to take place. The food we eat is broken down in about 6 hours using many enzymes. Without enzymes, digestion would take 15–20 years!

− ② Look at figure 2 on 'Enzymes in digestion'. Copy the headings of this table and complete it using figure 2.

Organ	Enzymes present
mouth stomach small intestine	

Naming enzymes

Most enzymes end in -ase and are named after the substance they act on and where they are produced.

- Enzymes which act on starches—amylases
- Enzymes which act on proteins—proteases
- Enzymes which act on fats—lipases

All sugars (carbohydrates) have their own enzyme which changes them into another type of carbohydrate.

- Enzyme maltase acts on maltose sugar to give glucose.
- Enzyme lactase acts on lactose sugar to give glucose and galactose.
- Enzyme sucrase acts on sucrose sugar to give glucose and fructose.

IT IS almost 500 years since Christopher Columbus "discovered" the pineapple, which he received in exchange for trinkets from Indians on the Caribbean island of Guadeloupe. Columbus tasted the fruit and instantly appreciated its commercial potential. He was also intrigued by its medicinal uses. The islanders drank pineapple juice as an aid to digestion and a cure for bellyache, particularly when feasting on meat; women used it as a cleansing agent to improve the texture of their skin.

NEW SCIENTIST 2 June 1988

Scientists now know pineapple contains a protease called bromelain. Fruit is still used today in skin care products

Eventually, all sugars, along with amino acids, fatty acids and glycerol are absorbed into the blood stream.

= ③ What does lipase do?
What does sucrase do?
List three enzymes which work on sugars.

Sensitive enzymes

Enzymes can only work if they are in the correct surroundings. The enzymes in our bodies work well around 40 °C. This is called the optimum (or best) temperature. The enzymes may be damaged at higher temperatures. They work much more slowly at lower temperatures.

Small amounts of poisons can destroy enzymes. Arsenic, strychnine and DDT in very small amounts cause serious damage. DDT is still used for killing insect pests in some countries although it is very dangerous.

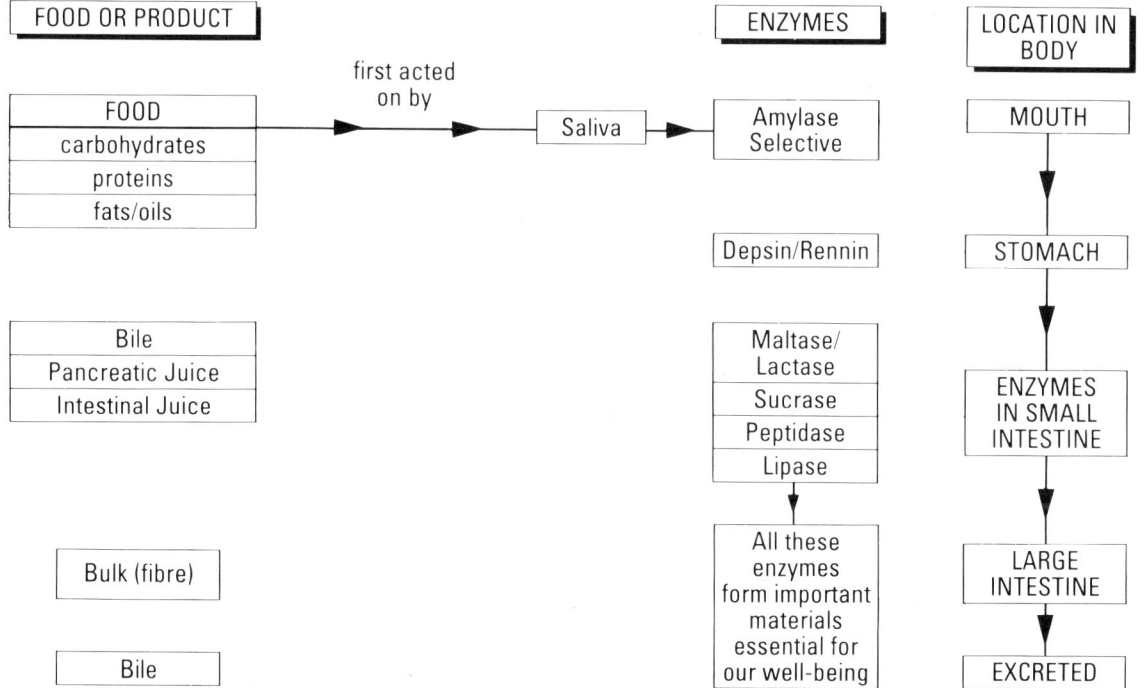

Figure 2 Enzymes in digestion

It is important to use the correct amount of enzyme for helping a chemical reaction. Only a tiny quantity is required. Too much enzyme can stop other enzymes from working.

Strong acids and alkalis are harmful to most enzymes. Most enzymes work best in a neutral solution (pH 7), but enzymes in the stomach work in a very acidic solution.

Large amounts of water are needed for enzymes to work well. Too little water can stop enzymes working at all.

Most enzymes only help one chemical change to occur.

≡ (4) Copy and complete this table using the section on 'Sensitive enzymes'.

Enzymes need	Enzymes cannot work when

Enzymes and locks

Enzyme molecules act like a 'lock'. The 'shapes' of their molecules exactly fit the shapes of the molecules on which they are reacting. In this way, each enzyme can bring about one (and only one) chemical change.

Look at figure 3.

Figure 3a shows 'models' of an enzyme molecule and a protein molecule. This protein molecule has four amino acid molecules of different 'shapes'. In 3b, the enzyme is reacting with two of the amino acids. See how the shapes of *only two* of the amino acid molecules fit the enzyme 'lock'.

Figure 3c shows the protein molecule split by the reaction with the enzyme. The two parts can go to other enzymes and be broken down further.

≡ (5) Look at the 'model' of a protein molecule in figure 4. Draw the enzyme molecule shapes so that the protein molecule can be split at A and B.

Could either of your enzyme shapes split the protein molecule at any other points? Explain how your answer also applies to real enzymes and proteins.

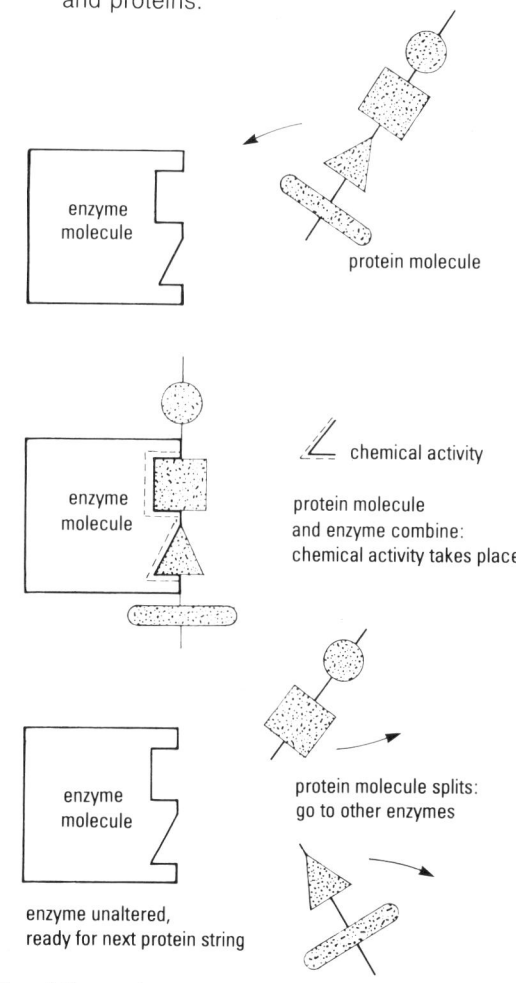

Figure 3 Enzyme shapes

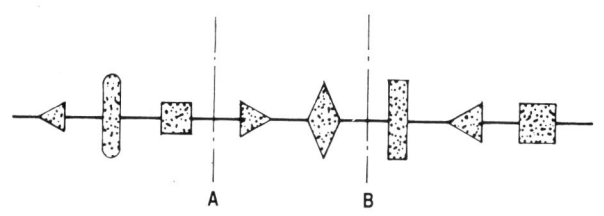

Figure 4 A protein molecule

13 USING ENZYMES

Enzymes have been used for thousands of years for making wine, bread and cheese. Recently, enzymes have been used for making medicines, detergents for washing and additives for petrol.

We all wear clothes and they have to be washed. Washing can be done in a lot of plain water, but it is very hard work. Automatic washing machines and detergents make life much easier. Some detergents contain enzymes.

In this chapter you can learn about enzymes and what they do to clothes.

Enzymes in detergents

Detergents in washing powders for the home are made from crude oil. Most washing powders contain *additives* which improve the effect of the detergent. Some additives just make the clothes look brighter. One group of additives **does** get clothes cleaner, often at a lower temperature than is usually used. These additives are enzymes.

When proteins, such as egg and blood, get on clothes they dry out to leave a stain. The stain is like a mesh which tightly links with fibres of the cloth. Ordinary detergents do not remove these stains easily. The washing water has to be heated almost to boiling point to remove stains. Such hot water often causes dyes to run and fibres to shrink.

Adding *protease enzymes* to a washing powder breaks down proteins into soluble chemicals. This allows the temperature of the wash to be as low as 40 °C. This saves energy because the water does not need to be heated as much.

The quantity of enzymes is important. Usually, about 1 mg of enzyme is used in 1 litre of washing water. So, adding enzymes seems a good idea!

Soon other enzymes will be added to detergents which will remove waxes, oils, fats, starches and sugars at low temperatures.

— ① Make a list of at least four advantages of adding enzymes to washing powders.

Figure 1 The addition of enzymes to washing powder now makes it easier for many people to clean their clothes

Facts on detergent enzymes

Enzymes today are extracted from cultures of bacteria, and these mainly act on proteins. Remember that other stains caused by fats or minerals will not be acted upon by protein enzymes.

Enzymes take a while to dissolve solid proteins, and for this reason, clothes have to be left to soak in a solution of the washing powder for several hours to make stain removal effective. They also act best at a warm temperature (about 40°C) and are destroyed at higher temperatures. Enzymes also work best in a definitive pH (acidity/alkalinity) of water—this varies with each enzyme. The pH of the washing powder will have been adjusted by the manufacturer—adding alkalis to the water will reduce its efficiency.

Wool and silk are fibres made from proteins and these may be affected by enzymes in washing powders; also the skin of our hands is protein, so wearing gloves is a good idea when washing with enzyme powder.

Problems with enzymes

Although enzymes give a cleaner wash, they do give problems. Some people working in detergent factories quickly developed skin rashes. Within weeks of new 'biological' powders being sold, some customers began to suffer with rashes too. The effect is called an *allergy* and can also occur with other things such as dust or pollen. You can read more about allergies in chapter 28 (Book 2).

One way of solving this problem is to surround each grain of enzyme with a soluble coating. In contact with water, the grains swell and burst, releasing the enzyme into the washing water. People should also be warned on the packet that it contains enzymes which can cause a rash. Some manufacturers advise that extra rinsing of the clothes is required.

= ② Describe a problem for some people in using washing powders containing enzymes.

Make up your own mind

Adding enzymes to washing powder makes them work better but can cause problems. Check the fact sheet on detergent enzymes and then answer these questions.

= ③ Look at the label from a washing powder packet in figure 1 (insert bottom right).

(a) Does it mention biological action, low temperature or all temperatures?

(b) Does it actually say that it contains enzymes?

(c) What wash temperatures do the manufacturers recommend?

(d) Does it give any precautions about using the powder? If so, what are they?

= ④ The normal human body temperature is 37 °C. Is there any connection between the temperature that enzymes work at in detergents and our body temperature? (**Hint**: check 'Sensitive enzymes' in chapter 12 (Book 2).

= ⑤ Write and draw an advert for a biological washing powder called 'Sudzyme'. You will have to make it clear that the powder may harm sensitive skins.

= ⑥ Write and draw another advert for a washing powder called 'Nozyme', that does not contain enzymes. Your advert has to explain why not.

Most clothes have labels similar to this, giving instructions on how to wash them

In some countries few people, if any, have washing machines

14 PHOTOSYNTHESIS

Photosynthesis

Plants which are green contain a green dye called *chlorophyll*. The chlorophyll is only found in very small areas of the leaf called *chloroplasts*.

So a plant needs chlorophyll, carbon dioxide, water and sunlight to make food. But what kind of food is a plant making? At first, *glucose* is formed and *oxygen* given off as a waste product. Glucose is a very simple carbohydrate molecule but this soon builds up into a larger *starch* molecule.

1. List the three factors which must be present for photosynthesis to occur in chloroplasts.

2. Here are the main words used in describing photosynthesis. Draw a flow diagram using all these words. Put each word in a box and use arrows to show the order in which photosynthesis occurs:

   Carbon dioxide, chlorophyll, glucose, oxygen, starch, sunlight, water.

Many musicians now use synthesizers to 'build up' complex sounds from simpler ones

Do you know what a synthesiser is? Perhaps you have watched pop groups using an electronic keyboard which blends sounds together and *builds them up* into a different sound. That's a synthesiser.

'Photos' means light and 'synthesis' means 'to build up' in the Greek language. Green plants use light energy to build up their food stores using carbon dioxide gas from the atmosphere and water from the soil.

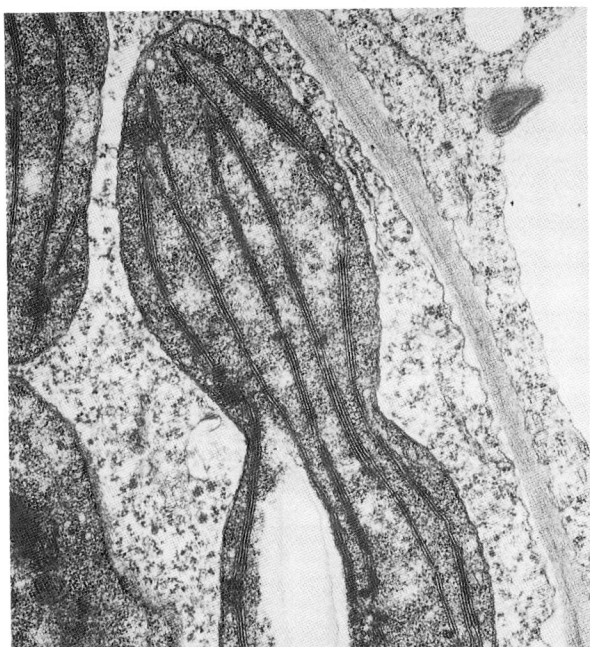

Chloroplasts are storage cells for chlorophyll. The photo shows a dividing chloroplast in the leaf of a pea plant

Did you know..........?

Roots, stems and leaves

Plants differ in size and shape but all plants have three main parts or **organs**

- stems or shoots
- roots
- leaves

- All three organs have a job to do. You have already found out that photosynthesis takes place in leaves. But leaves also give out or take in water vapour. This is called '**transpiration**'. The roots hold plants in the ground and take in water and dissolved food. Stems hold plants upright so that the leaves can obtain light for photosynthesis.

- In some plants, the organs have special shapes and may be very big or small. For example, the cactus plant has big swollen stems but leaves which are mere prickles. Pine trees have long narrow shiny leaves. These special shapes and sizes help the plant to survive in its particular environment.

- The shoots of a plant grow upwards towards the light and away from the Earth. Shoots are very sensitive to light and are attracted towards it. Perhaps you have noticed that indoor plants grow towards the window.

- Roots grow downwards away from the light and towards the Earth's centre. They are attracted by the pull of the Earth's gravity. But roots are also attracted by water and they can grow in any direction to find it. Sometimes roots even grow upwards towards the surface in their hunt for water.

- It does not matter which way up a seed is planted. If the root first grows upwards it will turn downwards. If the shoot faces downwards it will turn and begin to grow upwards.

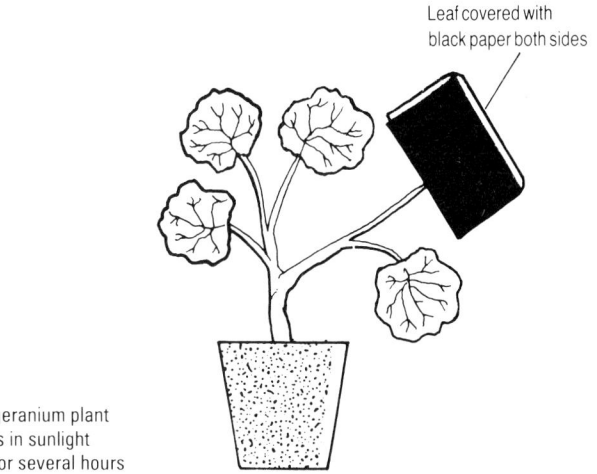

Figure 1 (a) Experiment to find out if light is needed for photosynthesis

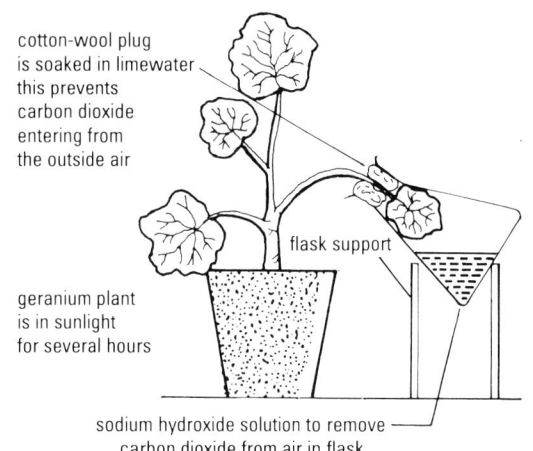

(b) Experiment to find out if carbon dioxide is needed for photosynthesis

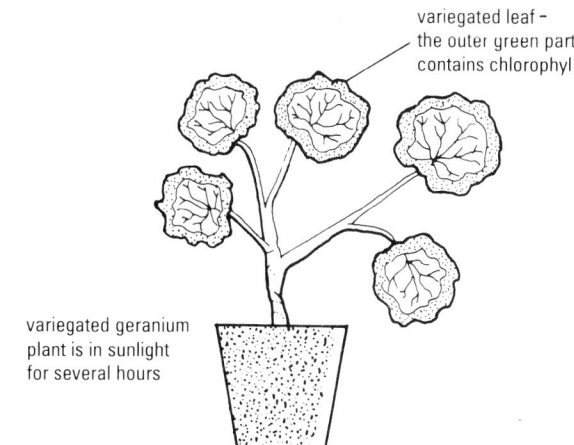

(c) Experiment to find out if chlorophyll is needed for photosynthesis

Three experiments on photosynthesis

Three geranium plants were placed in the dark for 48 hours. During this time, all the starch in their leaves would have been used up by the plants.

The three plants were then treated in different ways. Look at the three diagrams in figure 1. The treatments were:

Plant A   One leaf covered with black paper. No light could reach the leaf.

Plant B   One leaf inside a jar containing sodium hydroxide solution. No carbon dioxide could reach the leaf.

Plant C   A variegated leaf was chosen. Parts of the leaf were not green and contained no chlorophyll.

The plants were left on a sunny windowsill for 24 hours.

Preparing leaves for the starch test

A leaf from each plant under test was placed into boiling water to kill its cells. This stopped photosynthesis taking place.

The green colouring in the leaves was removed by placing the leaves in warmed ethanol (usually methylated spirits). The ethanol removes the chlorophyll.

Finally, the leaves were washed in water.

Testing for starch
When starch was found in any leaf, this proved that photosynthesis had taken place during the 24-hour test.

The test for starch was to place several drops of a special solution on each leaf. The solution contained a little iodine in potassium iodide solution.

Black patches on a leaf shows that *starch* is present.

Brown patches on a leaf shows that no *starch* is present.

= ③ Read through the last three sections and make a step-by-step list of instructions for setting up and testing plant A. Number each step and draw a diagram if this will help. Imagine that your instructions are for another student in your class who has not done the experiment and who has to do the experiment alone.

= ④ Copy and complete the following table for the experiment on each plant.

Plant	Treatment	Result of starch test	Explanation
A	leaf in dark		

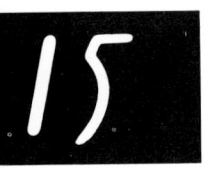

IMPROVING GREENHOUSES

Greenhouses are very popular for growing crops such as tomatoes and lettuce and for growing flowers. It is much easier to control the temperature, watering and feeding of crops in a greenhouse than in the open air. Pests and diseases are easier to control in greenhouses and plants can be protected from birds and small mammals.

The higher temperature in greenhouses helps the growth of crops. If you are not sure how a greenhouse 'collects' and saves energy from the Sun, read 'What is the greenhouse effect?' in chapter 35 (Book 2).

This chapter is about two new ways of improving greenhouses.

Helping plants to grow

A plant grows by making sugars in special cells in its leaves by a process called *photosynthesis*. For this process to occur, plants need sunlight, water and carbon dioxide. Warm temperatures also help growth.

In Great Britain, even in summer, there is not a lot of sunshine. The growth of plants is usually limited by the amount of light energy reaching them. In the next section, you can study some new designs of greenhouses which collect more light.

Supplying water for photosynthesis is no problem in Great Britain! But the supply of carbon dioxide is limited to the 0.03% in air. In the final section, you can study the effect on plant growth of increasing carbon dioxide in the air.

− (1) Light, heat, water and carbon dioxide are required for plants to grow. List at least *two* other things that plants need for growth. It may help you to check chapter 14 (Book 2) and chapter 18 (Book 2).

Changing the shape of greenhouses

Figure 1a shows a section through an ordinary greenhouse. This section is *symmetrical*. It has the same angle of roof on both sides. An *asymmetrical* greenhouse section is shown in figure 1b. Here, glass sheets at several angles combine to form a roof. This can increase the amount of light falling on plant leaves compared with ordinary greenhouses.

Natural light in ordinary greenhouses is only 50–60% of that outside. And in winter in Great Britain, there is no more than 30% or even 25% of the light required for good plant growth.

Look at table 1 which shows the results of an experiment using asymmetric and symmetric greenhouses growing the same plants.

= (2) (a) What was the average increase in night temperature for the asymmetric greenhouse when compared to the symmetric greenhouse, over the three test periods?

(b) What was the average increase in day temperature for the asymmetric greenhouse?

= (3) What was the difference in total plant mass for each greenhouse during the three test periods?

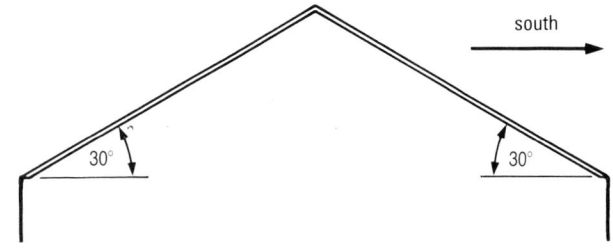

Figure 1 (a) A symmetric greenhouse

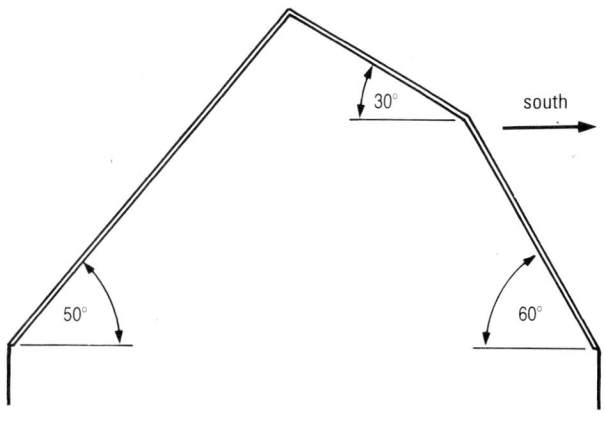

(b) An asymmetric greenhouse

Table 1

Test period	Average daily hours of sun	Average night temperature		Average day temperature		Total plant mass/g	
		A	S	A	S	A	S
6 Dec–15 Jan	1.4	15 °C	14 °C	16 °C	15 °C	2469	2217
17 Jan–30 Jan	2.8	16 °C	15 °C	17 °C	16 °C	3556	2728
2 Feb–24 Feb	3.3	16 °C	15 °C	18 °C	16 °C	10 009	9205

A = asymmetric greenhouse; S = symmetric greenhouse.

A more recent design is the *vertical south roof greenhouse*. In winter, in northern latitudes, the winter sun is low. Any low angle light striking the shallow sloping roof of the symmetric greenhouse will be reflected. Look at figure 2a.

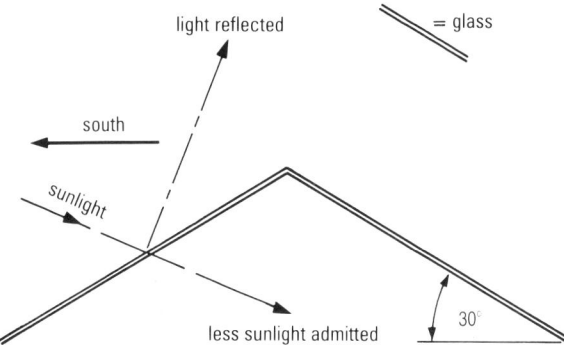

Figure 2 (a) A conventional greenhouse roof

If the south slope could be replaced by a vertical glass wall, more available light (and heat rays) would enter the greenhouse. This would be a big help in winter when they are most needed. Figure 2b shows how this works.

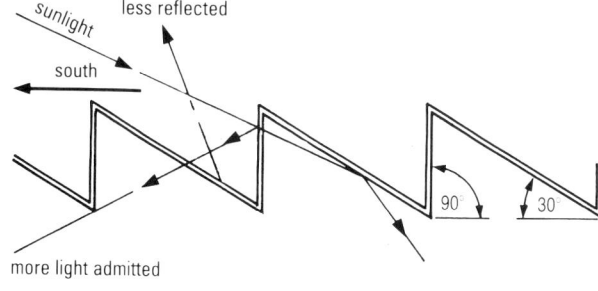

(b) A vertical south greenhouse roof

≡ (4) Using a protractor, ruler and pencil, copy in your notebook the greenhouse roof shape in figure 2b. Mark point X on your drawing. One ray of sunlight is shown in figure 2b. On your drawing, show rays reaching X at angles of 10°, 20° and 30° *above* the horizontal. Draw what happens to the rays after reaching X. Use your drawing to help you to explain *why* this kind of greenhouse helps to increase the light inside.

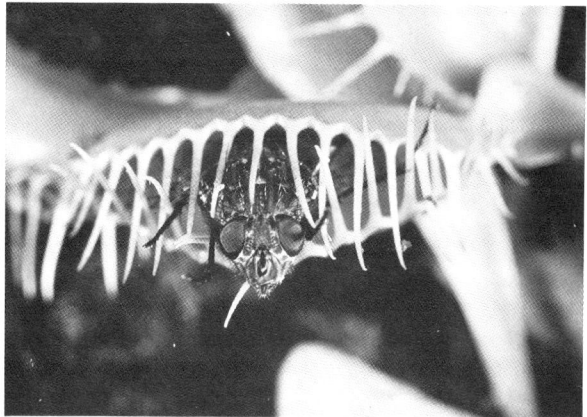

Some plants, such as 'flytraps' will only grow (and eat!) in the warm conditions of a greenhouse

Increasing carbon dioxide in air

Carbon dioxide gas is needed for photosynthesis. But carbon dioxide makes up only 0.03% of air. The rate of photosynthesis in plants would be higher if there were more carbon dioxide in the air. Increasing the concentration up to 1% in greenhouses brings about a big increase in crop growth.

Look at figure 3 showing how the rate of photosynthesis increases with carbon dioxide concentration.

= (5) Using figure 3, find the rate of photosynthesis in
(a) air,
(b) air with a carbon dioxide concentration of 0.06%.
Compare your two answers and explain the importance of the difference to people who grow crops in greenhouses.

Increasing the rate of photosynthesis increases plant growth. So anything which can do this, or a combination of things, will benefit plants. Figure 4 shows how the rate of photosynthesis varies with carbon dioxide concentration, light strength (energy) and temperature.

= (6) Use figure 4 to find the conditions which allow plants to carry out photosynthesis most quickly. List your values of temperature, carbon dioxide concentration and light strength.

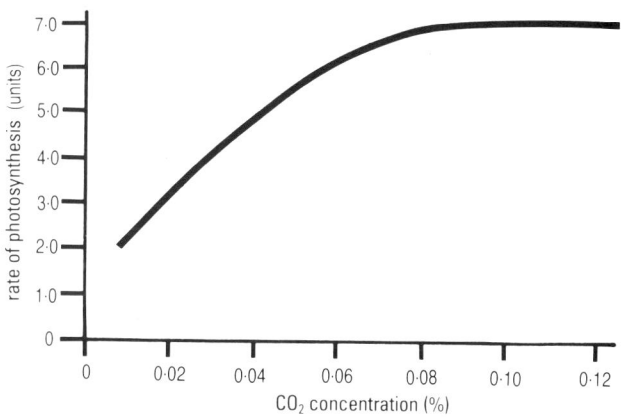

Figure 3 Rate of photosynthesis vs. CO_2 concentration

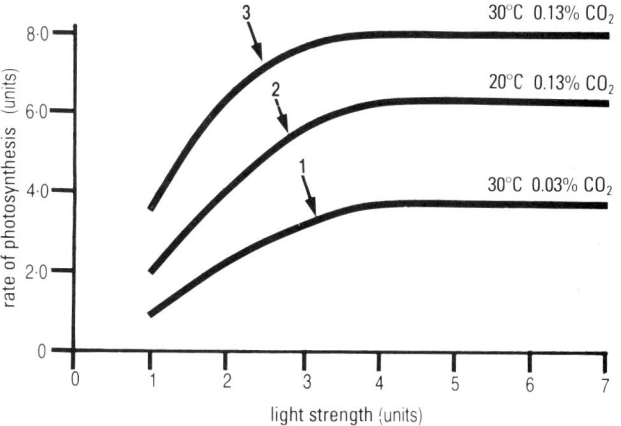

Figure 4 Rate of photosynthesis vs. light strength

16 FERTILIZERS AND NITROGEN

Harvesting wheat in Berkshire

We all need to eat! And there are more mouths to feed every year! Look at figure 1 showing the increase in world population since 1900. How can farmers produce more food each year to feed us all?

Farmers now use better machines, pesticides, better strains of plants for crops and huge quantities of fertilizers.

This chapter is about the need for fertilizers and how they help crops to grow better. Chapter 17 (Book 2) is about some of the artificial fertilizers and their effect on crops.

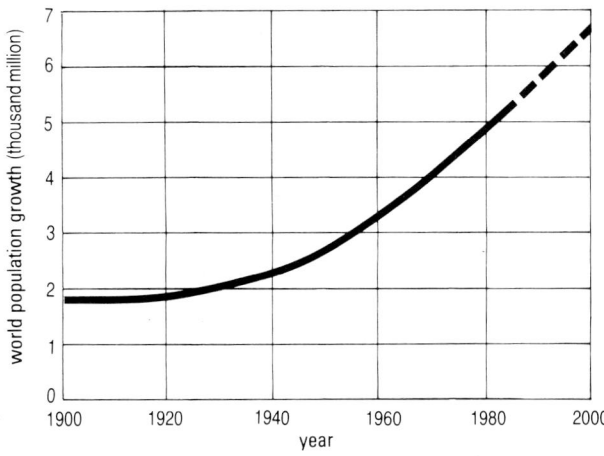

Figure 1 Increase in world population growth since 1900

Organic fertilizers

Since ancient times, people have known that animal manures help plants to grow. Gardeners still look for horse and pig manure. They can often collect it free of charge if they can stand the smell!

Some gardeners have a compost heap. They add grass cuttings from the lawn, kitchen waste and weeds. After a few months, bacteria break these down. The brown flaky compost is then spread on the garden.

Manures and compost are called 'organic' or 'natural' fertilizers.

Did you know..........?

- The world population by the year 2025 is likely to be 8000 million.

- Approximately 40 000 people die each DAY because of diseases related to lack of proper food.

- The world production of fertilisers in 1985 was 135 million tonnes. Half as much again will be required to produce food for the year 2000.

- Many fertilisers contain nitrates and these dissolve in water most easily.

Here the farmer is using nitrogen to feed his winter wheat

Inorganic fertilizers

Inorganic fertilizers are made in chemical factories. They increase the yield of crops much more than organic fertilizers when the same mass is used. They also work more quickly.

Why are fertilizers needed?

A natural ecosystem, such as an old woodland, does not need fertilizers. Animals eat plants and return most of the contents to the land in faeces and urine.

When plants and animals die, their remains are returned to the land.

But on farmed land, many chemicals from the soil remain in the plants when they are harvested. So these chemicals are lost to the soil. Fertilizers are spread on the land to replace them. Table 1 shows chemical elements needed by plants. Chemical compounds containing these elements are spread on the land in fertilizers.

Table 1 Chemical elements needed by plants

Large amounts	Small amounts
Nitrogen (N)	Manganese (Mn)
Phosphorus (P)	Zinc (Zn)
Potassium (K)	Copper (Cu)
Calcium (Ca)	Boron (B)
Magnesium (Mg)	Molybdenum (Mo)
Sulphur (S)	Chlorine (Cl)
Iron (Fe)	

— ① Explain why farmed land needs fertilizers.

Nitrogen and nitrates

Top of the list in table 1 is nitrogen. Plants need nitrogen to make the green substance *chlorophyll* used in *photosynthesis*. (See Chapter 14 (Book 2)). Leaves go yellow if the plant cannot obtain enough nitrogen. But 78% of the air is nitrogen! Why can plants not take it in? Sadly plants cannot use nitrogen from the air. They must take it in through their roots in nitrogen compounds called *nitrates*.

— ② Why are nitrates spread on farm land when plenty of nitrogen is in the air?

Look at figure 2 showing how fertilizers help plants to obtain nitrogen. This flow diagram is called the nitrogen cycle. The ammonium salts in the soil are compounds of ammonia gas (NH_3) which contains nitrogen atoms. (You may have smelled ammonia from wet nappies!)

= ③ Use figure 2 to draw a flow diagram with these words in boxes:

ammonium salts in the soil, death and decay, growing plants, nitrates in the soil.

Use your flow diagram to explain why grass cuttings put on a compost heap can help plants to grow. (**Hint:** Read again the paragraph 'Organic fertilizers').

= ④ Use figure 2 to draw a flow diagram with these words in boxes:

artificial fertilizers, growing plants, nitrates in the soil, nitrogen in the air.

Use your flow diagram to explain how artificial fertilizers help plants to take in nitrogen.

= ⑤ Use figure 2 to draw a flow diagram with these words in boxes:

ammonium salts in the soil, animals, death and decay, growing plants, manure, nitrates in the soil

Use your flow diagram to explain

(a) why spreading pig manure on a garden can help plants to grow.
(b) why a natural wood with plenty of animal life, does not need artificial fertilizers.

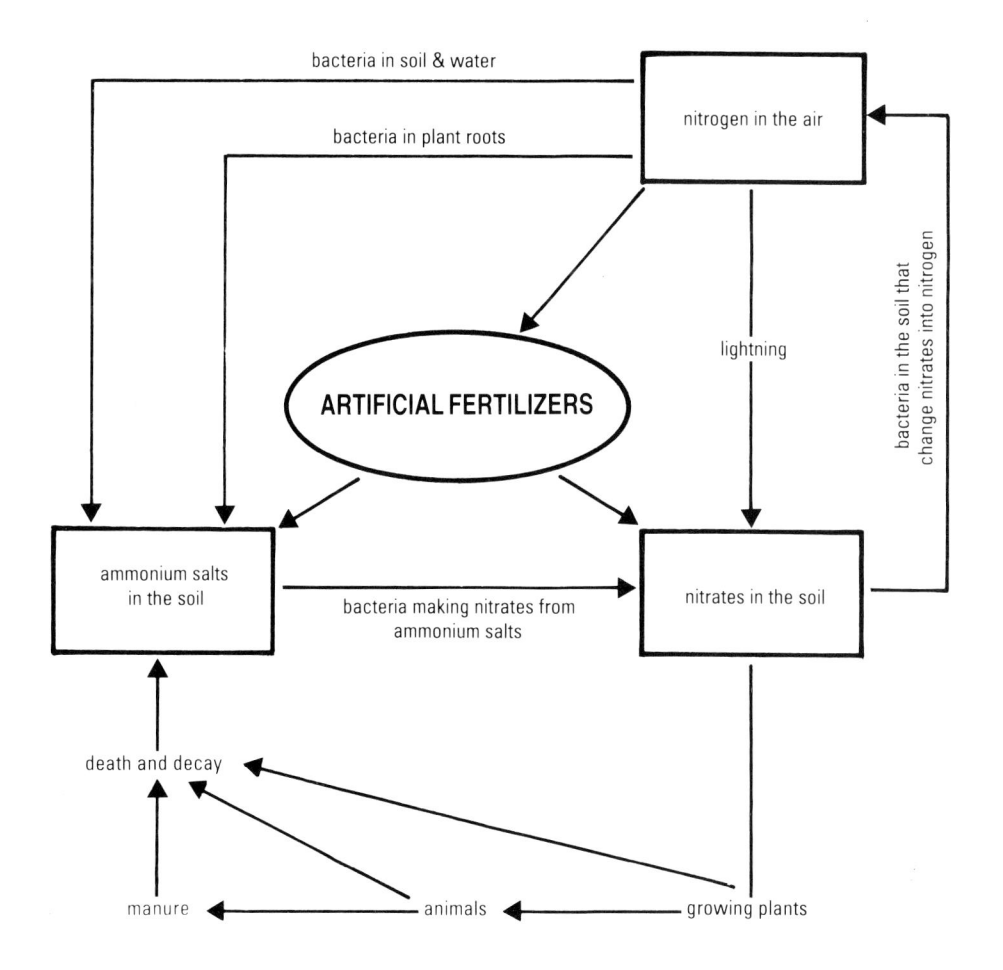

Figure 2 The nitrogen cycle

17. FERTILIZERS AND THE 'GREEN REVOLUTION'

If you do not know much about fertilizers and why they are used, you should read chapter 16 (Book 2) before reading this chapter.

In this chapter, you can study how the yield of crops can be increased by using artificial fertilizers. This yield is so great that the name 'green revolution' has been given to describe the farmers' success.

Natural or artificial fertilizers?

Natural, or organic fertilizers are made from manure or decaying plants. Before they act on crops, the manure or decaying plants must be broken down into substances which plants can take in through their roots. Artificial fertilizers work quickly because plants can take in chemicals in the fertilizers as soon as they dissolve in water.

Some common artificial fertilizers

Plants need nitrogen (N) and phosphorus (P) for healthy growth. Most artificial fertilizers contain each element in a chemical compound which easily dissolves in water. Another important element for plant growth in potassium (K).

A very popular fertilizer made by many companies contains nitrogen (N), phosphorus (P) and potassium (K) in chemical compounds. It is called 'NPK fertilizer'. The photograph shows one brand of NPK fertilizer.

How good are artificial fertilizers?

Fertilizers are tested on crops by the manufacturers. They can use the results to try and persuade farmers to buy their products. The farmers need to know how much of the fertilizers to spread on their crops. Farmers must also work out if the cost of the fertilizer will be paid for out of the extra crop yields. Here are the results of some tests.

Nitrogen fertilizers
Figure 1 shows the yield of wheat when different quantities of nitrogen fertilizers are spread. The area of the test wheat was 1 hectare, which is about the size of a football pitch.

= ① (a) What is the yield of wheat without fertilizer?

(b) What is the yield of wheat for 100 kg of fertilizer?

(c) How many tonnes *extra* of wheat does the farmer gain over using no fertilizer? What is the percentage gain due to using fertilizer?

② Imagine that Farmer Brown plants wheat in a field of 1 hectare. He then has to decide whether to spread fertilizer which costs £20 for 100 kg. He expects to be able to sell his grain for £40 per tonne. Use your answer to question 1 to work out if he should spread the fertilizer. What would his profit or loss be if he did?

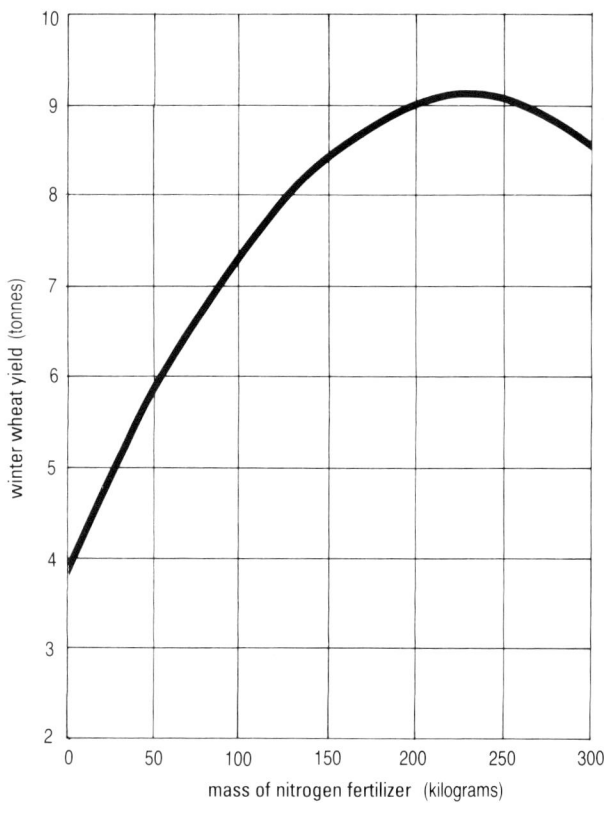

Figure 1 The effect of a nitrogen-containing fertilizer

= ③ Describe what happens to the crop yield if more than 150 kg of fertilizer is spread. Then explain

(a) why the farmer might not want to spread more than 150 kg.

(b) why the farmer would never spread more than 230 kg.

= ④ Find out from chapter 16 (Book 2) why nitrogen fertilizer helps crops to grow and, using information from both chapter 16 (Book 2) and this chapter how lack of enough nitrogen can damage plants. Now write an advert for a nitrogen fertilizer.

Phosphorus fertilizers
Table 1 gives data on the yield of barley and potatoes when using a phosphorus fertilizer. The area of the test was 1 hectare.

5 Which crop gains most from using the phosphorus fertilizer? Give your reasons. (Try to use in your answer the *percentage gain* in yield for both crops for 14 kg of fertilizer).

6 Write down the advice you would give to a farmer on how much phosphorus fertilizer to use per hectare on potatoes. Explain why he should not expect to increase his yield by spreading more and more fertilizer.

NPK fertilizer

Table 2 shows data on crop yields for wheat and potatoes when three fertilizers are used. The first three columns show the mass of nitrogen, phosphorus and potassium in each fertilizer. The first row shows yields *without* using any fertilizer. NPK fertilizer is number 3.

7 Using table 2 explain why fertilizer 2 is better used on potatoes than wheat. (Try to use in your answer the percentage gain in yield for both the crops).

8 Prepare an advert for NPK fertilizer (fertilizer 3) using *bar charts*, to show how much better it is than fertilizers 1 and 2. Criticize your advert for *not* mentioning possible dangers, hiding other facts, ignoring the high price of fertilizers or other reasons.

Table 1 Effect of phosphorus fertilizer

Phosphorus fertilizer/kg hectare	Yield/tonnes hectare	
	Barley	Potatoes
0	2.03	13
14	2.66	29
28	2.98	32
56	3.49	32

Table 2 Effect of different fertilizers on crop yields

Fertilizer	Mass of fertilizer per hectare kg/hectare			Crop yield tonnes/hectare	
	Nitrogen	Phosphorus	Potassium	Wheat	Potatoes
None	0	0	0	1.69	8.47
1	96	0	0	3.68	8.30
2	0	77	107	2.04	16.63
3	96	77	107	6.60	38.57

Source: Rothamsted Experimental Station.

Increasing numbers of people are now turning to organically grown produce

What's bad about artificial fertilizers?

Nitrates are very soluble in water and are easily washed into streams by rainfall. Some scientists think that there may be a link between nitrates in drinking water and stomach cancer. There may also be a link between nitrates and a fatal disease in babies called blue-baby syndrome.

In some lakes near farmland, a kind of reed has begun to take over. There could be a link between this growth and compounds containing nitrogen and phosphorus from fertilizers. Sadly, the spread of the weed can cause other plants and animals to die.

Some scientists believe that artificical fertilizers may eventually destroy soil.

So the 'green revolution' may not have a happy ending.

Farmer Brown and Farmer White

Farmer Brown 'You know, I'm an NPK fertilizer farmer! I spend a lot on NPK every year but my profit is huge. How about you George?'

Farmer White 'I've stopped using artificial fertilizers, Adam. I'm worried about polluting the streams running down to the drinking water reservoir. I only use farmyard manure!'

Farmer Brown 'I don't believe those tales about pollution. Nobody has *proved* that fertilizers do pollute. Anyway, in another 5 years I'll have made enough cash to retire. Somebody else can worry about pollution!'

Farmer White 'Perhaps nobody *has* proved yet that fertilizers do *cause* pollution, but *I think* that they do. I prefer to make a smaller profit and be sure that I'm not polluting the countryside. And people are now asking me if my crops are "organically" or "naturally" grown. It's good to be able to say "yes".'

Farmer Brown 'Maybe, but most people don't care *how* crops are grown. They just buy the cheapest!'

9 Copy and complete this table.

Farmer Brown's reasons for using NPK	Farmer White's response

If you were a farmer would you do what Farmer Brown does or what Farmer White does? Give your reasons.

18 GROWING YOUR OWN!

All living things must eat! Most people buy food from shops or supermarkets. But what would happen if there was no food available in the shops?

During World War II (1939–1945) imported food was scarce and the government asked people to dig up their gardens. It was called a 'Dig for Victory' campaign. Many people found that growing vegetables was easy and that gardening could be profitable.

Nowadays, more people are turning to home-produced food, if they have a garden which is large enough. A gardener who can produce enough food for himself and his family, with a bit left over could sell the surplus to buy seed and fertilizer for the next growing season.

This chapter is about growing some popular vegetables and their cost.

Planning the garden

Look at table 1. This lists data on eight popular vegetables. The table shows how much the Fletcher family of four eats per year, the cost in the shops and the mass in kilogrammes of each vegetable which can be produced per square metre of garden.

(1) Write out a table with these headings:

Crop	Mass eaten per year by family of 4/kg	Yield per m² of garden/kg	Area required/m²
	⋮	⋮	⋮

Fill in your table with data from table 1 and work out the area required in square metres for each vegetable. What is the *total area* required for all the vegetables?

Table 1

Crop	Mass eaten per year by family of 4 /kg	Yield per m² of garden /kg	Shop cost per kg /p
Cauliflower	27	4.5	40
Potatoes	200	2.5	30
Aubergines	30	1.5	25
Courgettes	15	1.0	120
Peas	30	0.75	40
Carrots	18	3.0	20
Onions	9	1.5	30
Runner beans	8	0.8	40

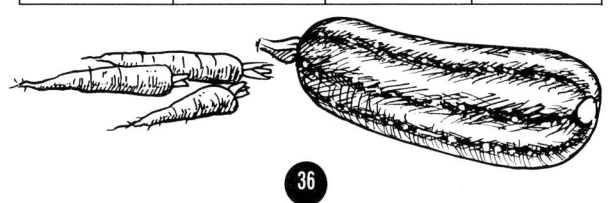

January: order vegetable seeds and potato tubers for planting: use (from previous year's crop), onions, carrots, potatoes. The vegetable garden needs to be planned now.

February: use carrots and onions; set out potatoes in trays, ready for planting in April/May.

March: use carrots and onions, sow onions and peas.

April: use carrots and onions, sow carrots, cauliflowers, more peas and aubergines. Plant early/main crop potatoes, stake peas.

May: use onions and sow runner beans and courgettes. Plant late potatoes, thin out carrots and onions. Stake peas and runner beans. Mound up early and main crop potatoes.

June: gather peas and thin out carrots. Stake runner beans.

July: thin out carrots and water runner beans.

August: gather runner beans, cut and protect cauliflowers. Pull carrots and onions, lift early potatoes.

September: gather runner beans, lift potatoes for storing.

October: gather last runner beans, lift potatoes for storing.

November: use carrots, onions and potatoes.

December: use carrots, onions and potatoes.

Growing your vegetables

Look at table 2. You will see that each vegetable needs a different time to grow from seed into a mature plant. The best times to sow also vary.

Table 2

Crop	When to sow	Harvest
Courgettes	May	September
Carrots	May	September
Cauliflower	previous September	November
Onions	previous August	August
Aubergines	February	January
Peas	April	September
Potatoes	April	October
Runner Beans	June	August

= ② Copy this table and fill in the vegetables which need to be
  (a) sown or,
  (b) harvested during each month.

Month	Vegetable sown	Vegetable harvested
January		
February		
March		
April		
May		
June		
July		
August		
September		
October		
November		
December		

Counting the cost

If the Fletcher family buy their vegetables the total cost per year can be calculated from table 1. If they choose to grow their own vegetables, they will need to pay for seeds, fertilizers and, perhaps, the cost of using the land.

Cost of seed

Seed for different vegetables costs different amounts. The total cost for the family was £18.

Fertilizer

Fertilizer cost the family £1 for each 3 kg bag. Each bag treats 20 m² soil.

= ③ Calculate the cost of fertilizer per year. (You need the total area of garden calculated in question 1).

= ④ Calculate the total cost of seed and fertilizer.

= ⑤ Use the data in table 1 to calculate the total cost of buying all the vegetables. Make up a table with headings like this:

Crop	Cost per kg /£	cost per year /£

Compare your answer with the cost of seed and fertilizer calculated in question 4. How much does the Fletcher family save by growing their own?

= ⑥ Look carefully at the cost of buying *each* vegetable. Which vegetable costs the most during a year?

Crop rotation

Gardeners must be careful in their planning not to grow the same crop on the same soil year after year. Each crop removes various nutrients from the soil. Nutrients are chemicals which help plants to grow. When the crop is harvested, these nutrients are often removed in the crop itself and in the rest of the plant.

Fertilizers can be used to replace nutrients but they cost money and usually do not help a crop to give as good a yield year after year. For example, potatoes rarely grow as well when planted in the same soil each year.

= ⑦ Here are some suggestions which the neighbours made to the Fletchers. For each, give your views on whether you think the advice is good. Give reasons for your answers.

FILL UP YOUR GARDEN EVERY YEAR WITH **POTATOES**. YOU WILL SAVE LOTS OF MONEY **AND** HAVE SOME POTATOES LEFT OVER TO SELL TO THE NEIGHBOURS.

DON'T GROW **RUNNER BEANS**. THEY TAKE UP TOO MUCH SPACE.

DIVIDE YOUR GARDEN INTO **THREE**. PLANT **POTATOES** IN ONE THIRD, **CARROTS** IN ANOTHER AND **CAULIFLOWER** IN THE REST. SWAP THE CROPS AROUND EACH YEAR.

19 SUGAR FROM THE GROUND

Sugar cane

Think of grass plants growing in a garden or by a road side and then think of that grass being 5–7 metres high! You will then have some idea of how a sugar cane plant looks.

Sugar cane belongs to the grass family and is easy to grow. It needs a well-drained soil that is rich and deep. It needs a hot, moist climate with a rainfall of about 150 cm per year.

Sugar cane uses a lot of minerals in the soil so fertilizers must be added to the soil. Fertilizers containing nitrates, potash and phosphates are used. (You can find out more about fertilizers in chapter 16 (Book 2) and chapter 17 (Book 2).)

The sugar yield from sugar cane is about 125 tonnes per hectare. (1 hectare is about the area of a football pitch). The yield depends on the climate, the water supply and the preparation of the soil.

Cane sugar production

Look at figure 1, showing the refining of cane sugar. Sugar cane must go through the crushers within 2 days of cutting. If left any longer, the sugar content drops and it becomes useless for refining. Cane growers plant the young shoots at different times so harvesting is 'staggered'. In this way, the sugar can be processed quickly.

The sap is boiled (4) to produce crude liquid brown sugar. This liquid sugar is called *molasses*. The next stages have to be carried out quickly to produce white sugar before fermentation begins. Fermentation is possible because of yeasts in the raw cane. The yeasts break down and destroy sugar producing ethanol (alcohol) and carbon dioxide gas. This process is used in brewing wine and beer.

In step (6), the syrup is concentrated by boiling and then filtered (9 and 10) leaving white crystal sugar.

World sugar production from cane is about 40 million tonnes per year. The main growing areas are Cuba, Brazil and India.

— ① Why do sugar cane growers plant young shoots at different times?

— ② Why is crude brown sugar quickly purified to produce white sugar?

Do you eat sweets? Nearly everyone does and most people like sugar in tea and coffee. In Great Britain we eat 1 kg of sugar per head per week!

For thousands of years, people have looked for ways to sweeten food and drink. The most obvious source of sweetness was honey. But bees have to collect pollen from flowers to make honey. As flowers only bloom for part of the year, the yield of honey is poor.

Then people discovered plants that contain sugar such as *sugar cane*. In more recent years, the *sugar beet* has been produced and can match the yield of sugar cane.

In this chapter, you can learn about the production of sugar from sugar cane and sugar beet.

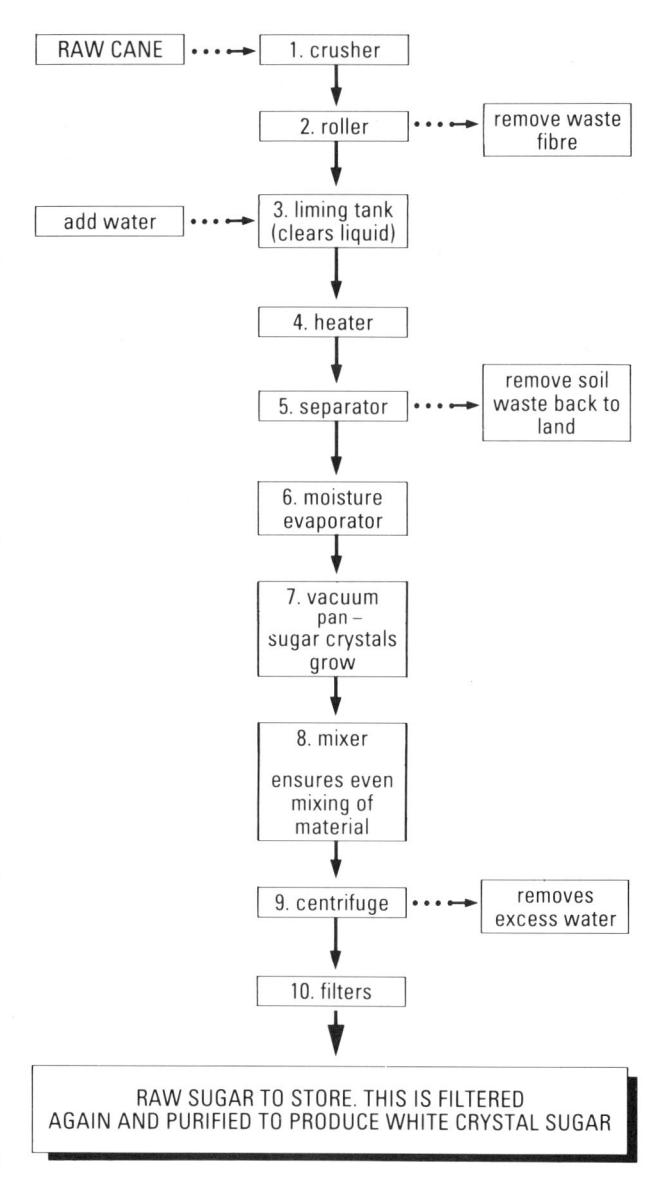

Figure 1 Flow diagram for refining cane sugar

RAW CANE → 1. crusher
↓
2. roller ···→ remove waste fibre
↓
add water ···→ 3. liming tank (clears liquid)
↓
4. heater
↓
5. separator ···→ remove soil waste back to land
↓
6. moisture evaporator
↓
7. vacuum pan – sugar crystals grow
↓
8. mixer ensures even mixing of material
↓
9. centrifuge ···→ removes excess water
↓
10. filters
↓
RAW SUGAR TO STORE. THIS IS FILTERED AGAIN AND PURIFIED TO PRODUCE WHITE CRYSTAL SUGAR

Sugar beet

Sugar beet

This plant is a relation of the mangold (see the photo). It has been specially bred from a natural plant called the sea-beet. Plant breeders in France and Germany selected and cross-bred beetroots until a plant containing 16% sugar was developed. Sugar beet now gives a yield of about 5 tonnes per hectare. Sugar beet plants need a fertile soil and warm summers. Potash has to be present in the soil, as this helps to increase the sugar content. The plant has deep roots and so can obtain water from below most other plant roots. This is important, because each plant needs about 150 litres in its life. Countries with a rainfall of greater than 50 cm per year will provide this.

Beet sugar production

After harvesting (called the 'campaign') the roots are taken to the processing factory, where they are cleaned and shredded. This material is boiled and centrifuged. The resulting 'raw juice' is further refined by adding calcium oxide to clear it. The calcium oxide is later removed by adding carbon dioxide. Further boiling renders the mixture down to white crystalline sugar. If brown sugar is required, caramel is added. About 3 tonnes of refined sugar can be made from 15 tonnes of beet plants.

(3) Look at figure 1 again. Using the information above, draw a flow diagram for the beet sugar process.

(4) Draw two columns; one for sugar cane, the other for sugar beet. On one side list the following: type of plant, rainfall per year, climate, soil type, fertilizers needed, crop yield per hectare and sugar gained from the crop yield. Complete the two columns.

(5) Use your table from question 4 to answer this question. Why is it better to grow sugar beet than sugar cane in England?

Sugar economics

The harvesting of sugar beet is done with expensive machinery. The roots are hardly touched by hand.

Sugar cane is best harvested by hand. So many people are needed to harvest sugar cane. For sugar cane companies to make money, they must have many workers who have no choice but to accept low wages.

In Great Britain, wages are high but machines can quickly harvest sugar beet. In India, wages are much lower and many people can be employed on sugar cane harvesting.

At present, Great Britain grows sugar beet and also imports sugar from sugar cane.

(6) Explain how Great Britain can produce sugar more cheaply than importing it from India.

(7) Here are two views on sugar cane.

(A) 'We should grow more sugar beet in Great Britain and stop importing sugar from India. This would create more jobs in Great Britain and reduce the money we spend on imports.'

(B) 'We should stop growing sugar beet in Great Britain and import sugar from India. Thousands of people in India depend on sugar production to live. Without these jobs they may not be able to earn a wage.'

State which of these views you support and give your reasons. (If you have a different view write this down). Then write a letter which you could send to your MP asking for your view to be put before Parliament. You need to state your view clearly and to give about three points supporting it.

***

Did you know.........?

- About a quarter of our calorie intake is supplied by white sugar, but they are 'empty' calories, having no minerals, vitamins or fibre.
- You would not call sugar an addictive drug, but it seems the more we have, the more we want.
- Sugar is needed, but in small quantities; a little will do you no harm, but some sugars are better for you than others. These are the different types:
- **White** or **Refined** sugar is more or less pure sucrose, with no fibre, vitamins or minerals. This is the most-used sugar.
- **Demerara** sugar comes in the form of large, sticky golden brown crystals and contains small amounts of B-group vitamins, which help us digest it, and minerals, such as calcium and potassium. (London Demerara or soft brown sugar is coloured white sugar)
- **Barbados** or **Muscovado** sugar can be pale or dark brown fine-grained crystals. This sugar is not as refined as Demerara and so has a higher vitamin and mineral content. It has quite a strong flavour. Muscavado means 'from the bottom of the pan'.
- **Molasses** or **Blackstrap** sugar is the least-refined of the sugars. It is very dark and sticky and contains traces of proteins, minerals and B-group vitamins. It also has only ⅕ of the calories of white sugar.
- **Honey** consists of 75% fructose sugar, which 'is considered to be better for you tha sucrose' Honey has A, C and B-group vitamins and a wide range of minerals. Energy provided by honey lasts longer than that provided by ordinary sugars. It also contains fewer calories.

20 ADDITIVES: ARE THEY IN OR OUT?

The label on the instant dessert packet boasts 'NO ARTIFICIAL COLOURS OR PRESERVATIVES'. Why is it important that some things are not in food whilst other things are added? Whatever the reason, you can bet that the manufacturers think it will make you buy their products. Otherwise they would not advertise it! Nowadays, consumers are more aware than ever before that what goes into food or what is left out is important to their health. If you want to know more about how food affects your health read chapter 22 (Book 2). To learn more about vitamins, read chapter 21 (Book 2).

Food additives

Nowadays we can buy a large range of foods from the supermarket. This is possible because of the mass production of food by the food industry. Chemicals are added to keep it fresh long enough to reach supermarkets and also to make it look appealing to the consumer (that's you). These are called food additives. Some additives are naturally occurring chemicals but most are made artificially.

Food additives; E's by gum!

The European Economic Community (EEC or 'Common Market') has made it a law that all European countries must label food additives with the same code; the letter 'E' followed by a number which identifies the chemical added. All food labels should show the contents as a list of 'E' numbers. The only trouble is that you have to look up a book to find out what each 'E' number stands for!

The Memo Pad gives a few examples of the types of additives which are put into our food. Beside each one there is the range of 'E' numbers which belong to that type of additive. Notice that none of them is of any use as a food source; they are 'non foods'.

— (1) Make a table like this

Type of food additive	Range of E numbers	Additives and numbers in chicken casserole mix

Complete the first two columns using the data below. Then check the food additives in the chicken casserole mix in figure 2 and write their numbers and names by your list of types.

INSTANT DESSERT TOPPING

Sugar *** Salt

Modified Starch Used as thickener. An umbrella term for 18 substances not defined by 'E' numbers.
Effects on Health No suggestion that they are harmful.

E477 Propane-1, 2-Diol Esters of Fatty Acids Used to emulsify or stabilise.
Effects on Health No known health risk.

Flavourings
Effects on Health Debatable, as no information is available. Many substances in this category are artificially synthesised; safety cannot be assumed.

E110 Sunset Yellow FCF Gives yellow colouring to product.
Effects on Health One of the azo-dye family which is recommended to be excluded from the diets of hyperactive children. Adults may have an allergic reaction with symptoms of skin rash, swollen blood vessels and gastric problems, especially if aspirin sensitive.

E102 Tartrazine Gives yellow colouring to product.
Effects on Health Has been implicated with causing sleeplessness at night in hyperactive and food-sensitive children. Symptoms including skin rash, hay fever, problems with breathing, blurred vision and purple skin patches are reported in susceptible people, particularly those who are aspirin sensitive or asthmatic.

Figure 1

Memo Pad —

PERMITTED COLOURS
E100 – E180 are used to make the product look attractive. Most are natural in origin.

PRESERVATIVES
E200 – E290 prevent the growth of micro-organisms and are considered to be safer than mouldy food!

PERMITTED ANTI-OXIDANTS
E300 – E321 prevent the oxygen in the air from making food unfit to eat. Oxygen, for example, can make fats go rancid or sour. Without this type of additive it would not be possible to have so many ready-packed foods.

EMULSIFIERS AND STABILIZERS
Some numbers between E322 and 494 are used to stop substances in mixtures separating out in foods like salad cream and sauces.

SWEETENERS
E420 – E421 are added to satisfy our sweet tooth.

CHICKEN CHASSEUR CASSEROLE
Sugar** *Salt***

621 Monosodium Glutamate
Enhances the flavour of foods containing protein by stimulating the taste buds or increasing degree of saliva produced in the mouth.
Effects on Health Responsible for symptoms of palpitation, headache, dizziness, nausea, muscle tightness, a feeling of weakness in the forearms, pains in the neck, and other, migraine-like symptoms in some people. This substance is recommended to be excluded from the diets of hyperactive children; it is also taboo in or on foods intended for babies and young children.

E150 Caramel Gives a brown colour to product and is used as a flavouring.
Effects on Health A question mark as to its safety hangs over this additive.

E155 Brown HT Gives brown colouring to product.
Effects on Health As a member of the azo-dye family this should be avoided by those who suffer from aspirin sensitivity, are asthmatic or have a tendency to allergies. It is recommended to be excluded from the diets of hyperactive children by the Hyperactive Children's Support Group.

E124 Ponceau 4R Gives red colouring to product.
Effects on Health One of the azo-dye family which is recommended to be excluded from the diets of hyperactive children. Adults who are aspirin sensitive or asthmatic may be affected.

Figure 2

Are additives safe?

Fortunately for us, most of them are ... but not all of them. Read the list of chemicals added to a chicken casserole mix. Look carefully at what is known about the effects of these chemicals on people's health.

— (2) For the chicken casserole mix, complete a table like this

Additive	Why it is added	Possible harmful effects

— (3) Make another table like that for question 2 and complete it for the instant dessert topping in figure 1.

= (4) Now that you have learned about the additives in a chicken casserole mix and instant dessert topping, explain how you feel about eating the two foods.

= (5) Read again the reason for adding E621 monosodium glutamate to the chicken casserole mix. Write a letter to the imaginary manufacturer explaining why the company should not add this substance to the product.

E numbers in nature

In case you are worried about E numbers, read the contents of **a fresh natural apple** in figure 3!

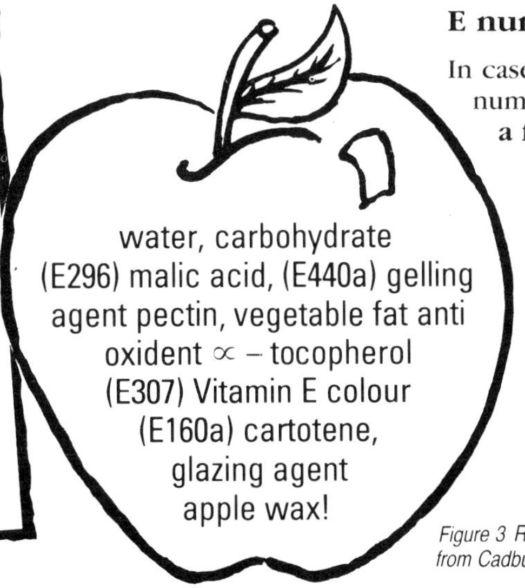

water, carbohydrate (E296) malic acid, (E440a) gelling agent pectin, vegetable fat anti oxident α – tocopherol (E307) Vitamin E colour (E160a) cartotene, glazing agent apple wax!

Figure 3 Reproduced with kind permission from Cadbury Schweppes Ltd

Controls on Additives

The manufacturer must show that the new additive will benefit the consumer – one that cannot be achieved by an old additive or by other means.

What kind of help? Six needs are taken into account.

- make it easier to present food attractively
- additives keep food fit-to-eat longer 
- extend peoples choice of foods
- making buying, packing, storage, preparation and use easier
- keep prices down by giving longer shelf-life.
- make it easy to supplement nutritional needs

21 VITAMINS: ARE THEY IN OR OUT?

Table 1 A guide to vitamins and their sources

Benefits	Sources	Shortage symptoms
B1 (Thiamin) Energy; nervous system; good muscle tone; digestion.	Wholegrains, such as brown rice and wholemeal flour; offal; watercress; beans; pulses and brewer's yeast.	Poor digestion and appetite; slow pulse rate; craving for sugar; tiredness and poor sleep; depression; beri beri.
B2 (Riboflavin) Energy production; vitality; growth; tissue maintenance; healthy red blood cells; longevity.	Milk; yeast; wheatgerm; meat; broccoli; grapefruit; watercress.	Bloodshot eyes; poor vision; sore mouth; oily skin. More B2 needed if taking Pill or pregnant (unborn babies can have B2 deficiency).
B3 (Niacin or nicotinic acid) Energy production; good skin; metabolism; helps regulate blood sugar and keep down cholesterol levels.	Oily fish; wholemeal bread; liver; fresh vegetables.	Irritability; tiredness; and in extreme cases, pellagra. More needed if you eat a lot of sugar and starch, or if you are pregnant.
B5 (Pantothenic acid) Energy; nervous system.	Most foods contain some. High in eggs, molasses and brewer's yeast.	Rare
B6 (Pyridoxine) Good circulation; metabolism; hormone system; helps prevent heart disease; relieves PMT and postnatal blues.	Wholegrains and cereals; dried fruit; liver; bananas; fatty fish; eggs.	Irritability; depression; anxiety; slow learning; poor dream recall; migraine. More needed if suffering from PMT.
B12 (Cyano cobalamine) Cell production; protein building; growth.	Animal and dairy products, particularly pig's liver and kidneys; eggs; milk; white fish; cheese.	Pernicious anaemia—vegans should take supplements.
Folic acid Similar function and benefits to B12.	Green leafy veg; lentils; pulses; boiled potatoes; nuts; wholemeal bread.	Megaloblastic anaemia. More needed in pregnancy.
Vitamin C (Ascorbic acid) Healthy tissues, arteries and bones; white blood cells; production of antibodies; prevents and treats infection.	Guavas; mangoes; oranges; lemons; rosehips; fresh vegetables.	Sore, bleeding gums; scurvy; easy bruising; tender joints; nose bleeds; wrinkles.

The fat-soluble vitamins (A, D and E) are stored in the body so they don't have to be taken daily. Because it is possible for fat-soluble vitamins to build up to a toxic level in the body, be careful when taking large amounts, particularly of vitamin A.

Vitamin A (retinol or carotene) Protects lungs, throat and digestive system from infection; keeps skin healthy, eyesight strong	Green and yellow vegetables, particularly carrots; fish liver oil; dairy produce; egg yolks.	Night blindness and light sensitivity; flaking skin; hair loss; ulcers. Skin turns yellow if too high doses are taken over a long period.
Vitamin D Helps healthy bone and teeth formation.	Sun (don't shower for 6 hours afterwards); oily fish; egg yolks; milk.	Osteoporosis; rickets; cramp; arthritis. More needed in winter.
Vitamin E (tocopherol) Good for cardiovascular system; helps wounds to heal.	Wheatgerm oil; sunflower oil; wholegrains; green leafy vegetables; shrimps; root vegetables.	Could lead to anaemia in premature babies, ulcers, poor skin. Deficiency can occur in alcoholics.

The above table is amended from Prima March 1987. (R.D.A. values deleted).

Have you seen 'added vitamins' on the cereal packet? Have you seen 'no preservatives' on the packets of 'pure' orange juice? Why should some things be *added* to food whilst other things are *not added*?

In chapter 20 (Book 2) you can read about some of the additives which are now labelled with 'E' numbers. In this chapter, we think about the need for vitamins to be in food.

Why are vitamins needed?

Vitamins along with some minerals are required in very small amounts to keep our bodies healthy. They allow many of the essential chemical reactions to happen in our bodies. Table 1 is a guide to vitamins, which foods contain them naturally and what can happen if you do not get enough of them.

– ① Look up vitamin D in table 1. How does this vitamin help the body?

= ② Look up vitamin C in table 1. List two problems we may have if we do not eat enough vitamin C. Then explain how we can be sure of eating vitamin C.

= ③ Look up thiamin and niacin in table 1. Describe what can happen if you are short of these vitamins. What foods supply thiamin and niacin?

= ④ Look at the main headings in table 1. Then complete a table with these headings

Vitamins to be eaten daily	Vitamins which need *not* be eaten daily

Vitamins in food

Mass produced food can be highly processed and food can lose some of its 'natural goodness'. Many vitamins are lost in this way.

Some manufacturers are proud of the fact that they add them back in again. You might wonder why they were taken out in the first place; so do a lot of other consumers!

A daily dose of vitamins

The Recommended Daily Amount (RDA) of some vitamins and minerals for an average adult has been calculated by doctors. This is the amount that is required to prevent any type of deficiency developing (plus an extra 10% just for luck!) The amounts are shown in table 2.

Some food manufacturers put the vitamin and mineral contents of their products on the label. The example in figure 1 shows the information on a packet of wholemeal bread.

Table 2 Recommended daily amounts of vitamins and minerals

	R.D.A. (for the average adult)
Vitamin A (Retinol)	750 ug
Thiamin (Vitamin B$_1$)	1.2 mg
Riboflavin (Vitamin B$_2$)	1.6 mg
Niacin (Nicotinic acid)	18.0 mg
Folic acid	300 ug
Vitamin B$_{12}$	2 ug
Vitamin C (Ascorbic acid)	30 mg
Vitamin D (Cholecalciferol)	2.5 ug
The minerals which may be claimed are:	
Calcium	500 mg
Iodine	140 ug
Iron	12 mg

Note:
$$1 \text{ mg (milligram)} = \frac{1}{1000} \text{ g}$$
$$1 \text{ ug (microgram)} = \frac{1}{1000} \text{ mg}$$

= ⑤ Look up table 2 and find the amount of thiamin (vitamin B$_1$) needed daily by an adult. Write down;
'Thiamin needed daily by an adult = _____.'

NUTRITION INFORMATION

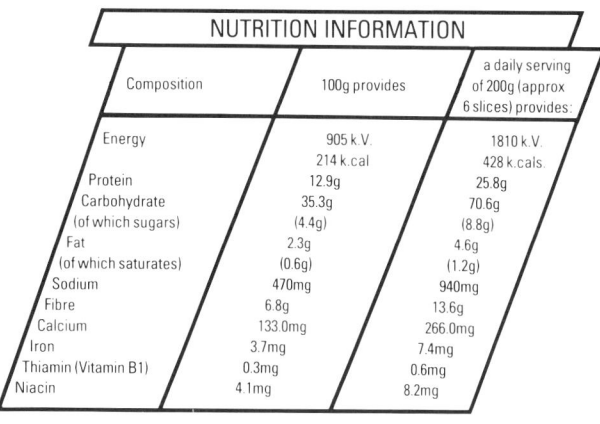

Composition	100g provides	a daily serving of 200g (approx 6 slices) provides:
Energy	905 k.V.	1810 k.V.
	214 k.cal.	428 k.cals.
Protein	12.9g	25.8g
Carbohydrate	35.3g	70.6g
(of which sugars)	(4.4g)	(8.8g)
Fat	2.3g	4.6g
(of which saturates)	(0.6g)	(1.2g)
Sodium	470mg	940mg
Fibre	6.8g	13.6g
Calcium	133.0mg	266.0mg
Iron	3.7mg	7.4mg
Thiamin (Vitamin B1)	0.3mg	0.6mg
Niacin	4.1mg	8.2mg

Figure 1 Label from a loaf of wholemeal bread

Using figure 1, write down and complete this sentence;
'Six slices of bread provide an adult with _____% of their daily need.'
Then write down and complete this sentence;
'The mass of thiamin in six slices of bread = _____ mg.'

= ⑥ Figure 1 includes data on three minerals containing metallic elements. Which metals are these? Try to find out why it is important for pregnant women to have enough of these minerals.

Do we need more vitamins?

Lots of chemists and health food shops now sell vitamin and mineral supplements in bottles. These are available so that we can take extra vitamins if we want to. But there is a lot of argument about whether or not we need them. High doses of some vitamins can even be dangerous.

= ⑦ Look again at table 1. We should be careful not to take too much of some vitamins. Design a warning notice with this information. Use the heading;

BEWARE vitamins can ruin your health!

≡ ⑧ Read the articles 'Yes' and 'No' in figure 2. Explain in a few sentences why Dr Brown thinks that we should *not* take vitamin pills and Mr Holford thinks we should. What do *you* think.

Figure 2

'YES'
Dr John Brown says, a nutritionist with the Health Education Council. "If your diet is bad, no amount of vitamin pills will help."

He reckons that provided you eat a fairly well-balanced diet you should get the vitamins you need.

"It is much better to get all the vitamins you need from nutrious food rather than, say eating a junk diet and than shelling out five quid on vitamins. The biggest problem with the British diet is not to do with vitamins but with consuming too much fat and not enough fibre. And if you're eating an awful diet you're going to get ill no matter how many vitamin tablets you take."

He goes on: "There are some instances where it is useful to take supplements – a doctor may prescribe supplements in pregnancy, for instance – but if you're sufficiently well organised to eat a healthy diet of fresh fruit and vegetables, there's no need even in pregnancy to take supplements. If you eat fresh fruit and vegetables, wholegrain cereal products and avoid processed food where a lot of the goodness has been removed – eat lean meat, for example, instead of meal pie which contains a lot of fat and salt – you will get all the vitamins you need.

'NO'
says **Patrick Holford, Research Director of the Institute for Optimum Nutrition.** "The majority of people lack some vitamins and minerals."

He believes that it is vitually impossible for the average person to obtain the correct nutrients without supplements.

"We did a study on 100 people and analysed what they ate. Thirty-two of them ate a perfectly well-balanced diet which met all the standard requirements for vitamin and mineral needs accordingly to the Department of Health's recommended daily allowance ... but out of that 32, 24 showed signs of multiple vitamin and mineral deficiency. It's probably an underestimate to say that two in three of the population are unlikely to be getting the recommended daily allowances because the need for nutrients varies from person to person according to their age, state of health and lifestyle – we've had people here whose need for a particular nutrient varies ten fold. So the recommended daily allowances are confusing because more and more people believe that you may need a vitamin supplement which, for optimum health, is way above the daily allowance.

PRIMA March 1987

22 WARNING: FOOD CAN DAMAGE YOUR HEALTH!

There have been many campaigns to inform the public of the need to lead a healthy lifestyle

When your parents were at school, people in Britain were encouraged to eat a *balanced diet* which contained proteins, carbohydrates, fats, minerals and vitamins. This was because many people were not getting enough of the right things to eat. They were suffering from *malnutrition*. Nowadays, most people in this country get enough food to eat. But some of the foods which we now include in our diets are actually making us ill. We are eating too much of the wrong things!

Did you know.........?
- Millions of people die from hunger each year? Many are not eating **enough** food, and are dying of **starvation**. Many are not eating all the right **kinds** of food and are dying of **malnutrition**.

Diseases caused by eating too much of the wrong thing

Here are some of the diseases which are linked to the food we eat.

Overweight or obesity
This may be caused by overeating or drinking too much sweet liquid and not taking enough exercise.

Dental decay
This is caused by eating too many things containing sugar and by poor care of the teeth.

High blood pressure
This may be reduced by losing weight and by cutting down on the amount of salt in the diet.

Liver disease
This may be caused by drinking too much alcohol (ethanol). (See chapter 26 (Book 2).)

Heart disease
Can be caused by smoking, lack of exercise, being overweight and too much saturated fat in the diet.

Bowel cancer
Can be due to a lack of fibre in the diet.

Food allergies
These occur when the immune system reacts against certain foods. Read chapter 28 (Book 2) to find out more about this.

All of these diseases can take a lifetime to develop. It is often too late by the time people realise that they could have prevented them. It is never too early to take care so read on carefully!

Table 1 Average mass of men and women

Height/m	Mass/kg Women	Mass/kg Men
1.42–1.45	45	
1.45–1.47	47	
1.47–1.50	49	
1.50–1.53	50	55
1.53–1.55	51	57
1.55–1.57	52	59
1.57–1.60	54	60
1.60–1.63	55	61
1.63–1.65	57	63
1.65–1.68	59	65
1.68–1.70	60	66
1.70–1.73	62	68
1.73–1.75	64	70
1.75–1.78	66	72
1.78–1.80	68	74
1.80–1.83	70	75
1.83–1.85	71	78
1.85–1.88		81
1.88–1.90		84
1.90–1.92		86

Cholesterol linked to British heart disease

By Andrew Veitch, Medical Correspondent

TWO thirds of adults in Britain run an increased risk of heart disease because of the level of cholestrol in their blood, specialists were told at a London conference yesterday.

One in four of these have cholesterol levels high enough to double their risk of dying of a heart attack or stroke, and one in 20 run four times the risk, said Professor Barry Lewis of St Thomas's Hospital, London.

Cholesterol levels help explain why Britain has the worst record for heart disease in western countries with more than 160,000 deaths a year.

In the US, where cholesterol levels and death rates from heart disease are lower, medical organisations have launched a "Know your cholesterol level" campaign. Dr James Cleeman of the US National Institutes of Health, the campaign co-ordinator, said.

The remedy in most cases, was a simple diet cutting down on saturated fat. For those most at risk doctors should prescribe cholesterol lowering drugs.

THE GUARDIAN Wednesday November 4 1987

How to take care of your diet

Doctors have made suggestions about what we can do to improve our diets. Here are some of them.

(1) Only eat and drink enough to keep your body mass within an acceptable range

— ① Look at table 1 and write down what your mass should be. Check other members of your class or family and make a list of their masses.

(2) Reduce the amount of fat you eat

The fats to cut down if you are overweight are called *saturated fats* which are found in animal products such as whole milk, butter, fatty red meat and fat for frying. These can be avoided by not eating fried foods, eating low fat products and using products high in 'polyunsaturated fats' which are less harmful to us.

Saturated fats increase the amount of a substance called *cholesterol* in the blood with serious results. Read the news item called 'Cholesterol linked to heart disease' to find out more.

— ② Write down the recommended remedy given in this article.

(3) Eat a lot less sugar

Sugar is in many of the foods we eat. It is even where we do not expect it! A bottle of tomato ketchup contains about 17 tablespoons of sugar. Soups, sausages, bread rolls and many breakfast cereals also contain sugar.

= ③ Check at home and see how many foods you can find which contain sugar. Sugar comes in lots of different disguises, here are a few so look out for them: glucose, fructose, galactose, sucrose, lactose, maltose, invert sugar, maltodextrin, dextrose, corn syrup.
This is a long list! Just remember that the names of most sugars end in *-ose* and you cannot go wrong.

Too much sugar may be harmful over a long period of time because it affects our teeth and our mass.

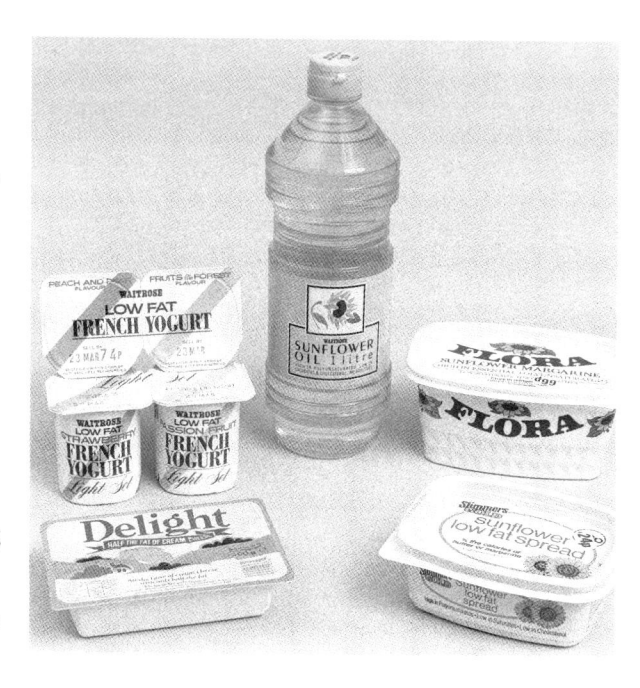

Sugar can also affect us in the short term. A mini chocolate cake contains about 12 teaspoons of sugar. It might stop us feeling hungry right away but its effect does not last long. Here is what happens when we eat a slice of chocolate cake.

—First of all the sugars are quickly absorbed into the blood through the digestive system.
—The blood glucose level rises very quickly.
—When the amount of glucose in the blood reaches a certain level, the body acts to store the extra glucose which it cannot use right away. This reduces the level in the blood.
—The sudden rise in the blood glucose level makes the body overreact and it takes too much glucose out of the blood. The blood glucose level goes *below* its normal level about an hour after the cake was eaten before reaching the normal level again.
—The person then begins to feel tired and hungry all over again.

What good has the chocolate been? ... Not very much! It has added extra joules of energy which end up being stored and has made the person crave for something else to eat. Several sweet things during a day will make blood glucose levels go up and down. This can account for changes in mood and behaviour as well as tiredness. Think about your own eating pattern, Do you give yourself 'sugar fixes' during the day? If you do, try an apple, nuts or a piece of bread instead. They will last you for longer and do your body more good in the long run.

= ④ Describe in your own words the effect on your body of eating chocolate cake. Make a list of five other foods which might have a similar effect.

(4) Eat more dietary fibre

The more refined or processed food becomes in the factory then the less fibre or 'roughage' it contains. Fibre comes only from plant materials such as *skins* of fruit and vegetables, *cereals* like wheat, and *pulses* like lentils and beans. Wholemeal bread contains more fibre than white bread, brown rice more than white rice, and baked potatoes more than mashed potatoes. Other good sources are nuts and salad vegetables. The fibre is not absorbed into the body as it passes through the digestive system. It holds moisture and so helps to keep the bowel or large intestine working properly.

(5) Cut down on the amount of salt

This is something very simple to do. Just do not add it to food when cooking or when it is being eaten. Watch out for the salt hidden in cooked ham, crisps and tinned food. You may not even know you are eating it!

People are changing their diets

= ⑤ Many people do seem to be prepared to change their eating habits.
 Write a letter to someone you know who you think has bad eating habits. Try to convince them to change. You might even like to give them your letter and see what they say!

= ⑥ What are your school meals like?
 Do they let pupils choose a 'good' meal?
 What do pupils actually choose to eat?
 Why don't you carry out a survey to find out?

23 SAVING A LIFE

Has anyone ever fainted at your feet? Would you know what to do if someone collapsed? A person might die if you did not.

Read what happened to John one day whilst at school.

A big problem in class

John found maths lessons on Wednesday mornings dull. He had his thoughts on the evening's football match; much more interesting than quadratic equations. 'Psst,' said Carl, 'want a sweet whilst he's not looking?' John took the sweet but pushed it into his mouth too eagerly as Mr Simpson turned towards the class.

Suddenly he felt the sweet lodge in his throat. He began to choke, quietly at first but afterwards quite violently. Carl thumped him on the back but to no avail.

Mr Simpson rushed to John and also tried thumping him on his back. This time the sweet flew out of John's mouth, but he still did not start breathing again.

Mr Simpson knelt by his side, put his cheek close to John's mouth, feeling for breaths and at the same time listening and looking along his chest ... nothing.

What could you have done to help?

Work through this chapter and find out how to help if you meet a problem like this.

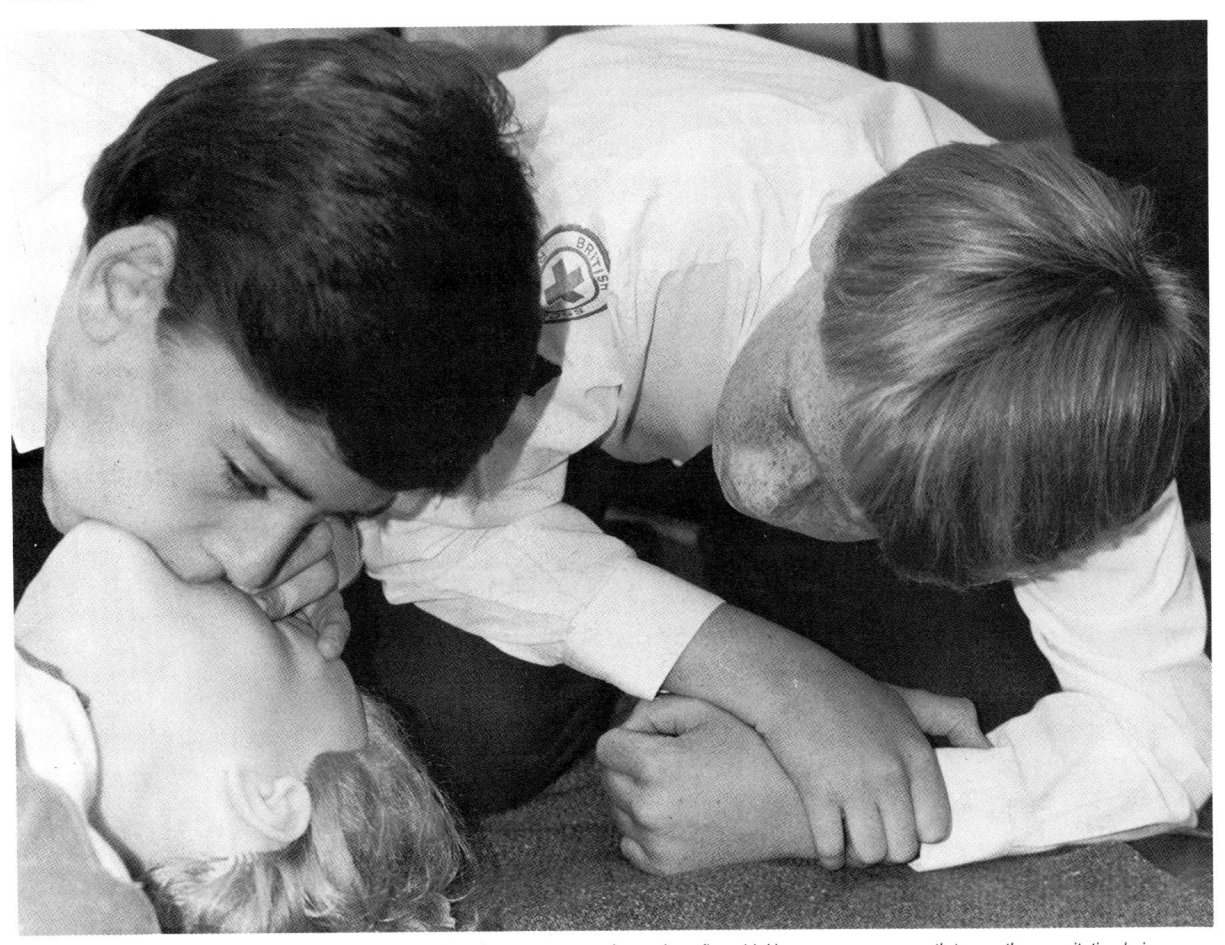

The Red Cross and St John Ambulance arrange courses for people wanting to learn about first aid. Here you can see mouth-to-mouth resuscitation being practised using a Rescussi Ann dummy

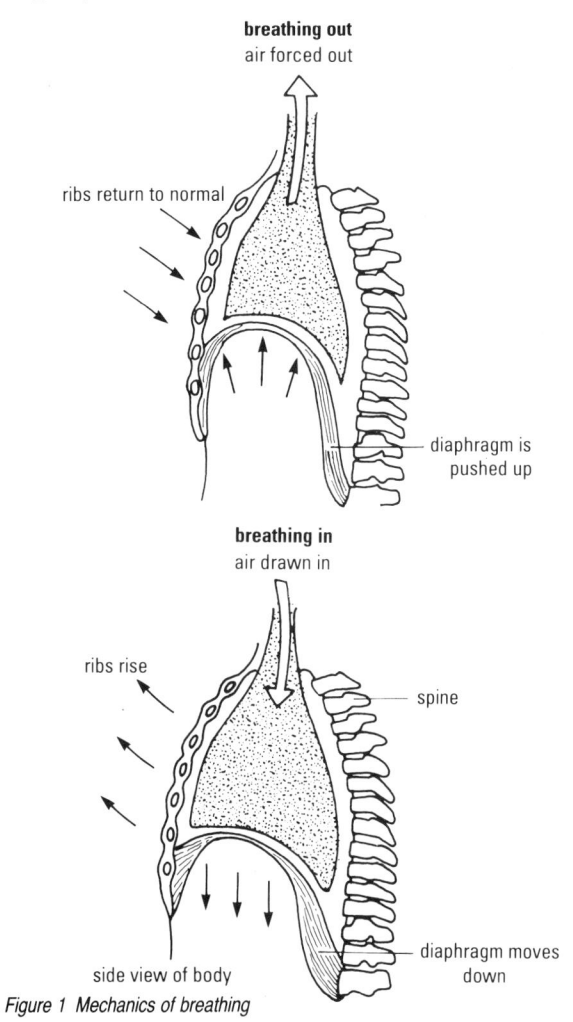

Figure 1 Mechanics of breathing

Some simple facts on breathing

(1) Every cell in the body needs a supply of oxygen.

(2) Cells in the brain start to die without oxygen after *only 3 minutes*.

(3) Oxygen enters the body via the nose and mouth, passes down the windpipe and enters the lungs.

(4) Once inside the lungs, oxygen passes into the blood and is pumped around the body by the heart to every cell in the body.

(5) Some of the oxygen is used by the cells and carbon dioxide is produced.

(6) The carbon dioxide is carried by the blood to the lungs where it is breathed out along with about $1/4$ of the oxygen breathed in.

Memo Pad —

HOW AIR PASSES THROUGH THE LUNGS.

Look at the diagrams in figure 1. When we breathe in, strong muscles pull down the diaphragm and increase the volume of the lungs. This action reduces the pressure in the lungs and air rushes in through the nose or mouth and down through the windpipe. Two branches, called bronchi lead to the lungs. When we breathe out, the diaphragm is pushed up and air leaves the lungs by the same route in reverse.

Figure 2 Mouth-to-mouth resuscitation

Starting up breathing again

Here are some simple instructions on how to help someone to begin breathing again. *You must not practise this on anyone* but you can practise on a model like 'Rescussi Ann'.

Step 1 Lay the patient on their back, with the fingers of one hand lift their jaw, and with the other hand on their forehead tilt the head backwards.

Step 2 If the casualty does not begin breathing, open your mouth wide and take a deep breath. Then hold the casualty's nostrils together, put your lips around the mouth and blow until the chest rises fully. (See figure 2.)

Step 3 If you can not force air into the casualty open their mouth and remove any obstructions such as a sweet, vomit or false teeth. Retilt the head and start again.

— (1) Why must the air way be opened up?

— (2) Why does your blowing cause the casualty's chest to rise?

Step 4 Take your mouth away and allow the chest to fall. Repeat at a rate of about 16 breaths per minute.

= (3) Why should you breathe into the casualty at this rate? Why not 4 per minute or 30 per minute?

Step 5 There must be no delay in carrying out the above techniques.

= (4) Why must there be no delay?

= (5) Now explain in your own words, the above sequence.

24 LUNGS AND BREATHING

If you cannot remember much about how humans breathe it may help if you read chapter 23 (Book 2) *before* reading this chapter.

Air and oxygen

We breathe in air and the lungs take out some of the oxygen. Oxygen enters the blood through the surface of the lungs in thin-walled air sacs called *alveoli* (see figure 1). The total surface area of these alveoli is about the same as the area of a tennis court! Even so, only a small amount of the oxygen that is breathed in is taken into the blood.

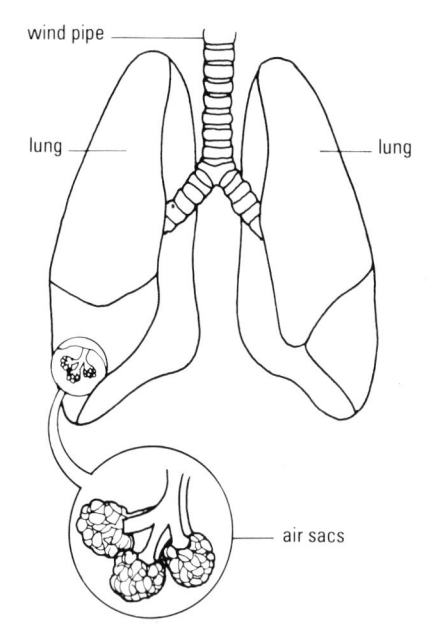

Figure 1 Air sacs in the lungs

Look at table 1 showing the content of samples of 1 litre of breathed-in (inhaled) air and breathed-out (exhaled) air.

Table 1 Content of samples of air

Gas	Breathed-in air/cm³	Breathed-out air/cm³
Total	1000	1000
Nitrogen	819	819
Oxygen	180	162
Carbon dioxide	1	19

- (1) Why does the volume of nitrogen gas not change?
- (2) Calculate the percentage of oxygen in both samples.
- (3) Calculate the percentage of the oxygen in the breathed-in air which is actually taken in by the lungs.

Our oxygen supply

The volume of air passing through the lungs must be enough to supply the body with oxygen for whatever the body is doing. When sleeping, only a small volume is needed; but much more is needed when exercising.

Look at the graphs in figure 2 showing the flow of air in litres per second for a person whilst sleeping and running. The horizontal scale is the same for both graphs and is marked in seconds.

The graph goes *above* the horizontal axis for breathing-in and *below* for breathing-out. The volume of air breathed-in is calculated from the *area* under one 'hump' of the curve. You just count up the number of squares and this number gives the volume in a breath. For example, 22.5 small squares have the same area as 0.225 big squares so the volume of air is 0.225 litres.

Now use the graphs in figure 2 to answer questions 4–7.

- (4) How many breaths *per minute* does the subject take when sleeping? (**Hint:** He takes 2 breaths in 10 s).

= ⑤ How many breaths *per minute* does he take when running?

Table 2

Activity	Breaths per minute	Volume per breath	Volume per minute
Sleeping			
Running			

= ⑥ Count the squares for one breath and calculate the volume of air *taken in* for the breath. Do this for both graphs. Then calculate the volume breathed-in during one minute for both graphs. Copy table 2 and enter your results.

= ⑦ Explain why so much more air is needed when running.

How cells use oxygen

All cells in the body need energy. This energy is used to make the body move and carry out all the body actions such as eating, drinking and breathing. Energy comes from simple sugars which reach the cells from food. But oxygen is needed to release all the energy from these sugars in a process called *respiration*.

Simple sugars burned with oxygen → carbon dioxide + water + energy

For one sugar, the chemical equation is:

$$C_6H_{12}O_6 + 6O_2 \rightarrow 6CO_2 + 6H_2O + energy.$$

≡ ⑧ Now look back at your answer to question 7 and give a fuller answer which includes the words; food, cells, energy and respiration.

Did you know.........?

Some people are unable to breath naturally and are kept alive in an iron lung? A case is fitted over the body and pumps are used to help them draw air into the lungs and expel it.
Some people have been helped by an iron lung for over 30 years.

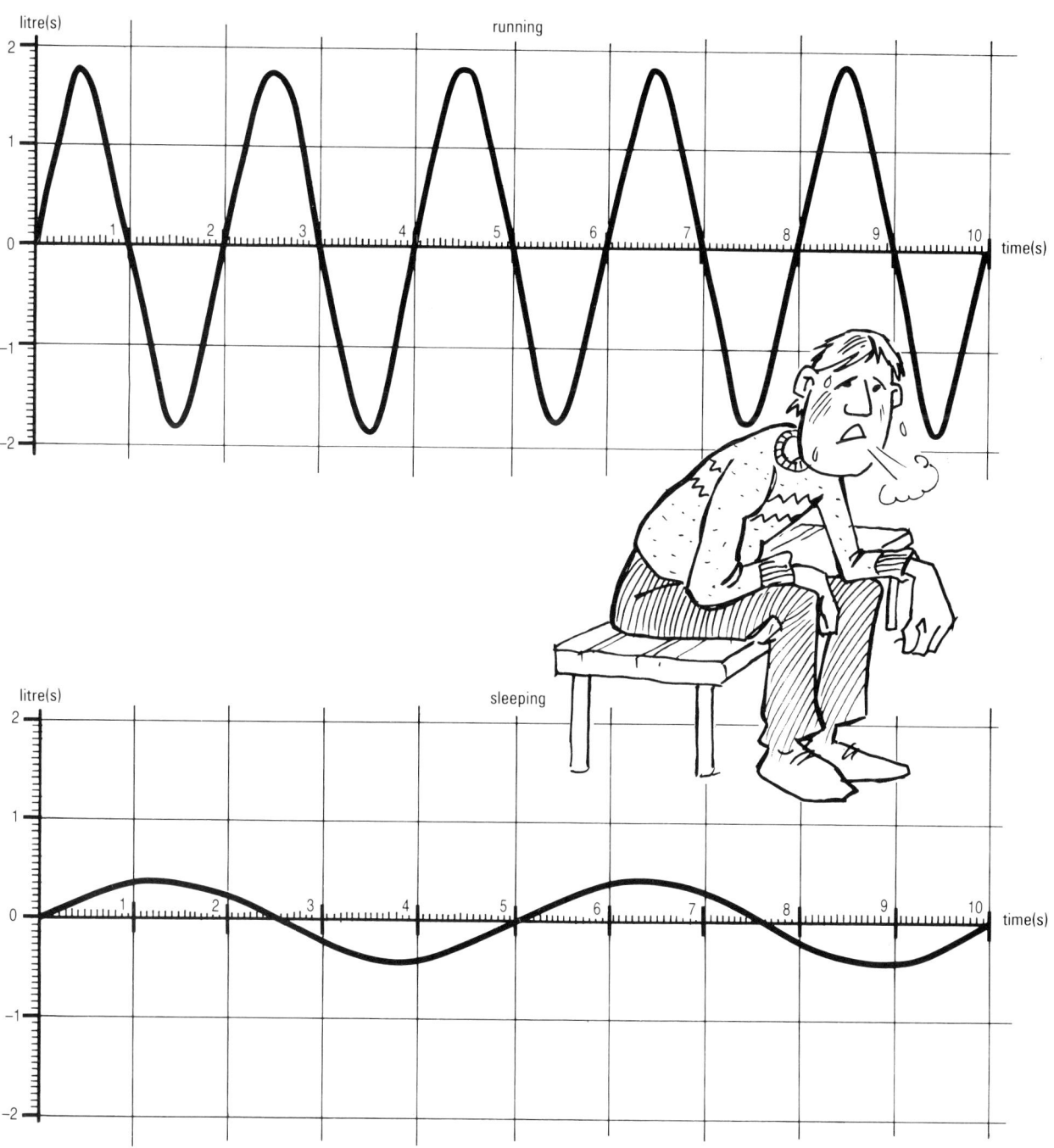

Figure 2 Breathing rate graphs

25 HYPOTHERMIA

London News: Titanic Sinks on Maiden Voyage

This was the sort of newspaper headline on April 15th, 1912 following the tragic accident of the luxury passenger ship *Titanic*. The ship struck an iceberg and began to sink into the ice-cold North Atlantic Ocean. Seven hundred and twelve people scrambled to lifeboats and were rescued, but 1489 people died in the water, despite most of them wearing lifebelts. So why did they die?

Heat loss and body cooling are very much faster in water than in air. After 30 minutes in ice-cold water most people die from *hypothermia*. Even the passengers who were excellent swimmers could not overcome the effect of the cold temperatures. The cold caused mental confusion and eventually they felt no pain.

① Explain in your own words why so many people died in the sea even though they were wearing lifebelts. The Memo Pad may help you.

Who gets hypothermia today?

The kinds of people most at risk from hypothermia on land are babies and old people. A lack of adequate heating and warm clothing may lead to severe hypothermia that can cause coma and eventually death. Babies do not have a fully developed system for controlling body temperature. In old people their system for control seems to slow down. Clearly a great deal of care is needed by both groups.

If you are reading this chapter in a warm room but outside is a cold winter's day, you might know someone who might be at risk from hypothermia.

Helping someone with hypothermia

First you need to know the *symptoms* of hypothermia. These are questions to ask yourself:

(1) Is the casualty shivering?
(2) Is the skin pale and dry?
(3) Is the casualty's temperature below 35 °C?
(4) Is the pulse and breathing rate slower than expected?
(5) Is the casualty confused?

If your casualty is sheltered, replace any wet clothes with dry ones then put the casualty in a warm bed. A covered hot water bottle in the left armpit helps blood to circulate better but do not place one near fingers and toes as this increases blood flow too rapidly. Hot drinks and energy-giving chocolate should be given.

If your casualty is out in the open, you must get them to shelter immediately. Cover them with whatever is available, e.g. blankets, newspaper, aluminium foil—even *your* own body!

② You and four of your friends are out on an expedition on remote, exposed moorland. You are lost! It is getting dark and the weather conditions are becoming quite worrying—snow, wind and the temperature is dropping quickly. Make a list of the do's and don'ts you and your friends must think about to avoid hypothermia.

Keep warm Keep well

Call the winter warmth line
FREE 0800 289 404
for a free booklet and advice, or write to:
Keep warm Keep well, FREEPOST, London EC1D 1BD

If you receive Income Support and are a pensioner or are sick or disabled or have a child under five, you may be entitled to extra benefit during very cold weather.

Memo Pad

If body temperature drops below 35°C we are said to be HYPOTHERMIC. Possible effects on the body include: Constriction (shrinking) of tiny blood vessels in the skin causes blood to circulate more slowly. Reduced blood flow at the skin surface increases shivering which helps the body to keep the skin and limbs warm, but even shivering stops when people become hypothermic.

Copy this table and complete it.

	What to do to avoid hypothermia	What *not* to do in treating hypothermia
(1)		
(2)		
(3)		

Hypothermia can be useful!

Hypothermia is not all bad news. It can actually be useful—sounds crazy but it's true. Surgeons sometimes give patients hypothermia when carrying out surgical operations. American surgeons Tauffic and Lewis first used the idea during heart surgery in 1953.

Their approach must have seemed very odd to patients when they were told that they were to be put into a bath of cold water for an hour!

Nowadays, if a surgeon needs the patient's body temperature to drop to 30 °C, it is a much simpler task. First the patient is anaesthetized (sent to sleep). Then an artery and a vein are connected to a large tube which is immersed in cold water.

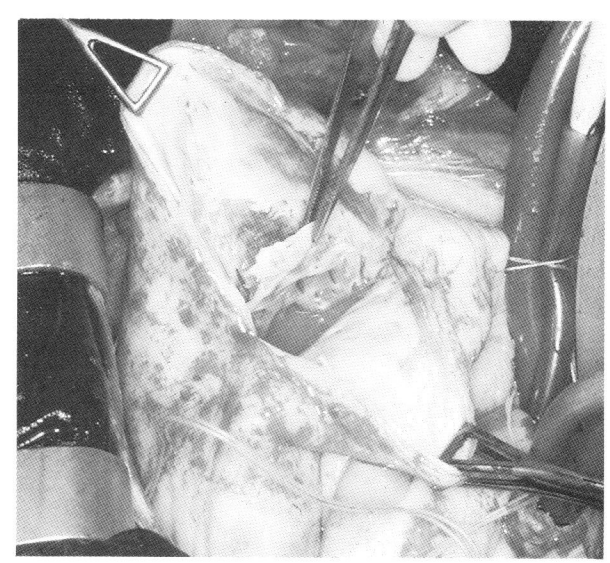

During major operations an artery and vein are connected to a 'cold' chamber via tubes. This lowers the body temperature and so prevents excess bleeding. The photo shows the technique being used during open heart surgery

Blood flowing from the artery is cooled as it passes through the coiled tube. As the cooled blood re-enters the body through the vein the body is cooled. During hypothermia, the body does not need as much oxygen or food so the body can work far longer without blood passing through.

= (3) Imagine you are visiting a sick friend in hospital. The surgeon has told you that your friend is to be given hypothermia before the operation. Write down the answers you would give to your friend when he/she asks these questions:

'What is hypothermia?'
'What will happen to my body?'
'Why is the surgeon doing this to me?'

Not to be confused with hypothermia—hyperthermia

Marathon day

A marathon runner needs to train very hard before a big race. Not just to build up muscles and energy levels but to learn how to control body heat. Controlling body heat is a very big problem for marathon runners. A good runner may produce kg of fluid during the 26 mile run. This is because up to 20 times more heat is generated than normal. If this heat isn't lost, then overheating will occur or *hyperthermia*. A person suffering from this becomes dizzy, fatigued and may collapse.

You may have seen runners after a race putting 'space blankets' on to **keep** warm ('space blankets' are large sheets of shiny plastic looking like aluminium foil) and they never seem to sit down and relax afterwards do they? That is because movement even if only slow, will prevent stiffness.

= (4) Why must a runner drink plenty of liquids before, during and after a marathon?

= (5) Why do you think a hot and humid day could be dangerous for a marathon runner—particularly one who has not trained enough?

= (6) How do the space blankets help the runners after a marathon?

Keeping warm after a race can be a big problem for marathon runners, so they are given 'space blankets' (made of aluminium foil), at the finish line to prevent their body cooling down too quickly

Did you know.........?

- Body heat is controlled by a 'temperature control centre' at the base of the brain. It works like a thermostat, automatically adjusting the processes that keep the balance between heat loss and heat gain.

- Temperature regulation may be poor or less effective in the very young or very old.

- Immersion in a cold sea leads to a rapid fall in temperature due to heat loss by conduction.

- Hypothermia is a general term for heat loss throughout the body. Frostbite is the name given to a local injury due to cold. Toes, fingers, the nose and ears are most prone to this.

- Lack of physical fitness, fatigue, dehydration and hunger will increase the risk of hypothermia.

26 THE LIVER

In chapter 22 (Book 2) you may have read that food can damage your health! You may also remember that this chapter mentioned the increase in liver disease due to drinking alcohol (ethanol). The liver's main job is helping with digestion but it also plays other roles.

The liver is the largest single organ in your body. It weighs about 2 kg and is built up of cells known as *hepatic cells* which are arranged in columns. Together these columns form liver lobules.

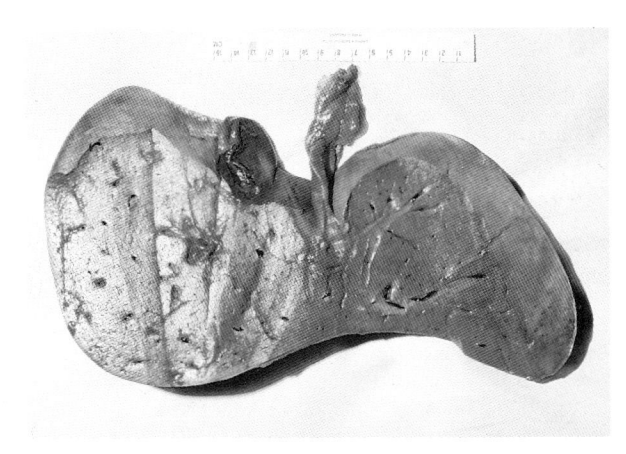

Figure 1 A healthy liver looks smooth and regular

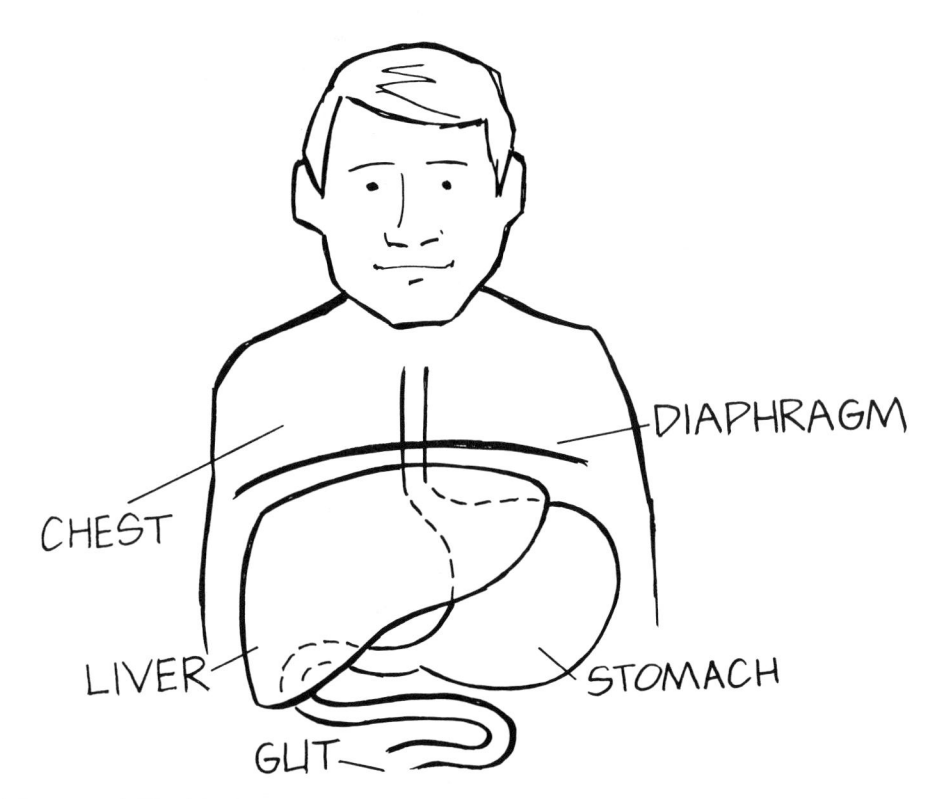

The liver is found in the upper part of the abdomen

Just how many functions does the liver have?

Claire's dad had just returned home to recover from a serious liver operation. The family had made his room warm and inviting in order to make him feel as comfortable as possible. The operation had not been an easy one and Dad was going to need quite a lot of care. What made things seem worse was that neither Mum nor Dad really understood why the surgeons didn't just take the liver out if it was going to cause such pain. Claire had learnt about the liver at school so she tried to explain.

'You see Dad, the liver stores nutrients from your digested food and changes them to a more useful form. You eat three meals a day but your body needs constant supplies throughout a twenty-four hour span; not just at meal times. So your liver releases the foods when necessary.'

'That sounds clever, but that can't be the only job it does, surely.'

'Oh no', said Claire. 'The liver is important for lots of body functions. Have a guess how long red cells in your blood live for.'

'Not a clue', said Dad.

'One hundred days,' said Claire 'or thereabouts. After that, the liver breaks them down into useful

Did you know..........?

- If part of the liver in a human is removed surgically, the liver cells begin to divide into new cells until the liver regains its normal size and shape.
- The liver performs over 500 functions including production, destruction and storage.
- Of the 2 kg liver in an adult, 16% is stored food.
- Up to two pints of bile are secreted daily by the average human liver.

and non-useful parts. For instance, iron is really useful in the body, so the liver recycles it and uses it to make something called bile.'

'Ugh! What on earth is bile?' asked Mum.

'Bile is a thick green liquid. It helps to emulsify fats, you know, make them dissolve in water. Then there are vitamins. How many times have we read the side of food packets in the supermarket to see what we're eating? And aren't we always being told it's good for us if we eat plenty of the right vitamins? Well, after we eat them the liver stores some of them until they're needed. It can store them for years. That's why the symptoms of lack of vitamins take so long to be noticed.'

'Well, I still don't see why the doctors couldn't just take my liver out and have done with it', said Dad.

'Well, we still haven't mentioned the job of purifying the blood. If poisons are taken into the body, the liver breaks them up so they are no longer harmful, but sometimes this is at the expense of the liver itself.'

'Oh very cheerful I'm sure', said Dad. 'Any more horror stories for me?'

'No, but I bet you're glad they didn't remove your liver after all', said Claire.

= (1) Make a list of the jobs which the liver has. Try to use your own words.

Figure 2 A cirrhotic liver looks enlarged and lumpy

Beware alcohol

People sometimes drink alcohol (ethanol) to feel good but alcohol is a depressant, affecting judgement and skills. But how does it affect the liver? This photograph shows a liver scarred by a condition known as *cirrhosis*.

In the first stages of cirrhosis, a fibrous tissue makes a network throughout the liver. This means that the liver cells cannot work properly and the whole organ becomes lumpy and much larger. Blood flow through it becomes very sluggish and eventually the liver just seems to collapse. We call this liver failure. There is no effective treatment for cirrhosis.

= (2) Use your answer to question 1 to help you list the problems a patient suffering from cirrhosis may have.

= (3) Read the article in figure 3. Then explain in your own words why polar bears may have sore heads!

Why the bear doesn't have a sore head

THE liver of the polar bear has long held a fascination for zoologists. Many animals stow unwanted vitamin A in the liver, but the polar bear is more industrious than most. Its liver is chock-full of the stuff — so full that when pioneering Arctic explorers first cooked it up for dinner, they took an overdose of the vitamin. As a result they suffered headaches, dizziness and diarrhoea.

Unless the polar bear has a permanently sore head, it must have evolved a way of dealing with this dangerous surplus. Canadian researchers now think they have found the answer. Their studies have focused on a type of liver cell called the Ito cell which are three to four times more numerous in the polar bear's liver than in ours, according to F. A. Leighton of the University of Saskatchewan and co-workers at the University of Alberta and the Canadian Wildlife Service.

The more vitamin A the bear tucks away in its liver, the larger are its Ito cells — suggesting that the cells simply act as a capacious storage depot for the excess vitamin.

All creatures at the top of the food chain suffer some accumulation of vitamin A. The polar bear is particularly vulnerable because it has a taste for seals, which are themselves high-living predators. By expanding its network of Ito cells, the bear neatly sidesteps any tendency to feel liverish. (Canadian Journal of Zoology vol. 66, p480.) SY

THE GUARDIAN Tuesday June 14 1988

Figure 3

27 SPECTACLES AND CONTACT LENSES

Our sense of sight helps us to detect our surroundings. But we all see objects differently. Some people are *short sighted* and cannot see clearly objects which are a long way from them. This chapter is about the eye and some of the aids to improve sight.

The inside of the eye

Look at the drawing in figure 1. This shows a section of an eye cut from top to bottom and looked at from the side.

Use the drawing to answer these questions.

1. Light reaching the retina has to pass through several parts of the eye. List three of these parts and give a short description of each.
2. Describe the retina and its functions.
3. What is the size and shape of the lens? What changes the shape of the lens?

Accommodation

The eye helps us to see distant objects at one moment and then close objects at the next. Stare out of the window or across the room and then quickly look again at this page. Did you notice that it takes the eye a short time to adjust before you can see the page clearly? Look at the two diagrams in figure 2.

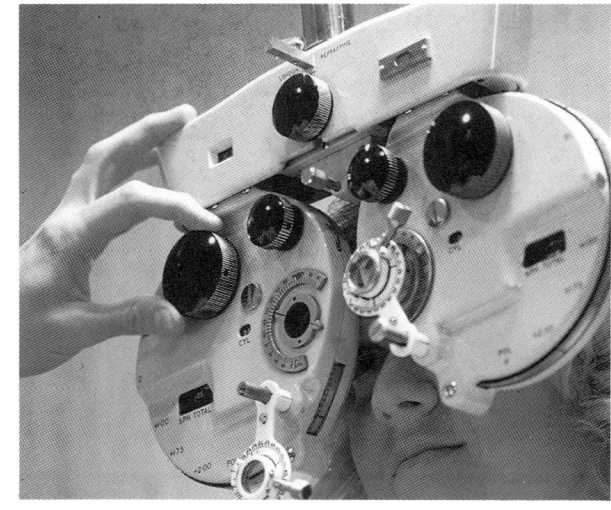

By turning the knobs on this machine the optician can choose different lenses until the correct ones are found and the patient can see clearly

In figure 2a light from a distant object enters the eye as a parallel beam. The converging (convex) lens of the eye brings the beam to a point on the retina. Light from a near object enters the eye as a diverging (spreading out) beam. The lens must make the light converge *more* than for a distant object to make it reach a point on the retina. The lens is made fatter in the middle, by using the ciliary muscles as in figure 2b.

The ability of the eye to change in this way is called '*accommodation*'.

a parallel beam   **b** diverging beam

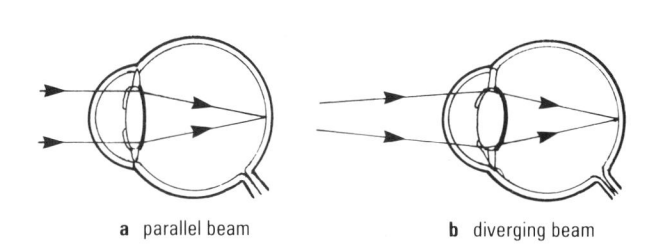

Figure 2 (a) Normal eye viewing a distant object
(b) Normal eye viewing a near object

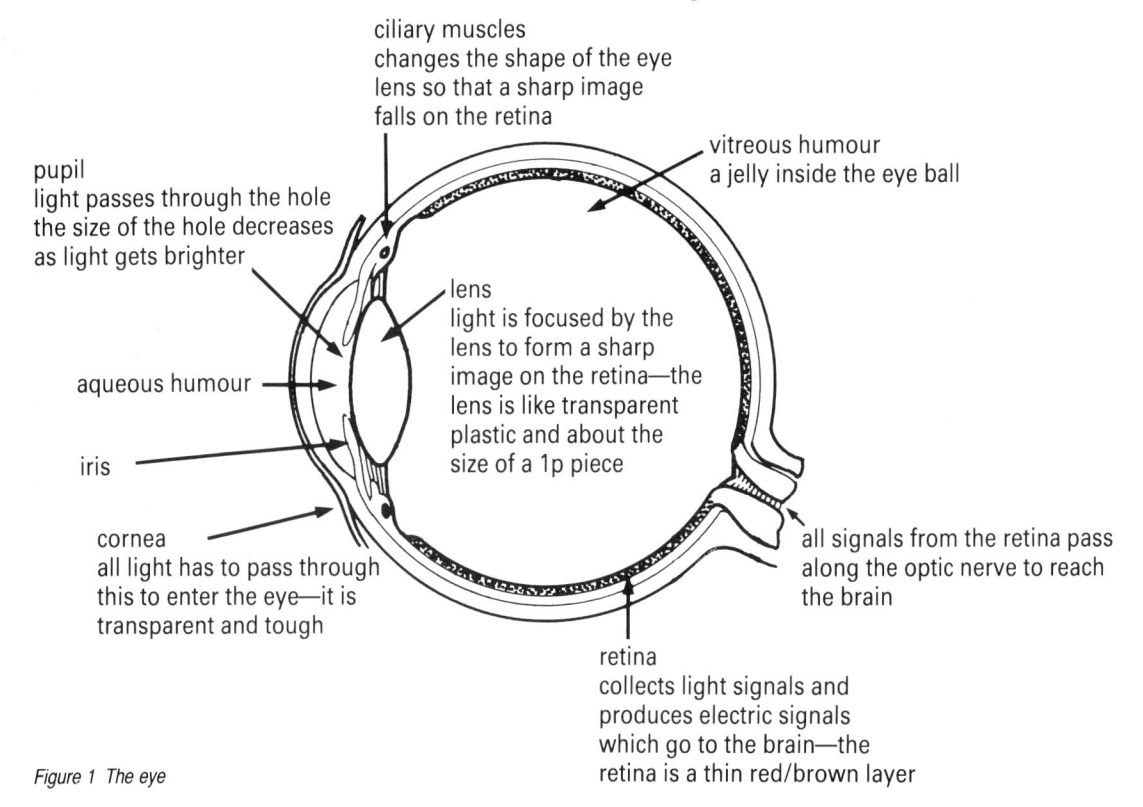

Figure 1 labels:

- **pupil** — light passes through the hole the size of the hole decreases as light gets brighter
- **aqueous humour**
- **iris**
- **cornea** — all light has to pass through this to enter the eye—it is transparent and tough
- **ciliary muscles** — changes the shape of the eye lens so that a sharp image falls on the retina
- **lens** — light is focused by the lens to form a sharp image on the retina—the lens is like transparent plastic and about the size of a 1p piece
- **vitreous humour** — a jelly inside the eye ball
- **retina** — collects light signals and produces electric signals which go to the brain—the retina is a thin red/brown layer
- all signals from the retina pass along the optic nerve to reach the brain

Figure 1 The eye

Short sight and long sight

Unfortunately, everyone does not have perfect lenses or eyeballs. Short-sighted people can see near objects but have difficulty seeing distant objects clearly. Look at figure 3a showing this problem. The eyeball is too long and images are formed in front of the retina. See figure 3b showing how an optician can correct this problem with a concave lens in spectacles.

Long-sighted people can see distant objects but have difficulty with near objects. Their eyeball is too short and images of near objects are formed *behind* the retina.

Now answer these questions.

= (4) Read again the last paragraph on long sight and draw diagrams like those in figure 3 for a long-sighted eye. What kind of lens would you recommend for correction?

= (5) As we get older, making the eye lens fatter becomes more difficult. Can you explain why older people often have to start wearing spectacles?

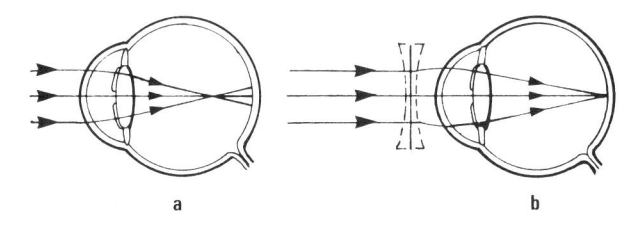

Figure 3 (a) Short-sighted eye
(b) Optician's correction for short-sighted vision

Contact lenses

Many people now use contact lenses instead of spectacles. Read the article in figure 4.

= (6) Describe *three* advantages and *three* disadvantages of contact lenses over spectacles.

= (7) At the end of the second paragraph in figure 4 it mentions a 'cosmetic purpose'. What does 'cosmetic' mean? Explain if you would want contact lenses for this purpose.

AS OLD AS LEONARDO

It was actually Loeonardo da Vinci who had the first idea for contact lenses! But it took another 400 years to develop the idea. Contact lenses, like spectacles are designed to correct defects of vision but unlike spectacles the lenses are positioned in direct "contact" with the eyes. They stay put because the thin layer of moisture which is always present can hold the thin lightweight lenses.

So why do we need contact lenses? Well, your field of vision is not restricted because when you turn your eye, the lens moves with it. All the images you see pass through the lens and so you get a much wider, unobstructed field of view than you would wearing spectacles. If you wear spectacles, you will know what it is like when they become misted over with condensation or rain. This is not a problem for contact lens wearers so sports are less of a problem. And of course contact lenses do serve a cosmetic purpose — for those who want it!

Contact lens wearers must keep their lenses very clean, otherwise, grit can get behind them and eye infection can occur. Some people find contact lenses difficult to get used to. Others find them expensive to buy.

Figure 4

Effect of brightness on the eye

Here is a simple experiment for you to try. You need a partner so that you can examine his or her eyes. Or you can use a mirror and examine your own eyes.

First, look at your partner's eyes for a few seconds looking carefully at the black circles in the middle. The circles are the 'holes' through which light passes and are called 'pupils'. Then ask your partner to cover up one eye for about twenty seconds. Finally, ask your partner to uncover the eye.

= (8) When an eye moves from the dark to the light, what happens to the size of the pupil of the eye?

≡ (9) Describe what happens to your eyes when you enter a cinema and have to find your seat in the dark. What happens to your sight after a few minutes?

Your pupils adjust the amount of light entering the eye so that the retina has just enough light to work correctly. Too much light can damage the retina and too little light does not give a clear image.

★★★★★★★★★★★★★★★★★★★★★★★★★★★★★★★★

Did you know..........?

There are three kinds of contact lenses

- **hard lenses** *made from perspex*
- **soft lenses** *made from hydrogel*
- **gas permeable** *hard (GPH) lenses which allow air to reach the cornea to keep the eye healthy*

Some people find hard lenses uncomfortable and prefer soft lenses. But soft lenses are not rigid and cannot be accurately shaped. GPH lenses are rigid and allow air to pass through to the cornea. But GPH lenses can cause dryness because they repel water.

A new kind of material for lenses is being made to combine the best features of the three kinds. The new material is called FSA (Fluoro-silicone acrylates). The makers claim that more oxygen from the air passes through than for other lens materials. This means that the lenses of FSA can be worn for up to seven days before they need to be removed. FSA also has low friction making it more comfortable when the wearer blinks.

28 HAY FEVER— A CASE OF MISTAKEN IDENTITY

I'M ALLERGIC TO WORK.

We all need to breathe! When we breathe to bring oxygen into our bodies, we also breathe in any small particles which happen to be in the air. Some of these are dangerous to us. The body has a superb defence system called the **immune system** which fights off these attackers. The invaders are called germs and are mainly bacteria and viruses. They can cause all kinds of diseases from colds and sore throats to whooping cough and bronchitis.

The immune system sometimes mistakes harmless particles such as pollen, fungal spores or house dust for dangerous invaders. It starts attacking them with unpleasant results. Hay fever and other *allergies* are a result of 'mistaken identity' by the immune system.

What substances cause hay fever?

Grass pollen

It is not just hay which causes hay fever. The most common cause is grass pollen which affects people in the spring and early summer; just around exam time! The last week in June and the first week in July are usually the worst in Great Britain. Daily radio broadcasts in spring and summer announce the pollen count for the day. That is the number of grains per cubic metre of air. When the count is above 50 grains per cubic metre, people begin to suffer. In 1964 the pollen count reached 820 grains per cubic metre in central London!

=① The pollen season gets later as you go further north through the country. The south of England is usually about two weeks ahead of the north and Scotland. Why do you think this is the case?

=② What effect do you think rain has on the pollen count?

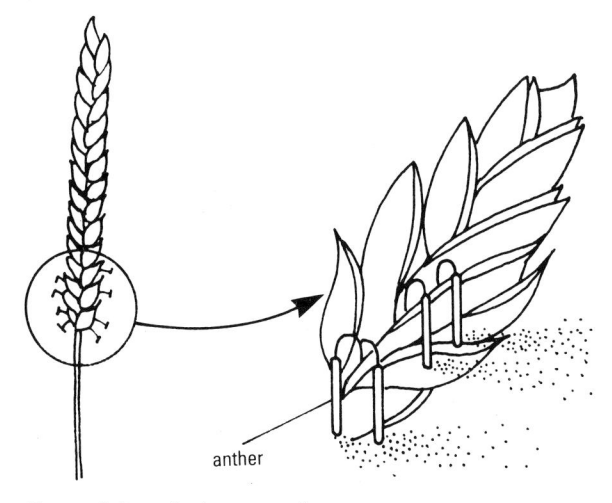

Figure 1 Pollen grains from a grass flower

MAKE SURE THE PERSON CAN BREATHE!

Figure 2

=③ If there was a way to keep the pollen away from the sufferer then the symptoms could be reduced. Suppose you are a designer. How about designing something for a hay fever sufferer to wear which would make life a bit easier? First of all, list down all the ways people are affected. Then list the ways pollen could be blocked from the person. Finally, let your imagination go and see what you come up with. Remember, the person must be able to breathe, see, speak, hear and move whilst wearing your hay fever protector. (See figure 2 for a hint!)

Other substances

Fungal spores and moulds may cause symptoms in the autumn. House dust mites which live almost everywhere can cause symptoms all the year round. These mites are especially fond of living in bedding where they eat bits of dead skin. They are microscopic and there is not a lot which can be done to get rid of them. It does not mean your bedding is dirty if you have them; everybody has them! Pets can also be a problem when people are allergic to their skin and coats.

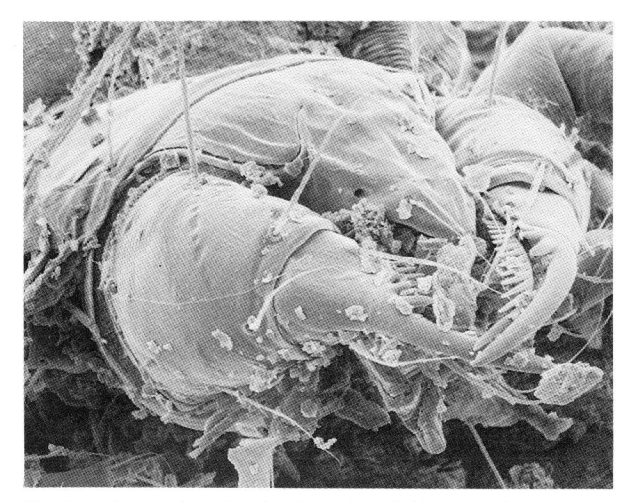

The photo shows a dust mite taken from a household vacuum cleaner

Table 1

Allergy	Description
Asthma	Affects the lining of the bronchial tubes in the lungs. Symptoms are coughing, wheezing and difficulty in breathing.
Dermatitis	Caused by skin coming into contact with irritants such as detergents, fabrics, perfumes, plants, industrial chemicals and dyes. Symptoms are itching, redness, flaking skin and blisters.
Eczema	Caused by a reaction within the body. Symptoms are similar to those of dermatitis.
Coeliac disease	Affects the digestive system and is a reaction to the protein gluten in wheat. It mainly affects children. Symptoms are wasting.

Treatments for hay fever

There is no easy cure. Injections or drugs can be given. Sufferers can take antihistamine drugs to counteract the effects of histamine. Nasal sprays or drops may cut down the irritation. Treatment for hay fever is not always effective. Sufferers may end up having to 'lie low' when there is a lot of pollen in the air.

How the immune system works

Hay fever is a result of 'mistaken identity' by the immune system. Let's try to understand what this means. First of all, let's look at what happens when the immune system gets it right, which it does most of the time. When it is working properly, the immune system attacks a dangerous invader directly or the poisons (toxins) which the invader produces. All cells, including our own have special markers on them called *antigens*. The immune system can instantly recognise whether antigens belong to the body or are foreign to it. If antigens turn out to be foreign, the immune system reacts by producing chemicals called *antibodies*. These 'knock out' the invader so that it can be surrounded and destroyed by special mobile cells called *white blood cells*. Each new invader needs different antibodies to attack it and so the immune system is kept on the go all the time. Most of the time we are not even aware of it. We only notice when things go wrong.

Read the last two paragraphs again and look at figure 3 then answer the questions.

(4) What is the immune system?

(5) What is an antigen and where would you find one?

(6) What do white blood cells do to help the immune system?

What is an allergy?

Allergies, like hay fever, occur when someone's immune system becomes sensitive to certain substances called *allergens* which may be harmless to other people. Instead of preventing the symptoms of infection such as colds or flu, the immune system actually *causes* symptoms which can be very unpleasant and even dangerous.

The victim may suffer from a blocked, running nose, hot, itchy eyes and attacks of sneezing. All in all the sufferer can feel pretty miserable.

Millions of people in Britain suffer from hay fever. Some doctors think that 20% of the population suffer from an allergy of some sort during their lives. Allergies are probably more common than we think.

(7) Explain how allergies are linked to the immune system?

(8) Describe the effects of an allergy. If you know someone with an allergy you can describe that problem. Look at table 1 showing some allergies.

antibodies antigen white blood cell

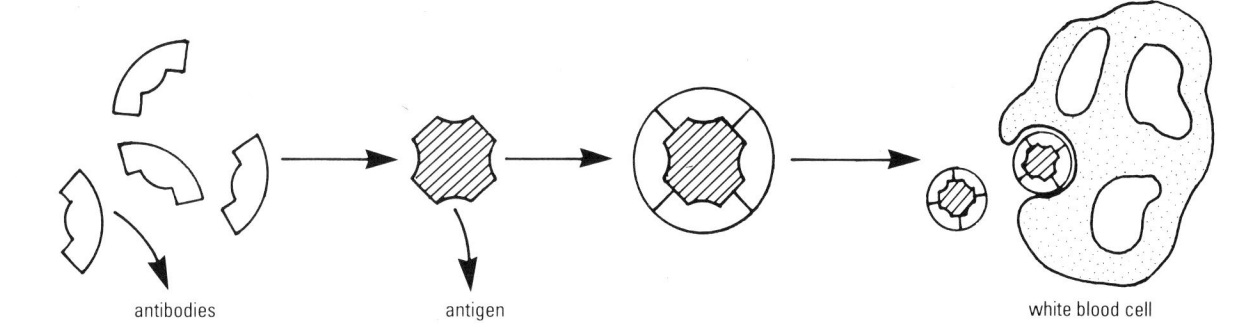

Figure 3 Antibodies surround antigen and the white blood cells 'eat' the invader.

29 SUNBEDS

Many people often use sunbeds to strengthen their skin before going on holiday

Sunbeds are used to give people a suntan. Many families have started using sunbeds in the last few years. Here are two reasons for sunbeds becoming popular.
- It is now the 'fashion' for people to have a suntan.
- Strong sunshine is not common in the UK! People going on holiday to hot Mediterranean countries can 'help' their skins to prepare for the sunshine by using sunbeds.

In this chapter you can find out about sunbeds and sunburn.

Did you know..........?
- The body needs UV radiation to make vitamin D.? This vitamin is used in the liver to take calcium out of food for building bones and teeth

What causes sunburn?

The skin absorbs a large quantity of ultraviolet radiation when exposed to strong sunlight. With too much ultraviolet radiation, the skin turns bright red and blisters may form. The skin then becomes very painful.

What is ultraviolet radiation?

Figure 1 shows the *electromagnetic spectrum* which includes lots of different radiations all travelling at 3.0×10^8 m/s, i.e. 300 million metres every second.

The ultraviolet region is divided into three separate parts labelled A, B and C (see figure 2).

UV-A from 315 to 400 nm
This passes through most types of glass and produces slight *erythema* (reddening of the skin). It is used to make some substances *fluoresce*. The colour they appear helps scientists to identify them.

UV-B from 280 to 315 nm
This also produces erythema of the skin.

UV-C from 100 to 280 nm
This can be very harmful to skin. UV-C kills germs and is used for sterilising foodstuffs and medical instruments. Lots of the fruit you buy has been exposed to UV-C radiation.

Sunlamps use either UV-A or UV-B. The skin is more sensitive to UV-B than UV-A.

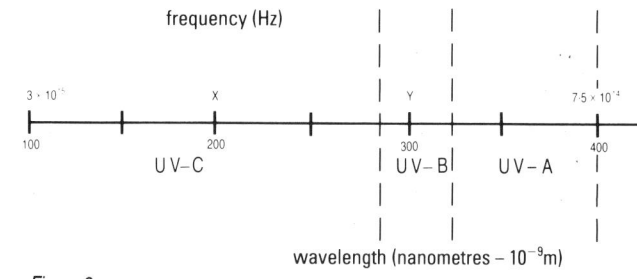

Figure 2

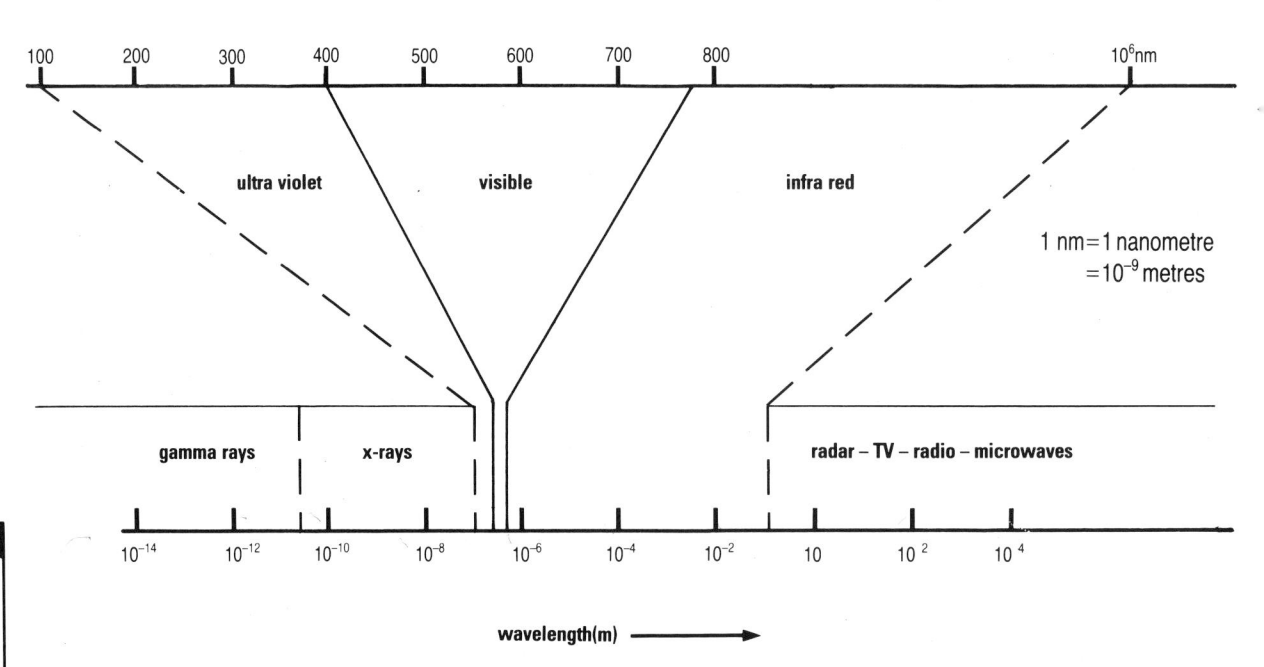

Figure 1

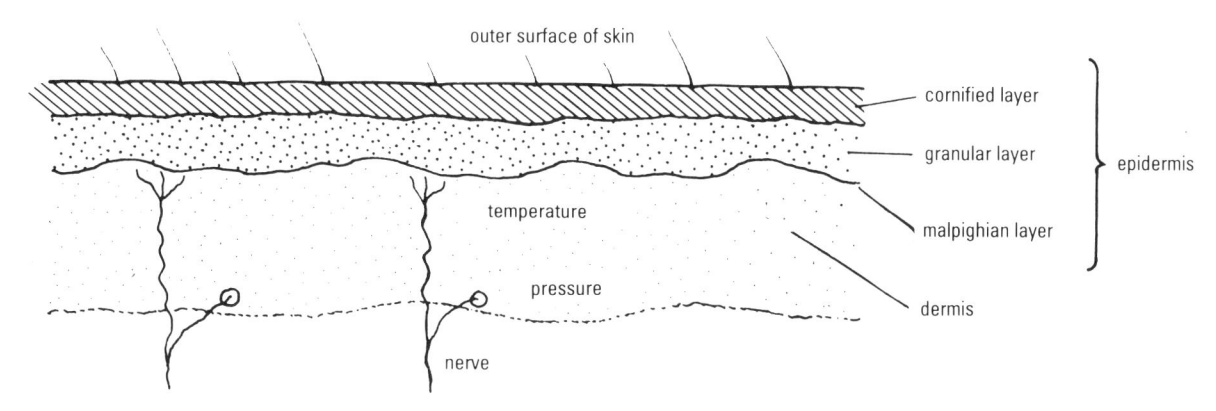

Figure 3

(1) Sunglasses protect our eyes from UV by filtering out the harmful rays. In winter, snow increases the amount of UV around us because it reflects ultraviolet light better than the soil does. Why do they wear sunglasses at the winter Olympics?

What in human skin reacts to ultraviolet radiation?

The Malpighian layer is a layer of cells (see figure 3) which is continually dividing to produce new cells. In this layer are pigment granules called *melanin*, which determine the skin colour. They go darker when exposed to sunlight. When they are dark, they protect the *dermis* from exposure to the ultraviolet radiation. If the dermis is exposed to too much radiation, it produces the blistering that we get with sunburn.

(2) Imagine that you are on holiday in a hot country.
   (a) Why should you expose yourself to strong sunlight for only a short time at the beginning of your holiday?
   (b) What happens in the skin as you sunbathe more and more each day?

(3) Some suntan lotions stop the ultraviolet radiation reaching our skin. These *sunblocks* have high protection factors of 'number 6' and above. Other suntan lotions claim to increase the speed with which we achieve a suntan. How do you think they work?

Sunbeds—how do they work?

Sunbeds are made using *fluorescent tubes* which produce lots of UV-A radiation and a small amount of infra-red rays. The infra-red radiation makes our skin feel warm when we are lying on the sunbed.

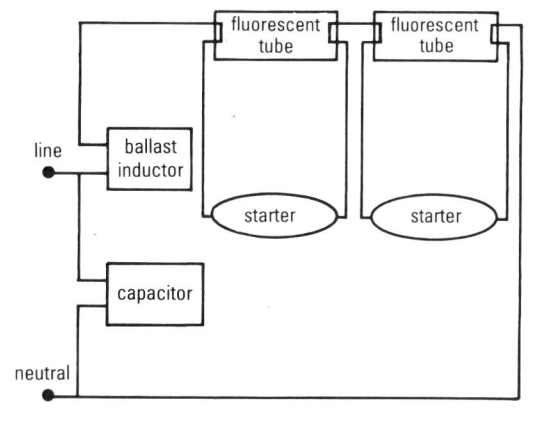

Figure 4

The more expensive sunbeds have fluorescent tubes above and below the person. The fluorescent tubes are similar to the ones used in kitchens and classrooms, except that they are designed to produce lots of UV radiation rather than visible light.

(4) Why do sunbeds use UV-A radiation and not UV-B or UV-C radiation?

Look at figure 4. When the lamp is first switched on, current passes through the tube electrodes via the starters. This warms up the tube to produce a gas of mercury. After a few seconds, a high voltage is made by the inductor and the capacitor. This voltage makes the fluorescent tube conduct and it emits ultraviolet radiation.

(5) Describe any possible electrical dangers present in sunbeds. How are we protected from them?

(6) How does the timer help us to use the sunbed properly? How will we know if we have had too much radiation?

Should we use sunbeds?

Some doctors say that too much exposure to ultraviolet radiation can make our skin grow old and wrinkly. It could even cause skin cancer. Perhaps we should find out more about these things before we use sunbeds or lie out in the sunshine.

(7) Write a short leaflet on the 'do's and 'don'ts' of sunbathing for people going to a hot country for their holidays. You might use cartoons to give your message.

(8) Write a questionnaire on sunbeds and analyse the results from at least 10 people you know. Each question should have only three possible answers 'Yes', 'No' and 'Don't know'. Here are some topics for questions:

Suntans and fashion.
Sunbeds may cause wrinkling or cancer.
Is the possible risk from sunbeds worth taking?

Find out if boys or men have different views from girls or women.

30 CLONING

Whom do you look like? Have people sometimes said 'You've got your mother's eyes and your father's nose!'? This is possibly true, because you are really a mixture of features from both parents.

In this chapter, you can learn about cloning and think about whether cloning should be allowed.

Genetics and fertilization

A new individual is produced when the nuclei of male and female sex cells join together. This process is called *fertilization*. The nucleus of the new cell contains 'strands' called *chromosomes*. These strands contain coded instructions called *genes*.

Genes help to determine your eye colour, height, whether you have straight hair or curly hair, and all your other features. *Genetics* is the study of inheritance and helps us to understand why living things look the way they do.

— (1) What passes on information from one generation to the next?

Parents and children

For humans, life begins as a cell whose nucleus contains all the genetic material needed to make a new human being. Half the 'information' has come from the father's sperm cell and half from the mother's egg cell. As the new human being grows, the genetic material in the nucleus is copied over and over again for all the developing cells.

= (2) Why does a child look partly like its mother and partly like its father?

What is a clone?

If you take a leaf or stem cutting from a plant it will contain exactly the same genes in the nucleus of each cell. So the cutting should grow into a new plant identical to its parent. This is said to be a *clone*.

= (3) Imagine that you are a clone of your mother. What would you look like? Explain your answer.

Cloning of sheep

Dr Steen Willadsen, a scientist from Cambridge, has produced clones of sheep from a single-cell embryo. He now works for a biotechnology company at Calgary in Canada. Here are the five stages he used.

Stage 1
A single-cell sheep embryo (A) has it's nucleus removed, leaving it 'empty'.

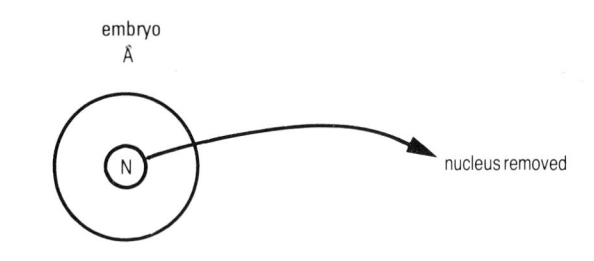

embryo A → nucleus removed

Stage 2
A second cell (cell 2) is fused with the empty cell 1. This cell has come from another sheep embryo (B) which was more developed. It had reached a stage of having 16 cells.

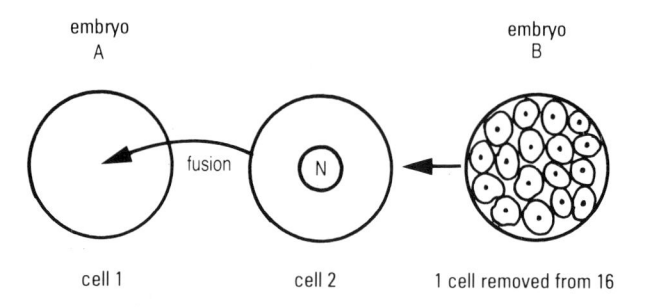

embryo A — fusion — cell 2 ← 1 cell removed from 16 — embryo B

cell 1   cell 2   1 cell removed from 16

Stage 3
Embryo A is placed in the womb of a female sheep and allowed to develop naturally.

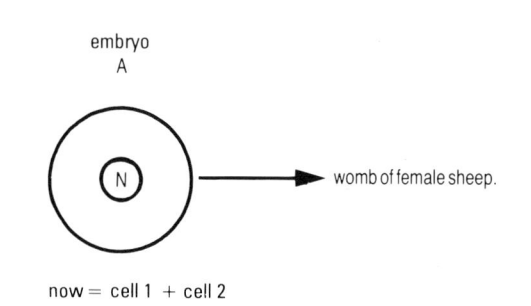

embryo A → womb of female sheep.

now = cell 1 + cell 2

Stage 4
Embryo B allowed to develop. Lamb is born.

Stage 5
Embryo A develops into a lamb. It is identical to B.

= (4) Describe in your own words how Dr Willadsen carried out the first three stages in his method.

= (5) Read the article 'Clone cows for farms' in figure 1. Do you think that the cloning of farm animals should be allowed? Explain your answer.

THE OBSERVER, SUNDAY 14 FEBRUARY 1988

Clone cows for farms

ROBIN McKIE ■ Science Correspondent

SCIENTISTS are on the verge of creating herds of genetically-identical cattle and flocks of sheep that are indistinguishable from each other.

The development will have a considerable impact on farming, but also threatens to trigger a protracted legal battle between British biotechnology firms and European patent lawyers.

The cloning breakthrough has also revealed that researchers are now much closer to the cloning of human beings than was previously thought.

'It is clear that cloning humans could be a practical consideration in a few years,' said Professor Barry Cross, of the Institute of Animal Physiology, Cambridge. 'However, I just don't see that there will be any demand for it — even if the practice was to be permitted, which is also extremely unlikely.'

Figure 1

Cloning of humans

Cloning of humans could be used to avoid genetic problems. Some people are born with a disease which they have inherited from one of their parents. Let us suppose that a man has a disease which can be inherited. The couple may choose *not* to have a child because of the very high risk of the child also having the disease.

If cloning were made possible, the woman could have a nucleus transplanted from one of her own cells to an egg cell. The egg cell would then be placed in the wall of her womb and allowed to develop as a normal baby. The child produced would be identical to her and would not inherit the disease from the father.

Should we allow cloning?

In figure 1 (second and third paragraphs), the writer says that cloning of humans may be possible in a few years. But Professor Cross does not think many people will want the cloning of humans.

A child could be cloned to be identical to one of its parents. A whole family of children could even be made identical. These children would not have their own 'identity'. The normal process of fertilization allows everyone to be different.

= (6) List the advantages and disadvantages in the cloning of humans.

= (7) Many people feel that it is wrong to interfere with nature and to 'design' a child. Write a letter which you might send to your MP explaining why cloning of humans should or should not be allowed.

****

Did you know.........?

Cloning and gardeners
*When a single-celled organism divides into two, the new cells are **identical** to the first. The two new organisms are clones of the 'parent'. This is an example of **asexual reproduction**.*

● *Gardeners and botanists use asexual reproduction to produce clones of plants. Pieces of stems or leaves are removed from a plant as 'cuttings'. They are kept moist to encourage root growth. Many cuttings survive and grow into new plants which are clones of the parent plant. Growing geraniums from cuttings is easier and quicker than growing from seed.*

● *Plants are also grown by a method called **tissue culture**. It is an expensive method and is only used for special plants such as orchids and palms. A few cells from the parent plant are removed and kept alive using plant hormones. The cells divide and multiply into many new cells each identical to the cells taken from the plant. Eventually a new plant is formed. All the information for the plant to develop is in chromosomes in the nucleus which are passed on as cells divide.*

61

31 TEST-TUBE BABIES

In July 1978, the world's first test-tube baby was born. Louise Brown was a perfectly formed little girl. Unlike other babies, she had *not* been conceived inside her mother's body. She was conceived by *in vitro* fertilization, or IVF for short (*in vitro* is Latin for 'in glass'). We say she was a *test-tube baby*.

In this chapter you can learn about several ways in which childless people can be helped to have a baby.

Conception of a test-tube baby

Scientists combined a female egg from Louise's mother and a male sperm from her father in a test tube. To remove the egg, the surgeon inserted a very fine tube into her mother's abdomen. The tube is made of an 'optic fibre' and allowed the surgeon to view inside her body without cutting her. Looking down the tube is like looking down a microscope. Through it, the inside of her uterus, oviducts and ovaries could be seen.

When the woman's ovary had been located the surgeon carefully removed an egg. This egg was then fertilized by a male sperm from her father outside the body in a test tube. The fertilized egg was then implanted in the mother's uterus to develop.

Since 1978, there have been nearly 4000 test-tube babies born throughout the world. Two thousand of these have been born in Great Britain.

Other methods of helping childless couples to have babies

Fertility drugs

Eggs are present in most women's ovaries from birth but they do not 'ripen' until puberty. Once they have reached puberty, around 12–13 years of age, women are able to have children. If a woman has no eggs or eggs which do not ripen at all, she is said to be *infertile*.

A woman who is infertile can try taking fertility drugs. Instead of only one egg being released each month, several eggs are released. The more eggs there are available, the greater the chance there is of her becoming pregnant. But there is a big risk of several babies being born. You may have read about multiple births in the 'news'.

A.I.D.

These letters stand for Artificial Insemination (by) Donor. Some men are sterile and so their sperm cannot fertilize an egg. In A.I.D., sperm from another man (the donor) is given to the woman. The woman may then become pregnant. The identity of the donor is never revealed to those involved. This method is also adopted by some women who wish to have a child without a partner.

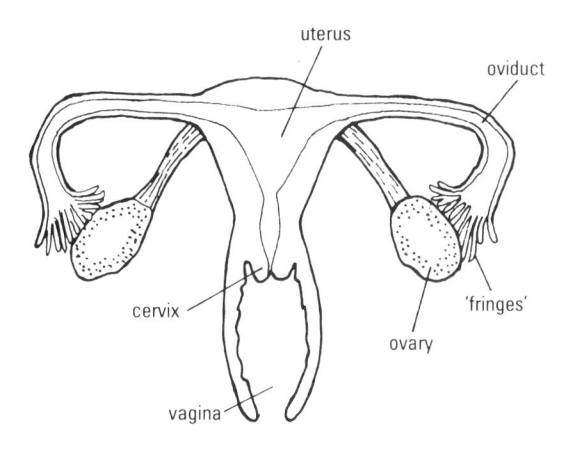

Figure 1 The female reproductive system

Surrogate mothers

In very rare cases, a woman may agree to 'leasing her womb' to another woman who is unable to have children.

The 'surrogate' mother is given sperm from a man whose partner is unable to have or carry a child. If the sperm and one of the surrogate mother's eggs join together, she is then pregnant. She will carry the baby until it is born and then give the baby to its father and his partner.

① Do you feel that childless people should be allowed to use artificial methods to have babies? Give your reasons.

② Here are the four methods described in this chapter. For each, explain their *disadvantages* and state whether you think that they should be allowed.

  (1) Test tube baby.
  (2) Fertility drugs.
  (3) A.I.D.
  (4) Surrogate mother.

③ Do you think that a child conceived by any of the methods described in this chapter has the right to know how he or she was conceived? Give your reasons.

Surrogates claim starts baby inquiry

THE Department of Health is to study a claim that some 100 surrogate babies have been born since 1980 and that many more are planned.

The claim has been made by Mrs Gena Dodd, whose Triangle organisation puts infertile couples who want to have children in touch with potential surrogates.

Mrs Dodd says that what she does is not unlawful because no fees are involved. But a Department of Health spokesman said reports of the surrogate births would be studied "in greater detail over the coming few days in the light of the Surrogacy Arrangement Act, 1985", which banned commercial surrogate motherhood.

Mrs Dodd, a Scottish housewife from Gruids, Sutherland – herself surrogate mother to four-year-old John – said there had been a lot of call for her work since she started the agency: "Since 1984, I have had numerous requests from childless couples desperately seeking surrogates. I cannot give childless couples any guarantee of ever having a potential surrogate for them, as there are always more childless couples than surrogates and I have to wait for women to contact me if they wish to help a childless couple.

"Surrogacy is not illegal. What I do is not illegal, as I do this on a voluntary basis and I receive no fee whatsoever.

"If the Government would let a non profit-making clinic set up to help childless couples and surrogates get proper counselling, advice and support, then organisations like Triangle would no longer be needed," said Mrs Dodd.

● Two of Britain's leading test tube baby clinics, Bourn Hall near Cambridge and Hallam Medical Centre, London, are joining forces to become the world's largest infertility centre.

THE GUARDIAN Monday July 25 1988

32 ANIMAL BREEDING

During the last 60 years, farm animals have steadily increased their output.

- The average mass of milk produced by cows in 1920 was 2500 kg. By 1980, the mass had increased to 4500 kg.
- The average number of eggs laid by hens in 1920 was 180. By 1980 the average number had increased to 280.

Although many people now insist intensive farming methods should not be used others still believe they are the most effective way to increase yield

There are several reasons for these big increases. The skills of farmers, vets and building designers have improved. And there are better foods and drugs to keep animals well fed and healthy. In this chapter, you can learn about the success of animal breeders.

What does the animal breeder do?

The animal breeder changes some features of animals by special breeding methods. For example, a breeder may want to increase the yield of milk from a cow or the number of eggs from a hen.

Features such as these are affected by **genes** which are passed from one generation to the next. If a breeder can change the genes being passed on to the next generation, features will be changed in all future generations.

Any animal has many features such as coat colour, mass and milk yield. Each of these is passed on by different genes.

= (1) Copy and complete table 1 assuming that the improvement continues at the **same rate** for the next 40 years.

Table 1 Gradual improvement of milk/egg production (per year)

Year	Milk per cow/kg	Eggs per hen
1920	2500	180
1940	3167	214
1960	3834	247
1980	4500	280
2000		
2020		

Selecting individuals for breeding

When a bull and a cow are mated, it is difficult to predict what the calf will be like. Let's imagine that a breeder wants to increase the yield of milk. The breeder will be successful if the mature calf gives more milk than its mother. So a bull will be sought that passes on genes which increase milk yield.

A breeder needs to test a bull for several years to see if its offspring pass on this feature. A bull may be 5½ years old before it is 'proved'. But once proved, the bull can be mated with many cows.

= (2) Explain why a bull must be tested before it is mated with cows to increase milk yield. Use the words **genes** and **features** in your answers.

= (3) Explain how a dog breeder could try to produce poodles with long legs.

64

Artificial insemination (A.I.)

A bull need not be mated with a cow to pass on its genes. Semen can be obtained from the bull and artificially placed in the cow. This process is called **artificial insemination** (A.I.). Semen can be collected from a bull and stored for many years. The semen can then be used even when the bull has died!

Artificial insemination allows many cows to be fertilized by a single bull. Only about 100 bulls are used to inseminate all the cows in Great Britain!

But great care must be taken in selecting these bulls. Otherwise thousands of calves and their offspring can be badly affected.

= (4) What is A.I. and why is it a useful process? Give one big disadvantage.

= (5) One bull, in one year, can produce 80 000–90 000 sons or daughters by using A.I. Why then, do you think, even 100 bulls are still needed to provide Britain's calves?
(**Hint:** Think about the many different **breeds** of cattle in Great Britain).

THE first all test-tube twin Calves, Frosty III and Frosty IV, were presented to the world yesterday by Philip Paxman, Chairman of Animal Biotechnolgy, which developed them, *writes Tim Radford.*

THE GUARDIAN Wednesday September 14 1988

Other ways of 'improving' animals

A hormone is a substance produced in an animal which 'triggers' the animal to behave or grow in a certain way. Scientists have 'switched on' growth hormones in mice which have caused the mice to double in size! It is possible that the size of pigs or cattle could be doubled by the same method.

You can read about *cloning* in chapter 30 (Book 2). This process leads to identical animals being bred. This seems a good idea if an animal is found to have 'perfect' features.

In Europe in the 1960's, *intensive* farming methods were introduced. Calves were kept in small crates to produce veal quickly. Chickens were crammed together to produce eggs in a very small space. Pigs were kept in dark sheds so that they gained weight quickly.

We now believe that these methods should not be used. Animals can suffer stress if they are kept in a small space and do not meet other animals.

= (6) Here are two views about animals:

(A) Animals can feel stress and pain and should be treated with care. Intensive farming methods should be *banned*.

(B) Some people can only afford to buy meat and animal products if they are cheap. Farmers should be allowed to use *any* method of food production as long as they can produce cheap food.

Write down A or B to show which view you share and explain why you believe this view to be correct.

33 THE SEA— Our biggest solution

About 97% of all the water on the Earth is in the oceans. Water has some special properties which affect the Earth. For example, water dissolves a far greater number of substances than any other common liquid.

What is dissolved in sea water?

Sea water contains about 35 g of dissolved solids in each kg. The most common elements in sea water are listed with their concentrations in table 1. These elements are present as parts of compounds and not as pure elements. The units are g/kg and the numbers show the mass in g of each element dissolved in each kg of pure water. Another important element present is oxygen dissolved as a gas as well as in water molecules.

= ① Use table 1 to draw a pie chart of elements dissolved in sea water. The third column gives the number of degrees for each element.

Table 1 Elements in sea water

Element	Concentration/(g/kg)	° for pie chart
Chlorine	19	195
Sodium	11	113
Magnesium	1.3	13
Sulphur	0.9	9
Calcium	0.4	4
Potassium	0.4	4
Other elements	2.0	22

With a salinity of about 200 g/kg it is virtually impossible to sink in the Dead Sea

Memo Pad –

a) Density in kg/m³ = $\frac{\text{mass in kg}}{\text{volume in m}^3}$

The density of a liquid increases if the mass of a certain volume of the liquid is increased.

b) An object will float in a liquid if the density of the object is <u>less</u> than the density of the liquid.

The memo pad for chapter 1.11 may also help.

Salinity of sea water

The *salinity* of sea water is the *total dissolved solids* in g per kg of water. Common salt (sodium chloride) makes up about 86% of the total dissolved substances. Dissolved solids *increase* the density of the sea water so high salinity water has a high density.

In open oceans, the salinity varies between 33 g/kg and 37 g/kg with a typical value on the surface of 35 g/kg. Here are some interesting variations:

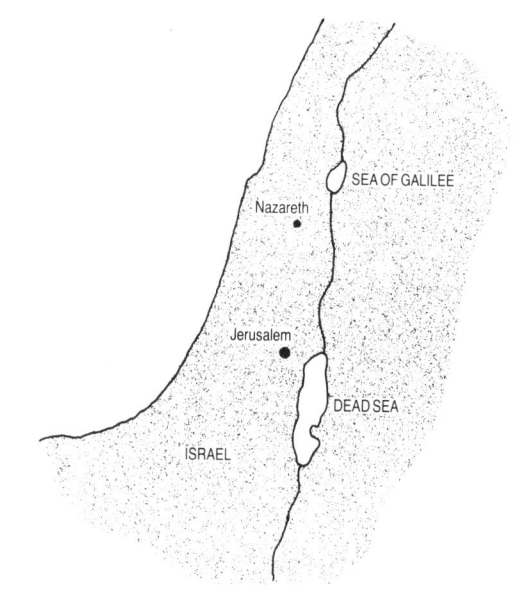

Dead Sea

Water only leaves the Dead Sea by evaporation. No rivers leave the Dead Sea as it is the lowest point on the surface of the Earth at more than 400 metres *below* sea level. The salinity is now about 200 g/kg. The density of water in the Dead Sea is so high that people can float with their shoulders and knees well out of the water and they cannot swim properly.

– ② Look at the map of the Middle East and look for the Dead Sea. What famous river flows into the Dead Sea from the North? What famous Sea does this river flow into on its way to the Dead Sea?

≡③ Calculate the mass of chlorine, sodium and magnesium which can be obtained from 1 cubic metre of average sea water, (1 m³ of average sea water weighs about 1022 kg).

=④ Why is the density of water in the Dead Sea higher than the density of pure water? Why do people float so high in the water of the Dead Sea? (The Memo Pad may help).

Mediterranean Sea

There is low rainfall and high temperatures in the Mediterranean Sea so the salinity is high. High salinity water has a high density. As the water *leaves* the Mediterranean at the Straits of Gibraltar, it sinks to the bottom of the channel whilst inflowing water with lower salinity and density enters.

=⑤ Why does water *leaving* the Mediterranean Sea flow at the *bottom* of the channel below the inflowing water?

Baltic Sea

There is high rainfall and much land drains into the Baltic Sea. This fresh water dilutes the sea water. So the salinity of the Baltic Sea is lower than in the oceans.

Oxygen in sea water

Oxygen in sea water is vital to marine life. Fish cannot survive without taking oxygen from the water. The oxygen is dissolved from the air by the sea water at its surface. The amount of oxygen in the air is about 200 cm³ per litre of air, but there is only about 7 cm³ of oxygen dissolved in a litre of sea water. Look at table 2 showing the volume of oxygen dissolved in sea water saturated with air at various temperatures.

=⑥ Using table 2, draw a graph of volume of dissolved oxygen in sea water against temperature.
   Plot volume in cm³ per kg as *y* (1 cm = 1 cm³ per kg).
   Plot temperature in °C as *x* (1 cm = 2 °C).

Use your graph to find the *difference* in volume of oxygen dissolved, (a) at 0 °C and 2 °C, (b) at 28 °C and 30 °C.
   Compare the two differences.
   About how big would you expect the difference in volume to be between 58 °C and 60 °C?

Table 2 Volume of dissolved oxygen in sea water at various temperatures

	Temperature of sea water/°C						
	0	5	10	15	20	25	30
Volume of oxygen/ cm³ per kg of sea water	10.2	8.9	7.9	7.0	6.4	5.8	5.3

Oxygen in the Atlantic Ocean

Look at table 3 which shows the average temperature of water at the surface of the North Atlantic Ocean at several latitudes.

=⑦ How does the temperature at the surface of the North Atlantic Ocean change as you move northwards?

≡⑧ Copy the table below and write in the data for columns 3 and 4. Use the notes below the table.

1 Place	2 Latitude /°	3 Ocean temperature /°C	4 Dissolved oxygen/ (cm³/kg)
Iceland	65		
Shetland Is.	60		
N. Ireland	55		
Lands End	50		
Azores	38		
Canary Is.	28		
Cape Verde Is.	15		
Equator	0		

Column 3; You can find the temperature of the surface of the ocean from table 3.
Column 4; Using temperatures in column 3, you can find the volume of dissolved oxygen from your graph for question 6 or from table 2.

Oxygen and fish

=⑨ Read again the first three sentences of 'Oxygen in sea water'. Then explain using your table for question 8, why big trawlers go fishing as far North as they can near the pack ice to catch cod and haddock.

You can read about more of the reasons for fish being found in special parts of the oceans in chapter 7 (Book 2).

Table 3 The average temperature of the surface of sea water at various latitudes in the North Atlantic Ocean

Latitude/°	Average temperature/°C
61–70	6
51–60	9
41–50	13
31–40	20
21–30	24
11–20	26
0–10	27

Did you know..........?

- The mass of silver which can be extracted from 1000 kg of sea water is 0.3 mg.
- The mass of gold which can be extracted from 1000 kg of sea water is 0.006 mg. Although the concentration of gold is very small there is about 20 million pounds worth in each cubic kilometre! But it would cost about as much as this to extract the gold!
- There is enough common salt (sodium chloride) in the sea to cover all dry land on Earth to a depth of almost 70 m.

34 COMMON SALT

Where did the U.K. salt come from?

The county of Cheshire produces 90% of the total U.K. output of salt each year (see figure 1). This total stands at about 8 million tonnes. Common salt, sodium chloride, was deposited in the U.K. when ancient inland seas evaporated. The Triassic Sea covered much of what is now mainland about 200 million years ago. The evaporation of this sea left behind valuable salt deposits.

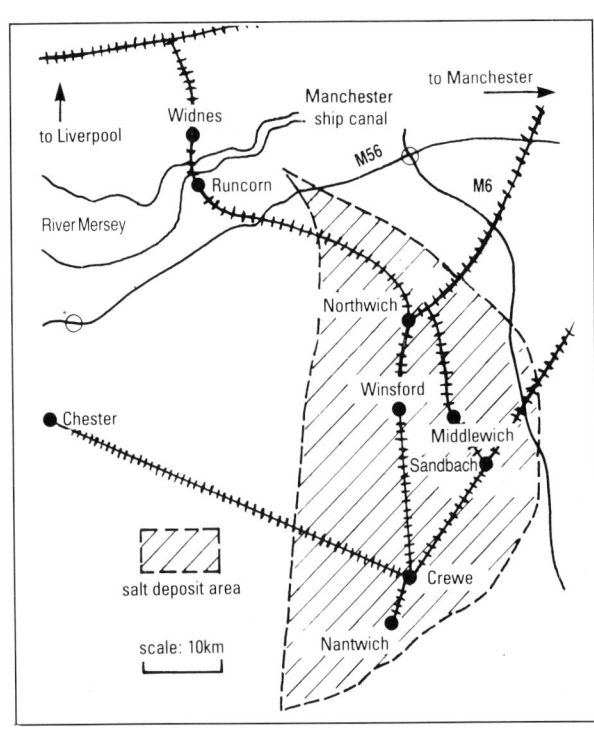

Figure 1 The Cheshire salt deposits

How is the salt mined?

The salt is 120 m below ground in the Meadowbank mine near Winsford in Cheshire. Large holes are cut leaving large columns of salt to support the roof. This is called the **room and pillar** method of salt extraction. Two million tonnes of the impure 'rock salt' are obtained this way each year for use on winter roads.

— ① Why do you think they choose 'rock salt' rather than pure salt for winter roads?

= ② How does salt help on winter roads? What damage can this salt cause?

In some areas the salt is already dissolved in natural underground water. The solution is called 'wild brine' and it is pumped out from below ground in the Sandbach and Middlewich areas of Cheshire. The brine can be evaporated to give salt crystals.

In the Holford area of Cheshire salt is removed using solution mining. A steel pipe is drilled down to the salt and then a narrower pipe is sunk inside. Water is forced down the outside and brine comes up the inside tube (see figure 2). The brine is evaporated to give a pure form of salt ideal for domestic and industrial use.

= ③ What are the three ways of getting salt out of the ground?

= ④ In hot countries, salt is often obtained by evaporating sea water. Why is this a poor way of producing pure salt? Is this method likely to be used in the U.K.?

Electricity transforms salt

Common salt contains sodium ions (Na^+) and chloride ions (Cl^-). Water also contains the hydrogen ion (H^+) and the hydroxide ion (OH^-). When two electrodes are placed in a solution of salt (called brine) and a D.C. voltage is applied, the ions move. The positive ions move to the cathode (negative terminal) and the negative ions move to the anode (positive terminal) (opposite charges attract). The result is that chlorine gas is given off at the anode and hydrogen gas at the cathode. The sodium and hydroxide ions are left in the solution making sodium hydroxide

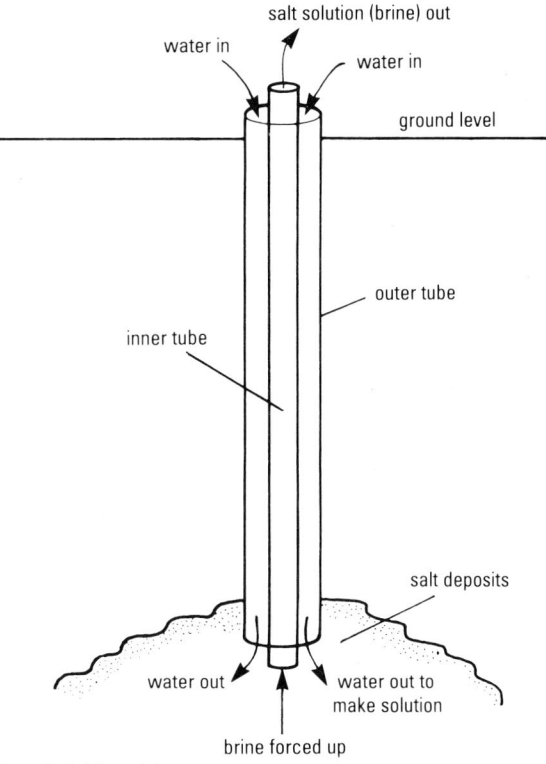

Figure 2 Solution mining

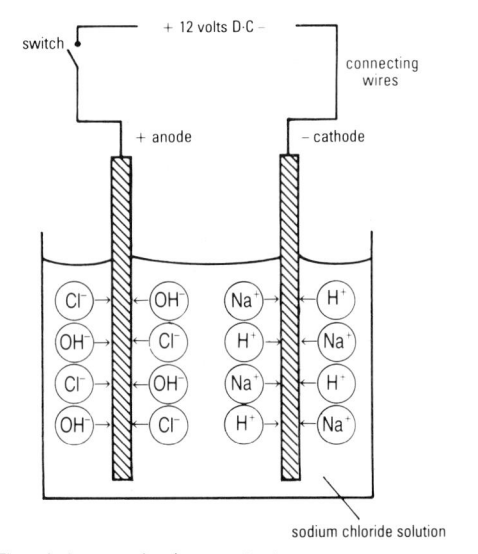

Figure 3 Electrolysis—opposite charges attract

(see figure 3). The sodium chloride solution has been broken down by the electricity. This process is known as **electrolysis**.

Which technology?
There are three main industrial processes for the electrolysis of sodium chloride solution. Each process is popular and they all use about 4 V, and a very high current of about 150 kA (kilo amp). For each tonne of chlorine made, there is 1.13 tonnes of sodium hydroxide and 0.028 tonne of hydrogen.

= ⑤ If 28 tonnes of hydrogen were obtained in the process, what mass of (a) sodium hydroxide and (b) chlorine could be expected?

Look at table 1 comparing the three processes and answer these questions.

= ⑥ Compare the three processes on
  (a) cost and ease of construction,
  (b) the need to replace parts,
  (c) the need for a constant current (not at all easy to guarantee in practice!),
  (d) environmental problems and
  (e) the quality of the product.
  Looking at the overall picture, which process is most likely to be favoured for future use?

Useful chemicals from salt

The chart in figure 4 shows that salt is a vital chemical that leads to so many other important chemicals. It should come as no surprise that huge chemical companies such as I.C.I. have set up factories not far from the salt deposits of Cheshire.

= ⑦ Look at the detailed map of the Runcorn area of Cheshire in figure 1 and answer the questions which help decide whether the area is suitable for a chemical factory.
  (a) Name a major port nearby, for exports and imports of chemicals.
  (b) Name any major roads and motorways passing through the area for transportation.
  (c) Name any major airport nearby.
  (d) Name any canals or rivers nearby for transportation or water supply.
  (e) Describe any rail lines and list any major stations nearby?

Table 1

Name of process	Construction	Operation of cell	Quality of product
Diaphragm cell	Relatively simple and inexpensive	Diaphragms need frequent replacement. Needs a constant current at 3.8 volts	Quite pure
Mercury cell	Expensive to construct	Mercury can be hazardous and must be reclaimed from the waste. Current can vary but needs 4.5 volts	Good purity
Membrane cell	Cheap to construct and install	Must start with high purity brine. Current can vary but needs 3.1 volts. Only change membrane every two years. No environmental problems	Very high purity

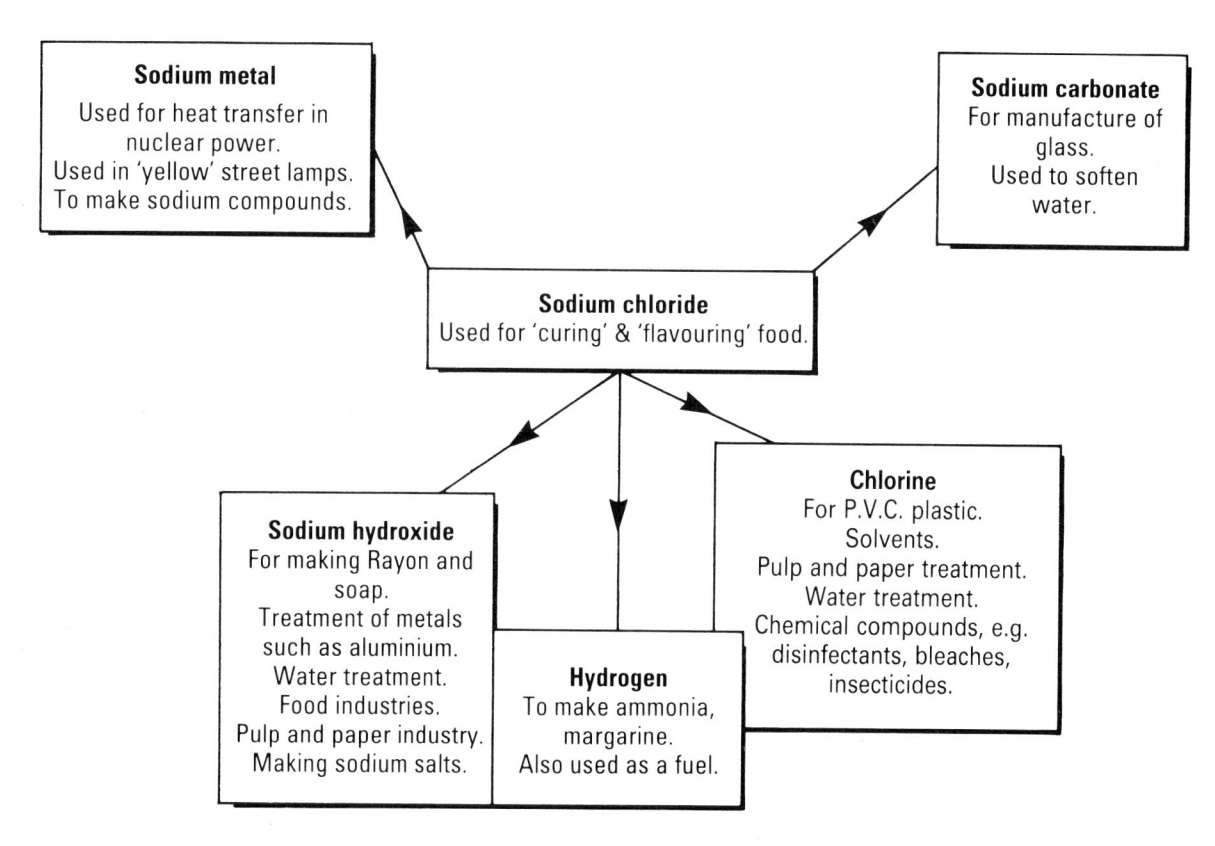

Sodium metal
Used for heat transfer in nuclear power.
Used in 'yellow' street lamps.
To make sodium compounds.

Sodium carbonate
For manufacture of glass.
Used to soften water.

Sodium chloride
Used for 'curing' & 'flavouring' food.

Sodium hydroxide
For making Rayon and soap.
Treatment of metals such as aluminium.
Water treatment.
Food industries.
Pulp and paper industry.
Making sodium salts.

Hydrogen
To make ammonia, margarine.
Also used as a fuel.

Chlorine
For P.V.C. plastic.
Solvents.
Pulp and paper treatment.
Water treatment.
Chemical compounds, e.g. disinfectants, bleaches, insecticides.

Figure 4 Useful chemicals from salt

35 CARBON DIOXIDE and the 'greenhouse effect'

- In 1972, Moscow had its worst drought for 300 years and there was a failure of the monsoon in India.
- In 1976, Europe had a record-breaking drought and the USSR had floods.
- 1983 was the hottest year on record for the average temperature in the northern hemisphere.
- In 1985, Ethiopia had a very serious drought and Band Aid went to the rescue.
- In 1988, the Sudan was flooded and many people drowned, and there was great concern in the USA about the Dustbowl Drought! (See the newspaper article on this page.)

These dramatic changes in weather have occurred during the last 15–20 years. During this time, there has been an increase in the average temperature in the northern hemisphere of about 0.5 °C. Some scientists believe that the average temperature will continue to rise. They also believe that the dramatic changes in weather are linked in some way with this temperature increase.

The 'greenhouse' hypothesis

Some scientists believe that these changes in the weather are due to the 'greenhouse effect' in the Earth's atmosphere. Read what Dr James Hanson says in the second paragraph of the newspaper article.

These scientists advise us to take action **now** to reduce the problem. But the action they recommend is difficult to take. It includes reducing the amount of coal burned to generate electricity and stopping the burning of tropical rain forest.

Greenhouse effect 'caused dustbowl'

By Charles Laurence in New York

THE "DUSTBOWL" drought in America is "99 per cent certain" to be an early manifestation of climatic changes, caused by pollution, which scientists have predicted for years, a leading space agency specialist has told a congressional committee.

Dr James Hansen said the evidence was that the "greenhouse effect" — expected to cause a rise in world temperatures and a series of droughts as infra-red rays from the sun are trapped in the atmosphere by carbon monoxide and other pollutants — had begun.

"It is time to stop waffling so much and say that the evidence is pretty strong that the greenhouse effect is here," said Dr Hansen who monitors both global temperatures and the contents of the atmosphere for the National Aeronautics and Space Administration.

Statistics compiled by NASA show, however, that the warming effect has gone beyond any previously logged variations. The expected results — drought, a drop in fresh water levels and an increase in the sea level as the ice-caps begin to melt — have already started.

"Global warming has reached a level such that we can ascribe with a high degree of confidence a cause and effect relationship between the greenhouse effect and observed warming," said Dr Hansen.

Senator Timothy Worth, chairing the Senate Energy and Natural Resources Committee, said:

"Now, we must begin to consider how we are going to slow or halt that warming trend and how we are going to cope with changes that may already be inevitable."

● **Roger Highfield**, Technology Correspondent, writes: Dr Phil Jones of the University of East Anglia's Climatic Research Unit was cautious about blaming the greenhouse effect for the drought.

"It almost certainly would have occurred anyway," he said. "There is no way you can say it is related to the greenhouse effect at all. The only thing you can say is that it might be slightly worse as a result."

But Dr Jones said there was growing agreement among scientists that the greenhouse effect would eventually occur.

"We should be doing things about it now at an international level."

THE DAILY TELEGRAPH Saturday June 25 1988

Work through this chapter and decide if you believe this hypothesis to be true and whether you agree that this advice should be followed.

= ① Why is it almost impossible to prove or disprove this hypothesis?

What is the 'greenhouse effect'?

Look at figure 1. Most of the energy radiated by the Sun is at wavelengths near to those of visible light. Our eyes have evolved to use these wavelengths.

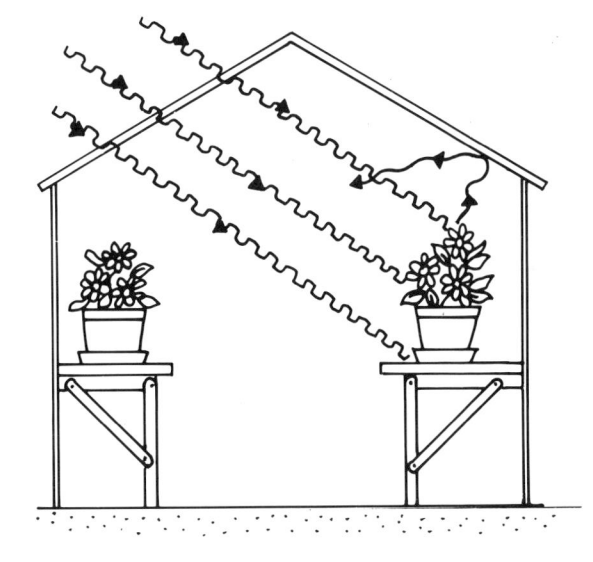

KEY: ⌐⌐⌐⌐ short-wave radiation   ➙ long-wave radiation

Figure 1 The 'greenhouse effect'

Light passes through the glass of a greenhouse and warms up the plants and other things. The plants and other contents then emit heat rays (infra-red rays) of longer wavelength. But these heat rays do not pass easily through glass. The rays are reflected back and trapped inside the greenhouse. This is called the **'greenhouse effect'**.

The 'greenhouse effect' in the atmosphere

Rays from the Sun pass through the atmosphere and warm the land and sea. Heat rays of longer wavelengths radiate from the land and sea, back into the atmosphere. Some of these rays are returned to the Earth by molecules of water vapour, carbon dioxide and other gases (see figure 2). So the Earth is warmed. The effect is called the *'greenhouse effect'*.

= ② Check the last two sections and explain why the name 'greenhouse effect' is used to describe the process taking place in the Earth's atmosphere.

= ③ What 'takes the place' of the glass in the 'greenhouse effect' in the atmosphere.

70

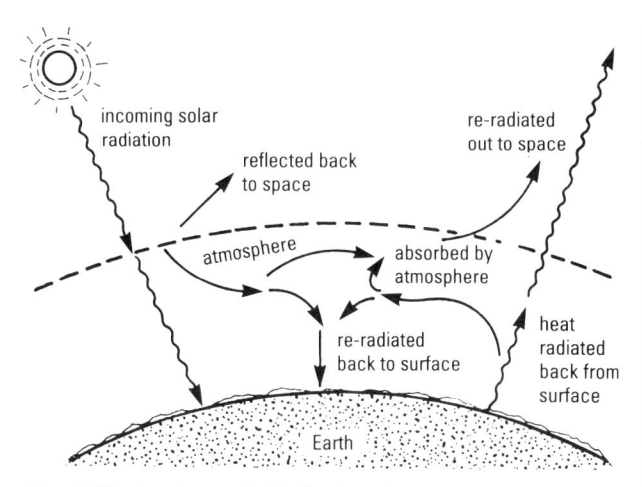

Figure 2 The 'greenhouse effect' in the atmosphere

Why has the 'greenhouse effect' become stronger?

Some scientists believe that the 'greenhouse effect' has become stronger over the last 15–20 years. They point to an increase in carbon dioxide in the atmosphere as the main cause. Look at the graph in figure 3. The gradient of the graph continues to rise.

= (4) Between which year and the present has the rate of growth been the biggest?

= (5) Use the graph to predict the year in which the concentration of carbon dioxide in the atmosphere will be *twice* the value before the industrial revolution (280 ppm).

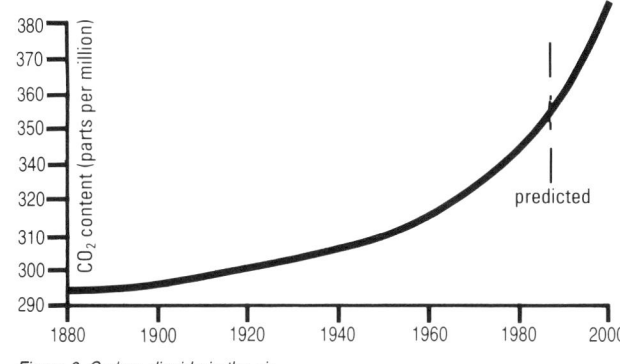

Figure 3 Carbon dioxide in the air

The use of coal to produce electricity is believed to be of one of the causes of the 'greenhouse effect'

What would happen to the Earth?

If the carbon dioxide concentration were to double, some scientists predict that these events would happen

- the average temperature of the Earth would increase by 2–3 °C.
- the average temperature near the North and South Poles would increase by 6–9 °C. Polar ice would melt and increase sea level causing flooding.
- the USA, Europe and USSR would have less rainfall and higher temperatures so reducing the yield of crops.
- India, China and Asia would have more rainfall.
- Winters in Europe would be colder.

Where has the carbon dioxide come from?

The increase in carbon dioxide in the atmosphere is blamed on two main causes; coal and oil. These have been used in huge quantities to generate electricity since the 1940's. The burning of these fuels is increasing throughout the world by 4% per year. The second cause is believed to be the burning of tropical rain forest. This *produces* carbon dioxide in burning. But trees *take in* carbon dioxide for photosynthesis so they can grow. With fewer trees carbon dioxide in the air cannot be reduced as much.

= (6) Explain why some scientists believe that burning coal to generate electricity is warming up the Earth.

= (7) Give two reasons why some scientists believe that cutting down tropical rain forests is warming up the Earth.

Another view

A few scientists do not believe that the 'greenhouse effect' is a serious problem. They argue that

- carbon dioxide makes up only 0.03% of the atmosphere.
- doubling the concentration would *not* cause heating of the Earth by as much as 2–3 °C. Some experiments suggest that the increase would only be about 0.2 °C.
- even if all the coal and oil known on Earth were burned there would still be plenty of oxygen for us to breathe.
- increasing carbon dioxide in the atmosphere would help plants to grow better.

What do you think we should do?

≡ (8) Read again 'The 'greenhouse' hypothesis'. Do you believe that it is true? Explain your answer.

= (9) Some scientists advise us to change our methods of generating electricity so that we do not burn so much coal. Write a letter which you could send to the Chairman of the Central Electricity Generating Board explaining why he should stop building new coal-fired power stations.

≡ (10) Read again 'Another view' and prepare a letter to Dr James Hanson of NASA (see the newspaper article), explaining why he may be wrong in what he says about the 'greenhouse effect'.

36 LEAD IN PETROL

Most petrol sold in Britain contains a small quantity of lead compounds. People talk about 'lead in petrol' when they mean lead compounds. In this chapter, you can read about the reasons for adding lead compounds to petrol and some of the problems.

What happens to petrol in the engine?

Petrol is a mixture of hydrocarbons which are compounds containing only carbon and hydrogen atoms. For smooth running, petrol should burn quickly and evenly in the engine. A small quantity of petrol in air should burn well to give cheap travel. Petrol with these ideal qualities is said to have a high octane number.

The hydrocarbons in petrol are of two kinds; those with a straight chain of carbon atoms and those linked like the bars in a children's climbing frame (branched). The branched hydrocarbons raise the octane number of petrol but are expensive to produce. Low octane petrol burns giving a metallic rattle (knocking) in the engine. The cheap way to make low octane petrol acceptable is to add lead compounds, such as lead tetraethyl, known as 'anti-knock agents'.

Dangers to health

Lead compounds in petrol leave motor car engines through the exhaust pipe and enter the atmosphere. Many studies have been done on the

Figure 1

effects of breathing in the lead compounds. In one study at Harvard University, USA the concentrations of lead in children's milk teeth were measured. The concentrations were then compared with the mental and physical abilities of the children. The scientists found that the children with higher concentrations of lead compounds were slower, less studious and had lower intelligence. They still could not prove that lead compounds in petrol were to blame.

Lead compounds can also enter the body from paint, food, cosmetics and the water supply. Paint now rarely contains lead compounds and careful checks are made for lead levels in all products as well as water.

= ① The scientists found a link between lead and human behaviour. Where could the lead have come from? Is it fair to blame petrol for the lead in milk teeth?

New regulations on lead in petrol

A Royal Commission on Environmental Pollution in Great Britain caused these regulations to be made:

(a) All new vehicles to run on lead-free petrol by 1990.

(b) Lead compounds in petrol to be reduced to 0.15 grams per litre from 1986.

(c) Unleaded petrol to be widely available for all vehicles by 1990.

Reduction of lead levels over the years have been: 1972, 0.84 grams per litre; 1981, 0.40 grams per litre; 1986, 0.15 grams per litre.

= ② Look at figure 1 which shows part of a leaflet from a petrol company issued to the public in 1987. Read carefully the answers to questions 1, 2, 3 and 4. Some members of the public found these answers difficult to understand. Write new answers in simple language.

Lead in Greenland snow

Look at figure 2 which shows concentrations of lead in Greenland snow. The lead must have been carried in the atmosphere to be deposited with the snow. The dates given on the scale were obtained by examining snow at different depths.

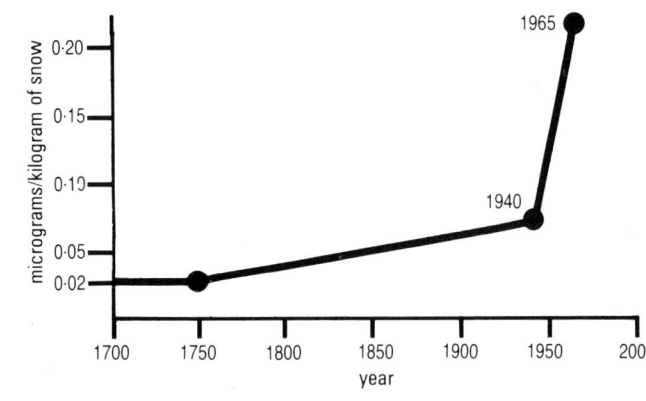

Figure 2 Levels of lead in Greenland snow

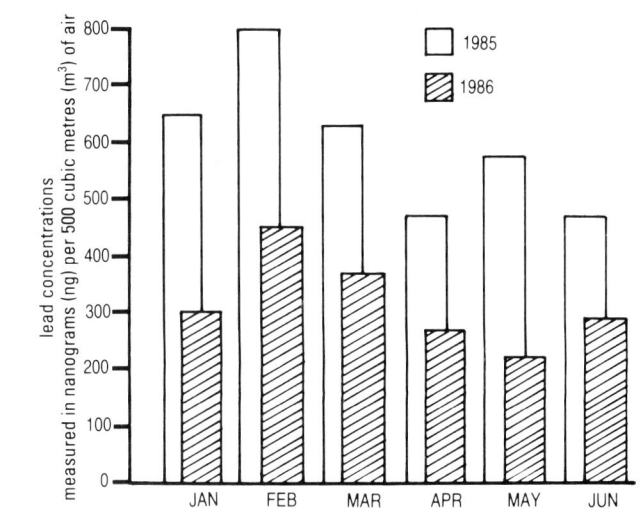

Figure 3 Monthly lead concentrations for 9 sites (Warren Spring laboratory)

= ③ Study the graph in figure 2 and suggest reasons for the change in lead level (i) up to 1750, (ii) from 1750 to 1940, (iii) from 1940 to 1965.

Monthly lead levels in the UK

Look at figure 3 showing lead levels in the air in the UK for 1985 and 1986.

− ④ Which month has the highest lead levels?

= ⑤ Are lead levels changing for the better?

= ⑥ Describe how much levels have changed between 1985 and 1986.

Lead and harmful gases

Petrol engines give out the harmful gases carbon monoxide, nitrogen oxides and several hydrocarbons. The graph in figure 4 shows how the level of these gases and lead compounds have changed between 1975 and 1985 in the UK.

= ⑦ Describe how the levels have changed for each of the gases and lead compounds and give reasons for each. (The nitrogen oxide changes are difficult to explain!) Why is there such a difference between changes in the levels of the gases and lead?

Catalytic converters

Platinum and rhodium metals in a car exhaust pipe can lower levels of carbon monoxide and nitrogen oxides in exhaust gases. They are known as catalytic converters and are costly but lower the pollution levels. Unfortunately, lead attaches to the platinum and rhodium ruining its chances of lowering pollution. You can find out more about catalytic converters in chapter 44 (Book 1) 'Catalysts are magic!'.

= ⑧ Why have catalytic converters been little used in UK vehicles despite the benefits of lower pollution? Why might catalytic converters become more popular in the UK after 1990?

= ⑨ It is costly to convert some cars to use lead-free petrol and even then the petrol is not available everywhere. Given the powers, how would you encourage car owners to convert their cars?

= ⑩ It is more expensive to make unleaded petrol. How did the Chancellor find a way in the 1988 UK budget of encouraging use of unleaded petrol?

= ⑪ Imagine you are a journalist. Write a newspaper article called 'Lead should be totally banned from petrol *NOW*'. Begin your article by saying whether or not *you* agree with this viewpoint. Use the information from this chapter to list reasons for and against this view.

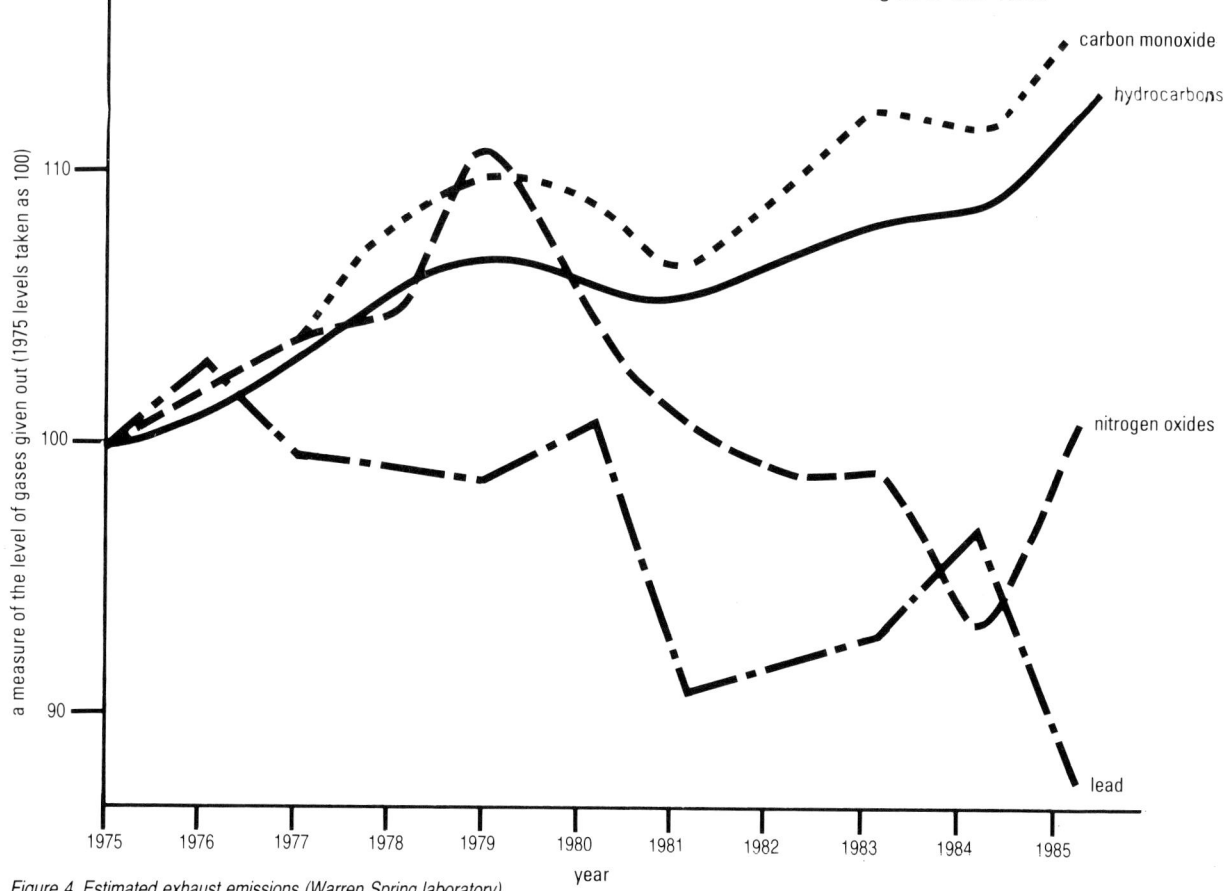

Figure 4 Estimated exhaust emissions (Warren Spring laboratory)

37 GAS FROM MORECAMBE BAY

Morecambe... an attractive prospect?

Most UK oil and gas fields have been found in the North Sea with its deep water and harsh weather. The idea of getting gas from the Irish Sea at Morecambe, with such shallow water, seemed a good idea. At low tides it is possible to walk out from Morecambe 20 km across the sand.

Sufficient gas at Morecambe?

Gulf Oil had been testing for gas at various sites in the North Sea. They tested for gas with 'echo-sounding'. Morecambe looked to them most unpromising. You can see a map of Morecambe Bay in figure 1. Echo-sounding involves sending sound waves to the depths of the sea and beyond. The echo received can give information about the rock formations below the sea.

Their echo-sounding results for the area did not suggest the correct rock formations beneath the sea for sufficient oil or gas deposits. Echo-sounding can be inaccurate in shallow water and the water was only 35 metres deep at the site. Also varying thicknesses of salt layers may have given misleading results.

Gulf Oil gave up the search. British Gas took it over after seeing Gulf's results. British Gas came to different conclusions and their gamble certainly paid off!

By 1985 the first gas was coming ashore from the Morecambe field. The gas field was huge covering an area of 8 km × 3 km and estimated to contain 140 000 million cubic metres of gas.

Figure 1 shows a map of the area with the Morecambe field being about 40 km west of Blackpool.

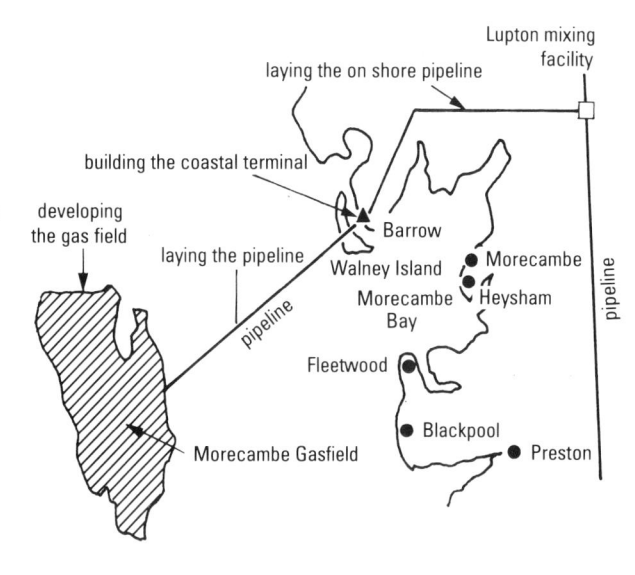

Figure 1

= ① List the reasons why echo-sounding can give wrong or misleading results.

Morecambe—a big challenge

What may have seemed a simple project in such shallow water turned out to be much more of a challenge! A trench prepared for the offshore pipeline filled in almost as fast as it was made. The tides and weather combined to destroy the trench. So a trench was dug to Barrow via Walney Island to avoid these problems. The gas pipe near the onshore terminal was repeatedly pushed up by a peat bog and so a concrete coating was applied to the pipe.

North Sea oil-drilling platforms are in deep sea. So the drill can reach many places in the reservoir of oil or gas. A small change in the angle of the drill changes the point of contact with the reservoir by a large amount. The shallow sea at the

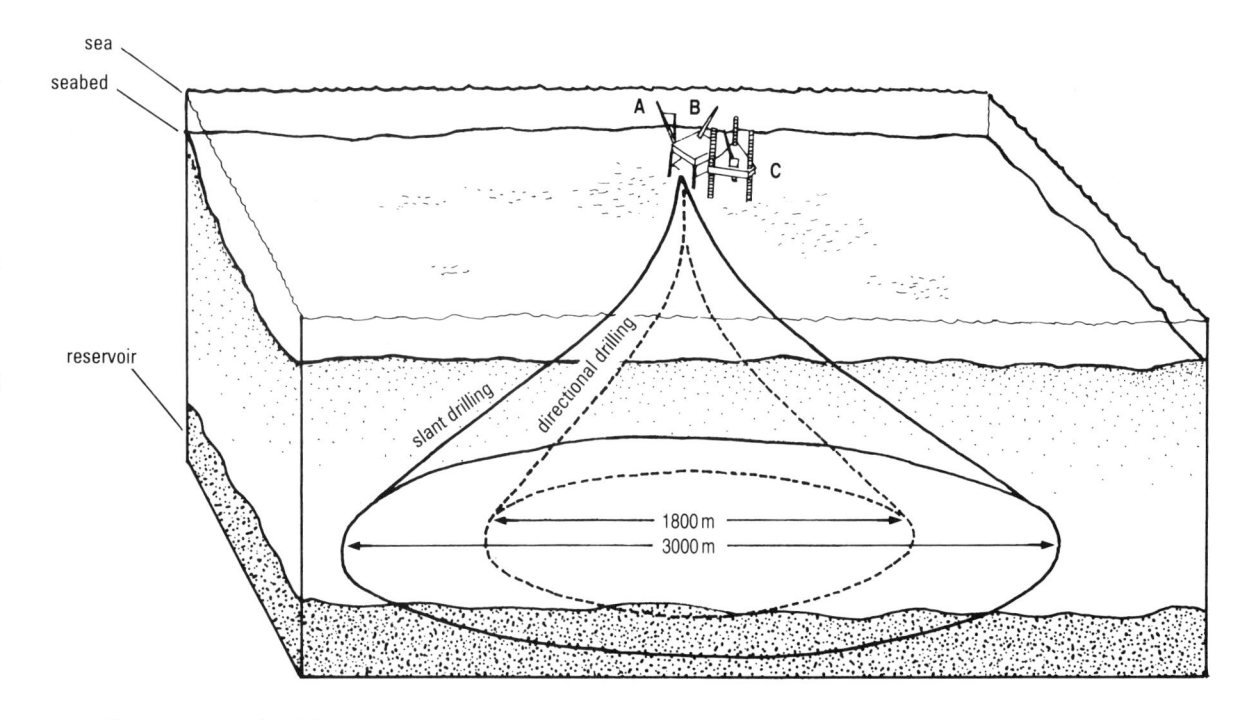

Figure 2 The advantages of slant drilling

Morecambe field meant that drills could not reach very far. They decided to use a fairly new method called **slant drilling**. They drilled at 30° to the vertical into the sea bed. Figure 2 shows the advantage of slant drilling. To their joy, the first slant drilling operation was only 30 m off target at a depth of 2286 m!

= ② List the problems found at the Morecambe field.

≡ ③ Look at figure 3 showing the line of a bore hole from a drilling platform. The hole reached 2200 m below the platform. The angle of the slant drilling was 32° (approximately). Draw a scale diagram using 1 mm = 10 m to find a distance X m between the end of the bore and the vertical line below the platform. Use your answer to explain the advantage of using slant drilling.

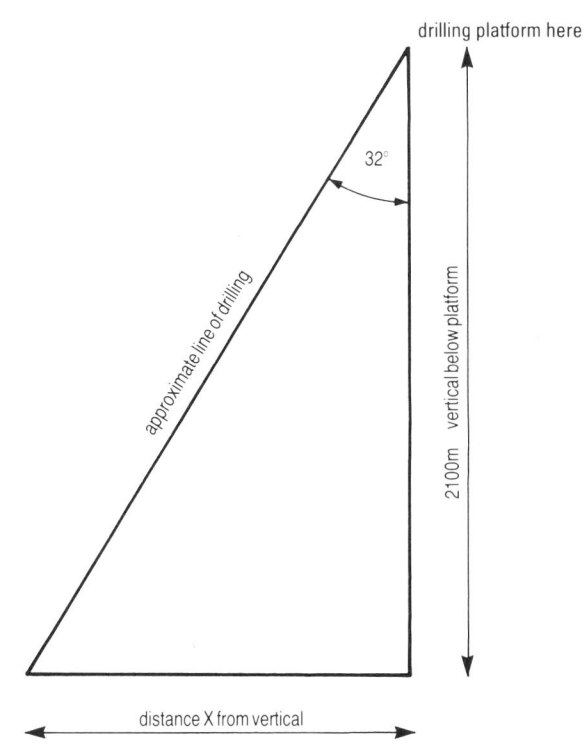

Figure 3 Line of the bore hole from the drilling platform

The offshore installations

The platforms and equipment used for drilling and collecting the gas are called **installations**. The accommodation, central processing and drilling/production platforms in the Morecambe field are shown in figure 4.

Figure 4 Installations at Morecambe Bay. From left to right accommodation platform, central processing platform and the drilling/production platform

= ④ Why is the accommodation platform separated from the central processing platform?

Onshore delivery

The gas comes to shore near Barrow which is next to a National Park. But the building has been cleverly designed to fit into the scenery. The 50 km length pipeline on shore is 1.05 m in diameter with thick walls to withstand pressures 70 times that of the atmosphere. The new pipeline joins the national gas system at Lupton, 12 km south-east of Kendal in the Lake District. Here, Morecambe gas is mixed with supplies coming southwards from the northern part of the North Sea.

Morecambe is designed to supply gas for peak demand in cold winter weather. It should provide 10% of the UK's needs at peak times. The cost of the whole project has been £1.3 billion.

= ⑤ Why is the Morecambe field only to be used during cold winter weather?

Gas *vs.* electricity

Mr Lee received his bills for gas and electricity in May 1988. The gas bill used 'therms' and the electricity bill, 'kilowatt hours' (kWh). He compared the two fuels by changing both to **joules** of energy. His comparison chart is shown below:

Gas: 182 therms, which is 19 200 MJ, cost £66.
Electricity: 2030 kWh, which is 7308 MJ, cost £106.

A MJ (mega joule) is 1 000 000 joules.

= ⑥ Work out the cost per MJ (mega joule) for each fuel.
If you had the choice of going 'all electric' or 'all gas' in your house, which would you choose on cost grounds alone?
List other factors that might influence your choice of fuel.

38. WHERE DID OIL REALLY COME FROM?

Crude oil is so valuable that nations have fought over it! Oil is an important fuel containing **hydrocarbons** which are used to produce thousands of substances including fertilizers, plastics and drugs.

Scientists agree on what oil is made of but disagree about where it came from. This chapter includes three hypotheses about oil and asks you whether you think they are true. If you do not know much about checking or testing hypotheses it may help if you read chapter 16 (Book 1) 'Hypotheses and feet' before reading this chapter.

Crude oil is a mixture of hydrocarbons. A hydrocarbon is a compound containing only the elements carbon and hydrogen. For example, methane (CH_4), propane (C_3H_8) and butane (C_4H_{10}) are all hydrocarbons found in crude oil. On this point all scientists agree.

Where did oil come from?

This is where scientists disagree. When they debate about where oil came from, they use words such as:

HYPOTHESIS—'a suggested explanation for a group of facts' (Collins English Dictionary).

THEORY—When a majority of experts agree on a hypothesis and it becomes more acceptable, it is re-named a 'theory'. A theory must be tested by experiments before it can be accepted. (You can read more about hypotheses in chapter 16 (Book 1).

① Explain in your own words how a hypothesis becomes a theory.

Three hypotheses on where oil came from

Here are three hypotheses on where oil came from. Read each in turn and then revise some facts about oil in the Databank. One of these hypotheses is completely untrue!

The Oilius productus *hypothesis*
Doctor Trebor Eel from Wallingham Polytechnic has discovered fossils of a plant which he believes once thrived both in the desert regions and at great depths in the seas and oceans. This plant, which he has named *Oilius productus*, had roots which buried themselves further into the ground than any other known plant. The roots often grew down natural gaps in the Earth's crust. The plant produced oil which it pumped out of its roots. Some rocks absorbed the oil and others did not. There is no new oil being made today because none of the plants have been found alive. Scientists are unsure why none of the plants exist today. Small numbers of the plant may have survived in rain forests.

Oilius productus

The Thomas Gold hypothesis
Thomas Gold of Cornell University, USA suggests that when the Earth was formed, materials were buried deep within it. These materials have 'cooked' for 4.5 billion years to make hydrocarbons. Critics say that the hydrocarbons would break down at the very high temperature found at the centre of the Earth. Gold says that the great pressures stop them breaking down. The oil is forced through rock to areas of lower pressure and temperature. Some of it does break up to form methane. Breaks in the Earth's crust allow a cool path for oil to reach the surface unchanged.

Drilling for oil was started at the Siljan granite crater in Sweden as a test for this hypothesis. Granite is formed by lava cooling slowly. If oil is formed from plants and animals, oil should not be found in granite. If this hypothesis were true oil should never run out.

The kerogen hypothesis
Plants and animals die and their remains collect at the bottom of seas, rivers and lakes. They form layers which get buried and compressed over millions of years. This happens particularly where rivers dump silt into the sea in sedimentary basins. The plant and animal remains make tar-like molecules called *kerogen*. The hydrocarbons in the kerogen are cooked under the high pressure and temperature. The pressure forces the oil out of the rock into more porous areas. The oil becomes trapped in a pool below a cap of rock that will not absorb it. Some of the oil breaks down to form methane.

The drill site at the Siljan Ring, Sweden

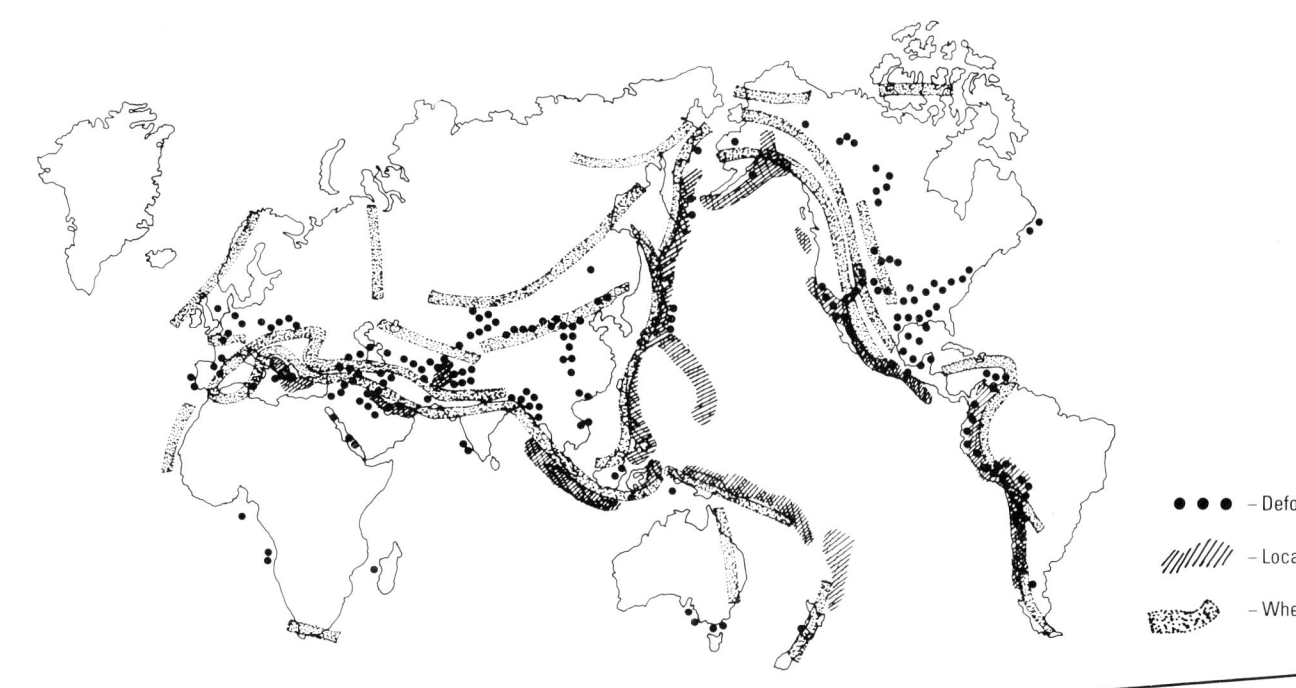

Figure 1 Most oil is found near fractures in the Earth's surface

- ●●● — Deformation belts (ripples in the earth's crust)
- ////// — Locations of major earthquakes.
- ▓▓▓ — Where oil is found.

Which hypothesis do you think is the best?

You have read the three hypotheses. You have also read some facts about oil.

≡ ② Take each hypothesis in turn and explain whether *you think it is true*. Include in your answer which parts of each hypothesis *you think* may be true.
Use a table like this for each hypothesis.

Hypothesis	Evidence for	Evidence against	Conclusions

≡ ③ Which hypothesis do you think is the best? Give your reasons in about four sentences.

= ④ One of the hypotheses is completely untrue. Which one do you think this is?

DATABANK

SOME FACTS ABOUT OIL

1. It is generally agreed that trees have made coal over millions of years. Coal also contains hydrocarbons.
2. Hydrocarbons are found in some meteorites which have never had animal or plant life on them.
3. The oil supplies do seem to be running out rather quickly.
4. Most oil is found near fractures in the earth's crust (rifts, faults and continental plates). See figure 1 for details.
5. Helium and mercury, two rare elements in the earth's crust, are found in rather large and variable amounts along with oil and natural gas. This suggests another gas (methane?) has carried and collected helium and mercury over a long journey.
6. The Guardian newspaper reported on 21st June 1988 that 60 kg of black sludge oil had been recovered from 6 km below the surface at the Siljan crater Sweden.
7. Oil reservoirs are often found stacked one above the other.
8. There are about 30,000 oil fields and only 33 of these contain half of the known oil reserves. The Middle East has 25 of these special 33 oil fields but surely could not have had all that extra plant and animal life!
9. Volcanoes give out lava which can tell us things about the centre of the Earth. Huge amounts of carbon dioxide are given off from erupting volcanoes. Perhaps this comes from burning methane.

39 NUCLEAR POWER

Omega is an imaginary island some 800 km off the coast of South America. Up until 20 years ago, it was a quiet agricultural community. Then industry began to grow and the population grew with the prosperity of the island. But the island has no coal, oil or gas resources of its own and has to import all the fuel it needs. The great oil crises in the 1970s and 1980s increased the costs of imported fuel. The Government has decided to build a new power station on the island. This will give a cheap reliable source of power for the future.

Figure 1 shows a map of the island with the main centres of population and the sites of the major industries. There is a high mountain range running down the centre of the island. The prevailing wind blows from a north-easterly direction.

Alpha, the island's capital, has a population of 15 000 and is the site for most of the island's light industry.

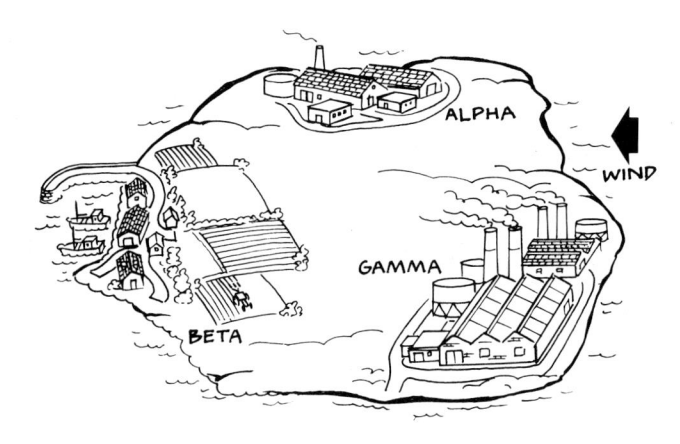

Figure 1 Map of Omega

The population of Beta is 80 000 and most people work in agriculture. There is also a large fishing community. Most of the industry is near Gamma which has a population of 70 000.

The island's government has to decide whether to build a coal-fired power station or a nuclear-powered station and where it should be built. The nuclear reactor they could choose is called the Pressurised Water Reactor (PWR) as used in the USA.

Information about the PWR

Figure 2 shows a diagram of a 600 MW PWR. This means that the maximum power it can produce is 600 MW. Reactors like these usually produce an average of 150 MW.

What happens inside a PWR?

Nuclear reactions take place inside uranium dioxide fuel rods and release a lot of heat. This heats water which surrounds the fuel rods. This water is kept at very high pressure inside a steel pressure vessel and it does two things.

(1) It acts as a moderator for the nuclear reactions.
(2) It passes heat on to cooling water in a heat exchanger. This hot cooling water is then used to make steam for the turbines which drive the generators.

In a PWR, about 32% of the heat released by nuclear reactions is used to make steam. The rest of the heat is lost warming up the pressure vessel and the air! Some of the energy of the hot steam is also lost in warming the turbines. The turbines have to be cooled by passing water through them. This cooling water is usually pumped from a nearby river or sea.

Cooling water from some power stations is used to warm large tanks of water in trout farms and other fish farms.

= (1) Look at the advantages and disadvantages of a coal-fired and of a nuclear-powered station shown in table 1, and decide which one you think should be built on the island.

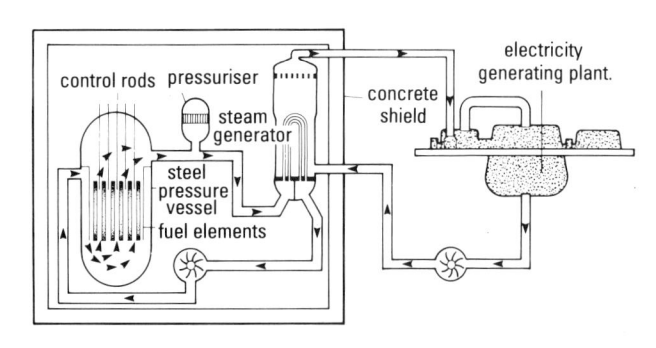

Figure 2 A 600 MW pressurised water reactor

= (2) It is a good idea to build a power station near a river or the sea. Explain in each case why this is so.

= (3) It is a good idea to build a power station far away from where people live. Explain why this is so for:
(a) a coal-fired power station.
(b) a nuclear-powered station.

= (4) Whereabouts on the island would you choose to build the power station? Explain your choice.

Table 1

	Advantages	Disadvantages
Coal fired	Cheap to build Ready in 4 years No radiation hazard	Coal is expensive to import Cost of electricity is high Pollution of the atmosphere from smoke and gases* Mining accidents
Nuclear	Cost of electricity is low No pollution from smoke or gases Very little fuel is imported	Expensive to build Ready in 10 years Radiation may escape Disposal of radioactive waste is difficult

* You can read more about pollution from power stations in chapter 35 (Book 2).

Sellafield nuclear power plant in Cumbria

Nuclear power plants and cancer—is there a link?

Read the newspaper articles in figure 3 and 4 about cancer and nuclear power plants.

- ≡ (5) In the last paragraph of figure 3 a hypothesis is stated. Write out, in your own words, what this hypothesis states. (It may help you to know that leukaemia is a cancer of the blood and that there are nuclear power stations at Sellafield and at Dounreay.)

- ≡ (6) Describe the extra evidence in the article which is claimed to support the hypothesis.

- ≡ (7) Explain, in your own words, two arguments given by Dr Taylor *against* the hypothesis.

There are usually three different opinions when people are asked whether we should build nuclear power stations.

(1) Yes, we should build nuclear power stations wherever they are needed.

(2) Yes, we should build nuclear power stations but only very far away from people.

(3) No, we should not build nuclear power stations anywhere.

= (8) Write a short paragraph giving your views on each of these three arguments. Explain whether you agree or disagree with each.

= (9) Do you think the island should have a coal-fired or a nuclear-powered station? Write a short paragraph to explain your decision.

New case takes cancer rate near nuclear plant at Sellafield to 'eight times national average'

Rob Edwards

ANOTHER young person with cancer has come to light in a small village next to the Sellafield nuclear reprocessing plant in Cumbria.

A 22-year-old women who went to school in Seascale and now lives in the village was last month diagnosed as suffering from a lymphoma or lymph cancer.

According to Mr John Urquhart, an independent nuclear risk analyst, this increases the cases of blood cancers among the under-25s in the area to eight over 22 years.

"This is very, very significant," he said yesterday. "The rate of these types of cancer in young people around Sellafield is now eight times the average." Three lymphomas among local under-25s were reported in six years, said Mr Urquhart, 20 times the expected rate. He felt this questioned the wisdom of encouraging families with children to visit the Sellafield exhibition.

The Government's advisory Committee on the Medical Aspects of Radiation in the Environment (Comare) had been informed of the case.

A report published by Comare in June concluded that the evidence tended to support the hypothesis that some feature of the nuclear reprocessing plants at Sellafield and at Dounreay in Caithness led to an increased risk of leukaemia in young people living near by.

THE GUARDIAN Wednesday October 3 1988

Figure 3

Nuclear facts store growing

THE risks of developing cancer as a result of exposure to radiation are usually grossly over-estimated in the minds of the general public.

Because it cannot be seen, heard or smelled, and because people associate it with atom bombs and cancer, radiation is viewed by many people with the same fear and suspicion that witchcraft evoked in the Middle Ages.

From health studies on groups exposed to radiation, such as the survivors of the Hiroshima and Nagasaki bombings and hospital patients who have been treated with radiation for various medical conditions, much is known about its effects on health.

Compared to the everyday hazards in life, the risks of cancer from radiation exposure are minute at the levels experienced by people living around our power stations or working in them.

Media controversy over the risks associated with eating irradiated "Chernobyl lamb" ignores evidence from the health records of many people regularly exposed to artificial radiation every day of their working lives.

News headlines followed the recent publication of the Comare report after six cases of leukaemia were found among young people living near Dounreay in Scotland — twice the national average.

However, investigations found that public radiation doses from Dounreay were much less than background radiation levels and were too low by at least a factor of 1,000 to have caused the cancers. The committee recommended fur-

DR DICK TAYLOR, above, head of the Board's health and safety strategy branch, examines the background to a major new initiative by the CEGB for a worldwide health study of nuclear industry workers.

ther research should be carried out.

The records for the two largest groups of radiation workers — those employed by British Nuclear Fuels and by the Atomic Energy Authority — have been analysed recently. On average, these workers receive more radiation than CEGB workers.

Not only do the findings show that they are as healthy as any other group of workers, but they are in fact healthier than the population as a whole.

POWER NEWS June 1988

Figure 4

40 THE ATMOSPHERE OF THE EARTH

The air we breathe comes from the atmosphere. It is difficult to believe, but the mass of the Earth's atmosphere is more than 5 million, million, million kg (5.27×10^{18} kg)! And we cannot even see it! This mass is about 1 millionth of the mass of the Earth itself and about 1 thousandth of the mass of the oceans.

Change in atmosphere with height

Have you ever noticed your ears 'pop' when riding in a motor car up a hill? If you have flown in an aeroplane you will have noticed your ears 'popping' on take-off and landing. The cause of the popping is the sudden change in the pressure of the atmosphere with height. Sucking a sweet, or just swallowing, helps to make the pressure inside your ear change to equal the pressure of the atmosphere. This soon lets the ear return to normal.

Look at table 1 and find the pressure of the atmosphere at an altitude (height) of 10 000 m. This is the height at which long distance aeroplanes fly. The pressure is 26.4 kN/m². You can see from the table that the pressure at sea level (0 m) is 101.3 kN/m². So the pressure at 10 000 m is only about one quarter of that at sea level. That is why the pressure in aircraft has to be increased to keep the passengers comfortable.

= ① (a) Draw a graph to show how the pressure of the atmosphere changes with height to 10 000 m. Plot on your graph as follows:
y-axis (vertical) for pressure using a scale of 10 kN/m² to 1 cm.
x-axis (horizontal) for altitude using a scale of 1000 m to 1 cm.

As the highest mountain in Great Britain, Ben Nevis has an altitude of 1343 m (4406 ft)

(b) Mark on your graph the altitude and pressure for,
(A) top of Ben Nevis (1343 m),
(B) top of Mount Everest (8848 m).

(c) Describe the shape of the graph and estimate the altitude for the pressure to reach zero. (Table 1 may help).

(d) Why do climbers on Mount Everest carry oxygen gas cylinders?

= ② Use the table to calculate the mass of 1 m³ of the atmosphere at altitudes of,
(a) 0 m (sea level),
(b) 1000 m,
(c) 10 000 m.

(The Memo Pad may help).

= ③ The temperature of the atmosphere decreases with height. Look at table 1 and answer these questions.

(a) At what altitude would you expect water to freeze?

(b) At about what altitude does the temperature begin to increase again?

Table 1 Pressure, density and temperature of the atmosphere

Altitude/m	Pressure/(kN/m²)	Density/(kg/m³)	Temperature/°C
0	101	1.22	15
500	96	1.17	12
1000	90	1.11	8
2000	80	1.00	2
3000	70	0.91	−4
4000	62	0.82	−11
5000	54	0.74	−18
6000	47	0.66	−24
7000	41	0.59	−30
8000	36	0.53	−37
9000	31	0.47	−44
10 000	26	0.41	−50
20 000	5.5	0.088	−56
30 000	1.2	0.018	−46
40 000	0.3	0.005	−23
50 000	0.01	0.002	−2

= ④ Imagine that you are taking part in a hot air balloon ascent to 20 000 m. Describe what precautions you would take to keep yourself comfortable.

Gases in the atmosphere

Most people know that about one fifth of the air is made up of oxygen and four-fifths of nitrogen. If you look at table 2 you will see that there are many other gases present also. But if you look

carefully at the third column, you will see that the volumes of these gases in 1 m³ of air are very small. In chapter 35 (Book 2), you can read how the percentage of carbon dioxide gas is increasing rapidly.

= ⑤ Draw a pie chart showing the proportions of gases in dry air. Show the separate 'slices' for oxygen, nitrogen and argon but group all 'other gases' together. Begin by completing table 3. (For the volume and percentage of other gases, use the information in *your* table rather than adding volumes in table 2).

≡ ⑥ Liquid oxygen and liquid nitrogen are produced by cooling air to low temperatures. Use the data in table 2 and table 3 to calculate the mass of liquid nitrogen and liquid oxygen obtained from 1 m³ of air. (The masses are the same for the liquids as the gases above their freezing points).

Table 2 Gases in the atmosphere

Gas	Formula	Volume
Air	—	1 000 000
Nitrogen	N_2	780 000
Oxygen	O_2	210 000
Argon	A	9300
Carbon dioxide	CO_2	300
Neon	Ne	18
Helium	He	5.2
Methane	CH_4	1.5
Krypton	Kr	1.1
Nitrous oxide	N_2O	0.5
Hydrogen	H_2	0.5
Ozone	O_3	0.4
Xenon	Xe	0.086

Volume of gas in cm³ in 1 m³ (1 000 000 cm³) of dry air.

Table 3

Gas	Volume	Percentage	Degrees
Air	1 000 000	100	360
Nitrogen	780 000	78	281
Oxygen			
Argon			
Other gases			

Where did the Earth's atmosphere come from?

Read this summary of the theory of the origin of the Earth's atmosphere which was described by two American scientists in 1965.

'The Earth was formed about 4 500 million years ago from small objects, such as meteorites, collecting together in space. The Earth had no atmosphere at all at this time. The large mass coming together caused heating and melting and there were many volcanoes on the Earth.

Volcanoes pushed out huge quantities of molten rock and gases. Gases from volcanoes include water vapour (up to 97%), nitrogen, carbon dioxide, hydrogen, sulphur dioxide and chlorine with much smaller quantities of methane, ammonia and other gases.

Enough water vapour has come from volcanoes to account for the total volume of the oceans. Volcanoes could also have produced all the nitrogen and other gases in the atmosphere—except for oxygen. No oxygen comes from volcanoes because it is combined with other elements in oxides and other compounds. So where did our oxygen come from?

Oxygen gas must have come from the break up of water molecules into hydrogen and oxygen. The hydrogen gas, being so light, would quickly escape from the atmosphere. At first, before life was formed, water molecules were broken up by ultra-violet light from the Sun acting on water vapour. Organic molecules (containing carbon) were formed in shallow pools on the Earth's surface through the energy of ultra-violet light. Early plant life was formed from these molecules about 600 million years ago. Then photosynthesis began in plants and this increased the oxygen in the atmosphere by releasing it from water.'

= ⑦ Why was there no oxygen in the early atmosphere? Why did hydrogen escape? What gas in our present atmosphere was not listed in the description?

≡ ⑧ Why is this description described as a theory? Write down a few ways in which proof of the theory could be found. (Think about the sentences on volcanoes and photosynthesis).

≡ ⑨ Using the theory of the origin of the Earth's atmosphere and table 2, write 300–400 words on the differences between the atmosphere about 600 million years ago and today.

Memo Pad

a)
$$\text{Density in kg/m}^3 = \frac{\text{mass in kg}}{\text{volume in m}^3}$$

So
$$\text{mass of 1m}^3 = \text{Density} \times \text{volume}$$

b)
$$\text{Pressure} = \frac{\text{Force in N}}{\text{Area over which force is acting in m}}$$

$$1 \text{ kN/m}^2 = 1000 \text{ N/m}^2$$

41 OZONE AND AEROSOLS

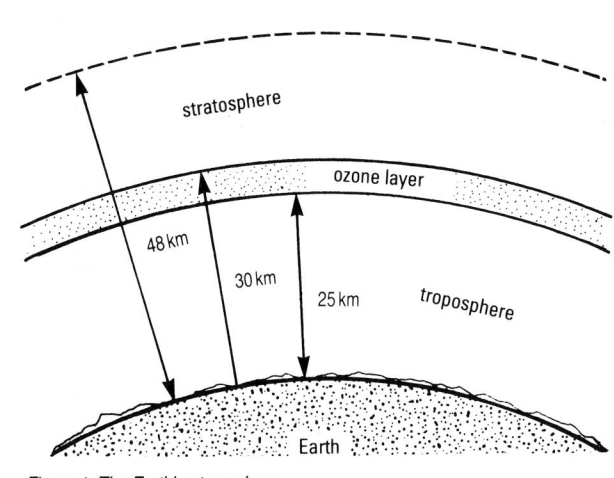

Why do we need ozone?

You may know that UV (ultraviolet) rays from the Sun give us a suntan. But UV rays can cause skin cancers. We need the ozone layer to reduce these harmful rays from sunlight. Scientists in the United States have calculated that a 1% increase in UV radiation would cause an extra 20 000 deaths from skin cancer every year.

More UV radiation reaching the Earth would also reduce yields of crops and could damage larvae of fish such as anchovies which are important as food. More UV radiation could also damage paint and plastics.

- (1) What is the difference between oxygen and ozone?
- (2) What would happen if the ozone layer disappeared altogether?

The balance of ozone

Ozone is used up when it gives oxygen atoms to other substances in the atmosphere. It oxidises these substances. The Sun's rays change oxygen into ozone in the outer atmosphere. Over millions of years the rate of production of ozone has matched the loss of ozone. The amount of ozone has become balanced. A new threat to this balance has come from substances which are used in aerosols.

How do aerosols work?

The contents of an aerosol can are under high pressure so that they come out as a fine spray when you press the top. To make aerosol cans work like this, a propellant is mixed with the useful substance. The propellant is a liquid when it enters the can under a high pressure but turns to a gas when it comes out of the hole as soon as you press the top. As soon as the useful substance leaves the can, the propellant drifts away and mixes with the atmosphere. Some scientists believe that some propellants from aerosols are beginning to destroy the ozone layer.

- (3) Explain in your own words why the propellant is needed in an aerosol spray.
- (4) Why must a propellant easily and quickly evaporate when it leaves the aerosol can?

Figure 1 The Earth's atmosphere

What is ozone and where is it found?

Oxygen molecules in our atmosphere have the formula O_2. Ozone has the formula O_3. So ozone has just one more oxygen atom in its molecule. Oxygen and ozone are very different. Oxygen is a life-giver whilst ozone is poisonous. However, we do need the protection offered by the ozone layer in the outer atmosphere.

Ozone is found in a layer very high up in our atmosphere. Look at figure 1. 'The Earth's atmosphere'. The layer containing ozone begins about 25 km from the Earth's surface and ends at about 30 km away. It is just as well that poisonous ozone is so far away that we cannot breathe it in!

The threat from aerosols

Many propellants in aerosols are made from the family of chemicals known as *chlorofluorocarbons* (CFCs for short). One member of this family is dichlorodifluoromethane which has the structure shown in the diagram in figure 2. The structure of methane is shown for comparison. Note how the

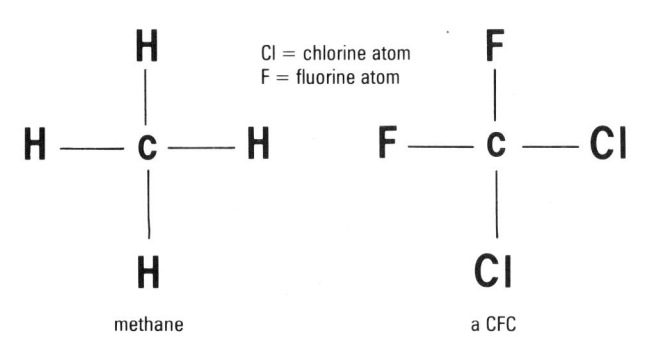

Figure 2 The chemical structure of (a) methane and (b) dichlorodifluoromethane

hydrogen atoms in methane are 'replaced' by two fluorine atoms and two chlorine atoms. Chlorofluorocarbons mix well with many other substances and do not combine with them chemically. They have no smell and change from gases to liquids easily when under pressure. So they make excellent propellants. But they can remain in the atmosphere for up to a century and they are known to destroy ozone under laboratory conditions!

Chlorofluorocarbons are also used for making foam rubber for chairs and beds; they are bubbled through the rubber as it solidifies from the liquid state. They are also used in refrigerators, air-conditioning and electronics.

Should aerosols be banned?

A 'big hole' in the ozone layer has been discovered over Antarctica. CFCs from aerosols and other products may be destroying the ozone layer. Banning CFCs as aerosol propellants may stop the hole getting bigger. Read the article from 'The Guardian' in figure 3 and then answer the questions.

5. Why is the ozone layer described as critical?

6. Name the two scientific groups involved in the ozone argument. Which scientist is a member of both groups?

7. List any points on which the two scientific groups agree.

8. List the points on which the two groups disagree.

9. Research into the damaging effects of CFCs is in its early stages. Produce arguments for delaying a ban on their use until more research has been done. What are the dangers of just continuing research?

What is being done? What would you do?
Sweden and the United States have already banned CFCs in aerosols. The Vienna Convention for the Protection of the Ozone Layer was signed by 28 countries in March 1985. This should lead to further investigations. The huge company Du Pont believes that substitutes could be found but it may take five years and cost a great deal of money. In Britain, the environmental group 'Friends of the Earth' have produced a list of aerosol products that do not contain CFCs. In February 1988, six major manufacturers of aerosol products stated that they would phase out CFCs.

Write a newspaper article with the title 'CFCs should be banned NOW'. Study the chapter including the newspaper articles and your answers to the questions to assemble your arguments.

OZONE OR NO ZONE

Friends of the Earth · The Body Shop
Helping the Earth fight back

Companies act on ozone threat

James Erlichman, Consumer Affairs Correspondent

BRITAIN'S biggest makers of aerosol toiletries announced yesterday that they are phasing out the propellant gas, CFC, which has been firmly linked with destruction of the earth's ozone layer.

"We have acted to protect the reputation of our products," said Mr John Sharpe, chairman of Elida Gibbs, the maker of Impulse body spray Harmony hairspray and five other aerosols which are propelled by CFC gases. Mr Jonathon Porritt, director of Friends of the Earth, welcomed the announcement. Leading scientists, including Dr Joe Farman at the British Antarctica Survey, believe that CFC consumption has to be cut by 85 per cent to stop the chemicals from doing further damage.

Sainsbury also said it has decided to end the use of CFC gases in all its own label products. Safeway has already removed CFCs from all its own label range. But neither supermarket is prepared to stop stocking branded products which contain the gases.

THE GUARDIAN Thursday February 2 1988

Aerosol carbon blamed for hole in ozone layer

By John Ardill, Environment Correspondent

British scientists are calling for an immediate 85 per cent cut in the use of chloro fluoro carbons (CFCs) used as aerosol propellants and foam-blowing agents after establishing that the chemicals are responsible for a big hole in the stratospheric ozone layer over antarctica.

The demand for the British Antarctic Survey will put extra pressure on the UK and EEC governments at an international protocol in Montreal next month to control CFCs. The ozone layer is critical in filtering ultra violet rays which cause skin cancer.

Latest research by the survey which discovered the hole, hardens a cautious stance by an official Stratopheric Ozone Review Group in its first report, published yesterday by the Department of the Environment. Dr Joe Farman, a member of both groups, who is reporting his latest findings and a call for action in a forthcoming issue of Nature, said that the ozone group report which was written months ago was already out of date.

He may not be supported by all members of the group. Met Office scientists said yesterday that the new findings would not necessarily change their view that the cause of the hole is not yet known.

Dr Farman said: "I was far too lax in agreeing to the consensus that is put forward. We should have stressed much more strongly that although there was little conclusive evidence in favour of the CFC theory at that time, really there was no evidence for anything else.

"Now I think we can safely say that the recent work does show pretty clearly that all the other suggestions really aren't on. It really is a 99.9 per cent probability that the CFCs are responsible.

"The situation is such that we shouldn't let the CFCs grow any more, which means in effect that we have to make an 85 per cent cut pretty sharply because at the moment we are putting them in six times as fast as nature is removing them."

The DoE said that the review group report showed that use of CFCs at present-day levels was unlikely to lead to a reduction of the ozone layer. The report says the cause of the Antarctic hole is unknown

THE GUARDIAN Friday August 7 1988

42 SPACE TRAVEL

So the space shuttle was developed and built, and first flew a manned mission in 1981.

Tragedy struck the shuttle programme in 1986 when the shuttle Challenger exploded just 73 seconds after launch, and it was 1988 before shuttle flights started again.

Before the Challenger disaster, the previous 24 shuttle missions had achieved a great deal. Thirty satellites for scientific research and for communications had been put into orbit around the Earth. Satellites in orbit have also been repaired by astronauts from a shuttle. A space station, called Skylab, has been built in space. Scientists from Earth will be taken by the shuttle to Skylab and will stay there for weeks or months carrying out experiments.

– (1) What persuaded the USA to end the Apollo programme and develop the shuttle?

= (2) The space shuttle has a mass of 30 tonnes (30 000 kg) half-way through its journey from Earth. In order to reach its orbit, the shuttle has to reach 8 km/s velocity. Using the Memo Pad, calculate its kinetic energy at a velocity of 8 km/s.

= (3) The shuttle has a mass much greater than 30 tonnes at take-off, but its mass decreases as it moves. Why do you think this is so?

= (4) Why do you think scientists wish to enter space and investigate other planets? Can you think of any day-to-day technology we have now thanks to space research?

Life in the space shuttle

Up to eight people can live inside the space shuttle. The eating and cooking area is 4 m by 3 m but has no furniture. In the **zero gravity** of Earth's orbit, walls and ceilings become floors as the astronauts float about. Exercise is important in zero gravity and an exercise bicycle is included. Sleeping is easy since there is no gravity. Sleeping bags can be tied anywhere, to the floor or the walls, and they are very comfortable!

Much of the food is **dehydrated** and takes about 20 minutes to prepare. Water is added and the meals are then heated in an electric oven. Figure 1 shows mealtime on a space shuttle mission. Drinks are **freeze dried** and hot or cold water is added when needed.

Figure 1

All the water for meals, drinks and for washing is produced as a by-product of the **fuel cells** that generate the shuttle's electricity. The fuel cells use liquid oxygen and hydrogen to produce electricity.

The astronauts can wash and shave but there is no shower on a shuttle! All rubbish and waste products are collected in a 'dustbin' under the floor. There is a toilet which uses a fan to produce a strong **airflow** to simulate the gravity of the Earth.

= (5) Explain, in your own words, the meaning of:
(a) zero gravity
(b) dehydrated
(c) fuel cell
(d) airflow

= (6) Can you explain why the space shuttle uses fuel cells to produce electricity instead of carrying lots of batteries.

– (7) Why do you think there is no shower in a space shuttle?

– (8) Why do you think that there is a need for simulated gravity in the toilet on a space shuttle?

The space shuttle

The biggest and most expensive American space project was the Apollo programme during the 1960s and 1970s which included man's only Moon landings. The Apollo programme was very expensive because each rocket was only used once. The cost of all these lost rockets was about £15 000 million.

The USA decided in 1972 to design a space vehicle which could be lauched from Earth on the back of a large fuel tank and booster rockets. After its mission in space, the vehicle could then return to Earth and land like a glider.

The future in space

People have visited space for almost 30 years. In the next 30 years there will be great changes. We must move away from expensive and wasteful rockets and develop space vehicles that can take off and land like aircraft.

In a space shuttle mission, 46% of the cost of a launch is lost when the fuel tank and boosters are used up. A vehicle that could take off itself would only cost half as much as a shuttle.

In order to go into its orbit around the Earth, any vehicle has to reach a velocity of 8 km/s. If a vehicle had to carry all its own fuel, like liquid oxygen and hydrogen, it would have very little space left for its crew and their equipment.

One answer is the British HOTOL, a 'horizontal take-off and landing' spacecraft designed by British Aerospace. Figure 2 shows what HOTOL might look like. The idea is that HOTOL would take off like an ordinary aircraft and use oxygen from the air together with liquid hydrogen from its tanks. This would take it to an altitude of 25 000 m, where there would no longer be enough oxygen in the atmosphere. HOTOL would then switch to its own supply of liquid oxygen to continue its flight into space.

HOTOL would have jet engines and fly like an aircraft. The shuttle has no engines and flies like a glider. HOTOL would be easier to land on Earth than the shuttle because the jet engines would make it easier to control.

Other programmes to build a space plane are being developed at present. The USA is planning its own version of HOTOL called the *Orient Express* and the European space agency is planning a small shuttle called *Hermes*. The next 30 years will be very exciting.

= (9) What do you think are the main commercial applications of being able to travel into space?

(10) What are the main benefits of a project such as HOTOL?

= (11) Explain why an ordinary jet engine cannot work at altitudes above 25 000 m.

= (12) Oxygen is about ten times denser than hydrogen. Explain the advantages of HOTOL being able to use oxygen from the atmosphere up to 25 000 m before switching to its own liquid oxygen.

Figure 2

Space: the next frontier

As America steps up the shuttle programme and the Russians seek joint ventures, ADRIAN BERRY asks: where do they go from here?

THE FLAWLESS flight of America's space shuttle Discovery has been aptly called a "return to the future". The five astronauts have not only restored faith in NASA's immediate shuttle ambitions (about 50 flights are planned in the next five years); they have revived hopes that man's journey into space is only beginning.

Within 30 years, the foremost experts believe, the reach of our technology will have extended from the present 22,300 miles — the height of communication satellites — to more than 40 million miles, the distance of Mars.

Permanently manned space stations, settlements on the Moon and Mars, the mining of the asteroids — all these will become possible with the assured safe access of people to space; and hydrogen-powered aerospace planes will eventually make the journey up into Earth orbit even cheaper.

THE DAILY TELEGRAPH Wednesday October 5 1988

Memo Pad

Kinetic energy = ½ × mass × (velocity)²

43 TALKING ROUND THE WORLD

Guglielmo Marconi (above) was born in Bologna in 1874. Before his death in 1937 he was awarded the 1909 Nobel prize, along with the German physicist Karl Braun, for the development of radio telegraphy

About 100 years ago, electric cables were laid along the bottom of the oceans to carry telegraph messages. Very soon, there were so many people wanting to send messages that the cables could not cope.

In 1901, Guglielmo Marconi sent a message by *radio* from Cornwall to Newfoundland over 3000 km away. The frequency of his radio waves was 1 MHz or 1 000 000 vibrations per second. Since then radio transmitters and receivers have been used in all countries of the world.

Table 1 Some distances on the Earth and in space

	km
London to New York	5760
London to New Zealand	20 000
Radius of Earth	6400
Radius of geostationary orbit	42 200
Earth to Moon	380 000

Radio and the ionosphere

Many people did not believe that Marconi could send a radio signal 3000 km *around the curvature of the Earth*. It was possible because of the *ionosphere*. This is between 80 and 400 km above the surface of the Earth. Ultraviolet rays from the Sun break up gas molecules and produce charged ions. It is these charged ions (hence *ion*osphere) which reflect radio waves.

Talking to New Zealand

= (1) Find a pair of compasses, a ruler and a sheet of graph paper for this question. The problem is to find the distance radio waves travel in taking a message from London to New Zealand. Look at figure 1 to help you to begin.

(a) Set the compasses for a radius of 64 mm and draw a semicircle with its centre half way down the left side of the graph paper. This semicircle represents the surface of the Earth with a scale of 1 mm = 100 km. (See table 1.)

(b) Mark London at the top of the semicircle above the centre and New Zealand at the bottom of the semicircle. London and New Zealand are directly opposite to one another on the other sides of the Earth.

(c) Now draw another semicircle with a radius of 67 mm having the same centre as before. This represents the ionosphere at 300 km above the surface of the Earth.

(d) Imagine radio waves being sent from London to New Zealand and being reflected by the Earth's surface and the ionosphere. They travel in straight lines and are reflected like light.

(e) Measure the total length of the path of radio waves in mm. Then multiply the number of mm by 100 to obtain the distance in km. (You should find a distance of about 22 000 km.)

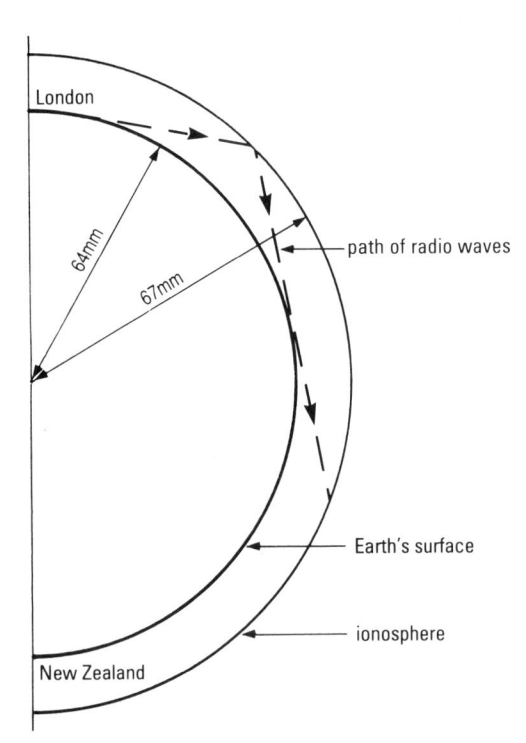

Figure 1 Radio waves around the Earth. (Not to scale)

Communications satellites

Some radio waves are *not* reflected by the ionosphere and can escape completely from Earth. Radio waves in the range of frequency from about 15 MHz to 3000 MHz can escape and frequencies in this range are used when sending messages via satellites.

Since the 1960s, communications satellites have been taken into space by rockets to reflect radio waves back to Earth. Many of these satellites have been placed in *geostationary orbit*. This means that they stay above the same part of the Earth all the time. (Actually they move once around their orbit in 24 hours which is the time taken for the Earth to spin once around its axis).

Communications satellites have an orbit of radius 42 200 km with its centre at the centre of the Earth. (See figure 2.) There is a satellite above the Atlantic Ocean so that messages from Europe can be reflected to the United States.

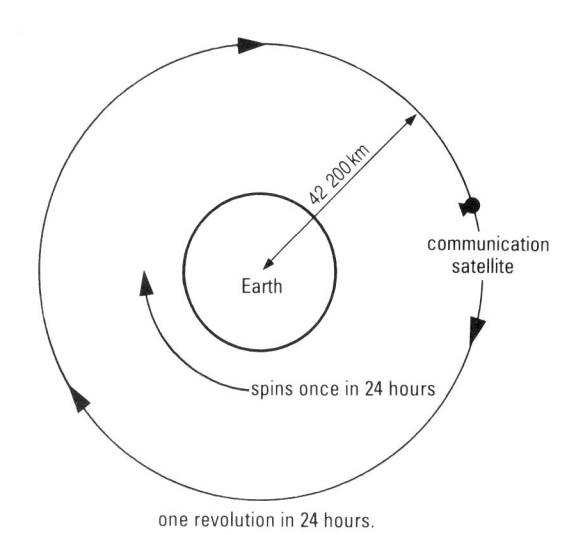

Figure 2 A geostationary orbit. (Not to scale)

Earth — 42 200 km — communication satellite — spins once in 24 hours — one revolution in 24 hours.

Talking to New York via satellite

=② Find a pair of compasses, a protractor, a ruler and a sheet of graph paper. Mark a point half way down the left hand side of your graph paper for the centre of the Earth. Look at figure 3 to help you to begin.

(a) Copy this table into your notebook. It will help you to work out distances using a scale of 1 mm = 400 km. Fill in the top two rows using table 1. The distance on the graph is the distance in km divided by 400.

	Distance /km	Distance on graph/mm
Radius of Earth		
Radius of geostationary orbit		

(b) Using your compasses draw a semicircle for the surface of the Earth. Mark London at the top and New York at 52° from London.

(c) Mark a communications satellite A in its orbit at 26° from London.

(d) Draw in the path of radio waves from London to New York and measure its total length in mm. (Calculate the distance in km by multiplying by 400.)

(e) Calculate the time taken for radio waves to travel this distance by using the Memo Pad. (You should find the time to be about a quarter of a second.)

It is not possible for someone in London to talk to someone in New Zealand using just one satellite because of the curvature of the Earth. In question 3, two satellites are used.

Talking to New Zealand via satellite

=③ (a) Carry out the same instructions as for question 2a. Then mark London on top and New Zealand at the semicircle representing the Earth. Look at figure 4 to help you.

(b) Mark a communications satellite B in its orbit at 45° from London. Mark another satellite C in its orbit at 135° from London.

(c) Draw in the path of radio waves from London to B, from B back to Earth at the equator, from the equator to C and finally from C to New Zealand. Calculate the distance in km by multiplying your path by 400.

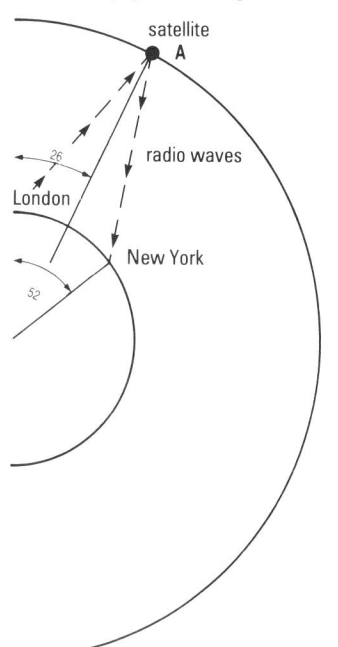

Figure 3 Using a satellite to New York. (Not to scale)

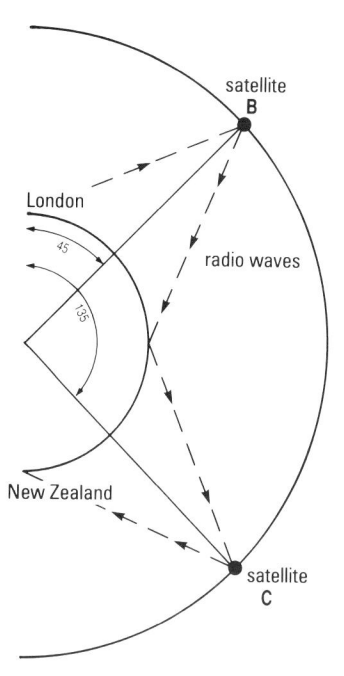

Figure 4 Using satellites to New Zealand. (Not to scale)

(d) Calculate the time taken for radio waves to travel this distance by using the Memo Pad. (You should find the time to be about half a second.)

When you speak over the telephone to someone in New Zealand there is a minimum gap of about 1 s between your question and the other person's answer. This can be annoying until you become familiar with the problem. But it is a small inconvenience when you think that your words have travelled a distance equal to over half the way to the Moon!

=④ Explain why there is a minimum gap of about 1 s between a question and an answer during a telephone call between London and New Zealand.

Memo Pad

$$\text{Time taken} = \frac{\text{Distance travelled in km}}{\text{Speed in km/s}}$$

For light and radio waves, speed is 300 000 km s^{-1}.

44 LISTENING TO SPACE

People have been watching the stars ever since the human race emerged. Records of astronomy began over 2000 years ago. But serious study probably began with Galileo and his small 50 mm diameter telescope about 350 years ago. He showed the ancient beliefs that the Sun revolved around the Earth, and that Earth is at the centre of the Universe, to be wrong. Until about 1925, it was still believed that our solar system with the Sun at the centre and the Earth and other planets around it, was at the centre of the Universe. And it was thought that the Milky Way *was* the Universe!

Huge telescopes built during the last 50 years show us that there are about 100 000 million stars in the Milky Way. We also know that the Milky Way is one of many *galaxies*, or groups of stars in the Universe. Our sun with its planets is also a long way from the centre of our galaxy.

Radio astronomy

Although astronomy is a very old science, radio astronomy began only about 50 years ago. And it began almost by accident.

Karl Jansky, who worked for Bell Telephone Laboratories in the USA was studying the interference or 'crackle' in long distance radio communication. You can hear interference when you are tuning in your radio to a weak signal. Whatever he did to cut down the interference, he could always hear a crackle in the background. But of much more interest was his clever conclusion that the changes in *strength* of the crackle repeated themselves every 23 hours and 56 minutes! This is the time taken for the Earth to rotate once about its axis with respect to the stars.

= ① Write down the conclusions which you think Jansky made from these observations. Give your reasons.

Following Jansky's observation, special telescopes were built to receive these weak radio signals. Look at the photograph of the huge radio telescope at Jodrell Bank in Cheshire, south of Manchester. The 'dish' has the shape of a parabola and is 76 m in diameter.

= ② Why do you think the dish has the shape of a parabola. (**Hint:** Think about the shape of the shiny reflector in a torch, bicycle lamp or car headlamp).

Wavelengths and frequencies

In chapter 43 (Book 2) you can read about radio waves from Earth being reflected back by the *ionosphere*. This is part of the atmosphere a few hundred km above the Earth's surface. It contains millions of charged ions which reflect radio waves.

Table 1 Strengths of radio signals at 73 cm wavelength from Andromeda

Declination (y) →		55	50	45	40	35	30	25
	44	3.5	4.0	2.5	1.8	1.0	0.0	0.0
	43	2.5	4.8	6.0	3.5	1.8	0.5	0.0
	42	2.0	4.0	7.5	5.8	4.0	2.8	0.1
	41	2.8	5.5	8.2	16.0	7.0	4.0	0.5
	40	1.5	4.0	6.0	6.0	5.0	3.0	1.0
	39	1.0	0.0	2.0	2.5	1.8	5.0	1.0
	38	1.2	1.0	0.8	2.0	2.0	1.0	0.0

Right ascension (x) →

A very important range of frequencies which can pass through the ionosphere is **15–3000 MHz**.

1 MHz is 1 000 000 vibrations per second and is pronounced 'megahertz'. The radio telescope at Jodrell Bank was designed to work for *wavelengths* as short as 21 cm.

(3) Copy this table in your notebook and use the Memo Pad to help you complete the table. Remember that radio waves are part of the electromagnetic spectrum and travel at the speed of light.

Wavelength	Frequency	Notes
21 cm		Received at Jodrell Bank
1 m		Received at Jodrell Bank
	104.8 MHz	Radio 1 (VHF) from London
1500 m		Radio 4 longwave

(4) Using your table and the information in 'Wavelengths and frequencies' explain why VHF (Very High Frequency) radio signals cannot be received at large distances from the transmitter which sends out the signals whereas Radio 4 on 1500 m can be received in France and Germany.

What do radio telescopes 'hear'?

The 'picture' of space shown by radio telescopes is quite different from that which we see with our eyes. Some bright objects in space seem to send out hardly any radio waves. And radio telescopes have detected very strong radio waves from objects which can hardly be seen by the most powerful light telescopes!

One kind of information from radio telescopes is used to draw 'maps' of space. The maps are like contour maps or Ordnance Survey maps.

To give you an idea of how a map is drawn, table 1 shows some data for the galaxy Andromeda. The different numbers show areas which have different strengths of radio waves. The higher the number, the greater is the signal received. This galaxy is rather like our galaxy in shape. In question 5 you are asked to use this data to plot the strength of radio signals of wavelength 73 cm on a grid.

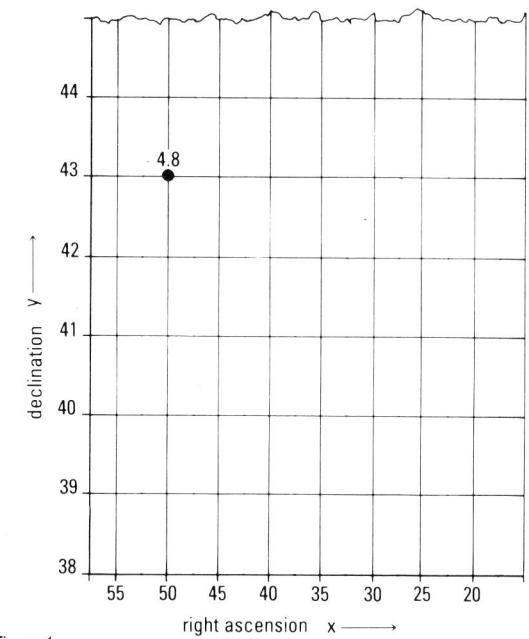

Figure 1

(5) Draw a radio map of Andromeda at 73 cm wavelength using these steps.
(a) Draw a grid on a sheet of graph paper like that in figure 1. You will see that y is for *declination*, giving angles above the Earth's equator. You will also see that x is for *right ascension* giving angles across the sky from right to left.
(b) At the point x = 50, y = 43, write the number 4.8 as shown in figure 2.
(c) Check on the table that at the point x = 50, y = 43. Then write down the numbers at the correct points for all the other data in the table. You now have the strengths of radio signals at all the points on your map.
(d) Draw a 'contour' line for strength 8 on your grid. All points *inside* your contour line must have a *greater strength* than 8. Make sure that your line passes near to points which are close to a strength of 8.
(e) Draw contour lines for strengths 4 and 2.
(f) Mark on your chart, a cross where you think the centre of Andromeda occurs. Write down, under your chart, the co-ordinates (x, y) for the centre of Andromeda.

Memo Pad –

WAVELENGTH, FREQUENCY AND SPEED

For all waves in the electromagnetic spectrum

speed = frequency × wavelength

$$\text{frequency} = \frac{\text{speed}}{\text{wavelength}} = \frac{300,000,000}{\text{wavelength in m}}$$

$$\text{wavelength} = \frac{\text{speed}}{\text{frequency}} = \frac{300,000,000}{\text{frequency in Hz}}$$

For example, radio waves of frequency 100 MHz have a wavelength of

$$\frac{300,000,000}{100,000,000} = 3.0 \text{ m}$$

45 WHAT ARE STARS MADE OF?

The life story of stars is fascinating. Just like people, stars are born, they live a long, steady life and then they die.

One difference is that stars live a very long time. They live for many millions of years. Because they live such a long time, it is difficult to see the changes that occur to stars.

When was our sun born?

Stars like our sun, were born out of the gas which fills the whole of space. This gas is mainly hydrogen atoms with some helium atoms. In some parts of the Universe, the gas occurs in denser clouds called *interstellar gas clouds*. (Interstellar means 'between stars').

About 5000 million years ago, the forces due to gravity in this cloud caused the atoms to come closer and closer. Hence, the *density* of the cloud increased and it also became hotter. Soon the temperature at the centre of this compressed mass of gas reached 10 million °C. This was enough to start *nuclear reactions*. These reactions turned hydrogen into helium and released huge amounts of energy.

As a result, the gas began to shine and the Sun was born. The Sun has about another 5000 million years before it dies.

There are a great many stars in the *Universe*. Imagine a star to be the size of a pin head. Think of the number of pin heads that would fill a warehouse of volume 8 m × 8 m × 8 m. That is the number of stars in our galaxy alone!

Figure 1 shows a giant elliptical galaxy about 41 million light-years away. Our galaxy looks like this.

— ① If a pin head is 1 mm across, how many pin heads fit into a length of 8 m?

Figure 1

= ② How many pin heads fit into a volume of 8 m × 8 m × 8 m? So about how many stars are there in our galaxy?

= ③ What happens to a gas when it becomes compressed? (If you have ever pumped up a bicycle tyre, this may help you answer this question).

= ④ Why does our sun shine?

What type of star is the Sun?

The mass of a star is fixed at the time it is born out of gas. It is the mass of a star which determines how it lives and how it dies. If we use our sun as a reference, stars vary in mass from 0.07 Suns to 100 Suns. Heavy stars are the hottest, brightest and most compressed. The surface of our sun is at about 6000 °C. For some stars, the surface temperature is 30 000 °C.

Scientists arrange stars in a list called the *main sequence* depending on the brightness of the star. Our sun is in the middle of the sequence with a surface temperature of 6000 °C and the brightest at the other end around 30 000 °C.

The heaviest stars have the shortest lives. The Sun has a life of about 10 000 million years. The heaviest stars have lives of around one thousandth of this, the lightest about one hundred times longer.

Figure 2 shows a photograph of the clouds of very hot gases at the surface of the Sun.

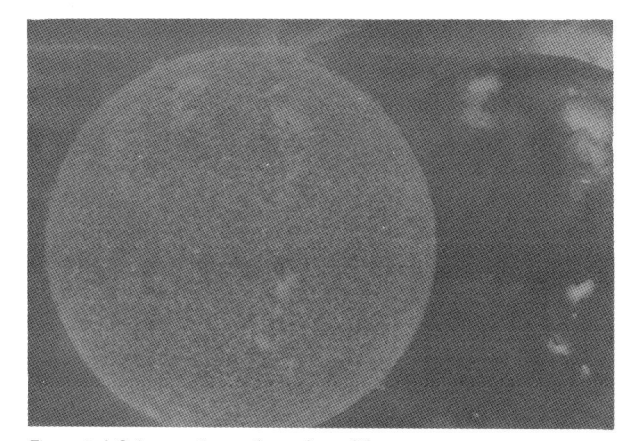

Figure 2 A Solar eruption on the surface of the sun

How will the Sun die?

When a star dies it does not just suddenly stop shining.

An average star like the Sun starts to swell up and becomes a *red giant*. A red giant is a rather cool star and the outer layers of gas soon drift off into space. The only part of the star left is the core which is about the size of the Earth. It is so hot that it shines white-hot and is called a *white dwarf*. A white dwarf does not release any new energy, so it gradually cools down and eventually fades away completely.

How do heavy stars die?

The heaviest stars have much more dramatic deaths.

As this type of star swells up into a red giant, nuclear reactions continue in the core because it is so hot. The core becomes very unstable and within a few seconds collapses. The star blows apart in an enormous explosion called a *supernova*.

Astronomers in 1987 were very excited to see a huge supernova that was so bright it could be seen in daylight with the naked eye.

What happens after a star dies?

A supernova does not just mean the death of a star. The blast from a supernova sweeps through space and gathers up gases into clouds. So new stars can start to be produced.

When a star dies it sends out into space all the new elements it has created from hydrogen during its life. Elements such as iron, carbon, silicon, gold and uranium are produced.

Astronomers believe that when the Universe began there was only hydrogen and helium. Dying stars have produced all the other elements, that form the Earth. So really life itself depends on the birth and death of stars like our sun.

= ⑤ Describe what will happen to the Sun when it starts to die.

= ⑥ Describe what you think will happen to the Earth when the Sun starts to die. How do you think people will be affected when this happens?

Stars and planets

Now read this newspaper article about the discovery of the first planet outside our solar system.

Astronomers detect giant planet in outer space

By Pearce Wright
Science Editor

Astronomers have discovered the existence of a giant planet, 30,000 times bigger than the Earth, orbiting a star outside our solar system.

The object is so close to its own star that it orbits once every 84 days. Mercury, the planet closest to the sun, has an orbit of 87 days.

The discovery was announced by Dr David Latham, from the Oak-Ridge Observatory in Massachusetts, to a conference in Baltimore.

He described how his team had found the planet by accident while conducting instrument tests using a star known as HD114762. The characteristics of the star are so well known that astronomers have used them for years as a standard against which they can compare measurements when they are looking for basic types of star.

Their instruments detected a slight wobble in the motion of the star that could only be caused by a nearby orbiting body.

Dr Latham said that the planet would have to be massive, about 20 times larger than Jupiter, which is the largest planet in the solar system, in order to give the star such a wobble.

Dr Latham believes the discovery indicates that "companion bodies", or planet-like bodies orbiting stars, may be more common than was previously believed, which would provide plenty of chances for an Earth-like planet.

The new planet is probably lifeless, because it would have a surface temperature of hundreds of degrees.

"It is much hotter than an oven", according to Dr Latham.

THE TIMES Thursday August 5 1988

= ⑦ How do scientists know that there is a large planet orbiting star HD114762?

= ⑧ Could there be life on this planet?

= ⑨ Do you think there are other planets in the Universe just like the Earth? How does the discovery of this new planet help you answer this question?

INDEX

accommodation, 54
acidic, 13
additives, 40
ageing, 11
A.I.D., 62
alcohol, 38, 53 (see also *ethanol*)
alkaline, 13
allergy, 27, 44, 56, 57
Amazon Forest, 17
amino acids, 25
ammonia, 33
amylases, 24
antibodies, 57
antihistamine, 57
artificial insemination (A.I.), 65
astronomy, 88
atmosphere, 70, 72, 80, 82

bacteria, 32
badger, 20
biogas, 7
biomass, 4, 6
biomes, 4
birth rate, 10
breathing, 46, 47, 48
breeding, 64

cancer, 79
carbohydrates, 22, 24, 44
carbon dioxide, 14, 28, 48, 81
carbon monoxide, 73
catalysts, 73
census, 10
cereals, 22, 45
CFCs, 82
cheese, 23, 26
chicken, 23, 42
chlorofluorocarbons, 82 (see also *CFCs*)
chlorophyll, 28, 33
chloroplasts, 28
cholesterol, 44
chromosomes, 60
cirrhosis, 53
cloning, 60, 65
common salt, 66
compost, 32
conception, 62
consumers, 4
contact lenses, 55
coppicing, 6

cornea, 54
crop rotation, 37
cyanide, 21

DDT, 5, 24
Dead Sea, 66
death rate, 10
density, 66, 81, 90
deserts, 5
detergents, 26
diaphragm, 46
diet, 44, 45
digestion, 24
distribution, 19
diversity, 2

Earth, 80, 85, 88, 91
EEC, 42
echo-sounding, 74
economics, 39
ecosystems, 4
electricity, 71
electrolysis, 69
electromagnetic spectrum, 89
embryo, 60
emigration, 9, 10
environment, 16
enzymes, 24, 26
erythema, 58
ethanol, 29, 38 (see also *alcohol*)
eye, 54

Friends of the Earth, 17, 83
fats, 22, 24, 44, 45
fermenting, 6
fertility drugs, 62
fertilization, 60, 61
fertilizer, 7, 14, 16, 32, 34, 36, 37
food, 2, 22, 36, 38, 40
foodchains, 5
fuel, 6, 84
fuel cells, 84
fulmar, 8

galaxies, 88
Galileo, 88
garden, 36
gas, 74
genes, 64
genetics, 60
geostationary orbit, 86

glucose, 28
grain, 7
gravity, 84
green revolution, 35
greenhouse, 30, 70
greenhouse effect, 17, 70
guanay, 16
guano, 16

habitats, 2
hay fever, 56
hepatic cells, 52
heron, 8
histamine, 57
hydrocarbons, 72, 73
hyperthermia, 51
hypothermia, 50, 51
hypothesis, 19, 70

immigration, 9, 10
immune system, 56
in vitro fertilization, 62
ionosphere, 86, 88
ions, 68, 86

Jodrell Bank, 88

lactase, 24
law, 20
lead, 72
lens, 54
life expectancy, 8
lipases, 24
liver, 52
long sight, 55
lungs, 47, 48

malnutrition, 44
malpighian layer, 59
maltase, 24
manures, 32
medicines, 2
meteorites, 81
Milky Way, 88
minerals, 23, 43, 44
molasses, 38
Moon, 87
mortality, 8

nanometre, 58
natality, 8

neutral, 13
nitrates, 33
nitrogen, 32, 33, 34, 35
nitrogen cycle, 33
North Sea, 14, 74
NPK fertilizer, 34
nuclear power, 69, 78
nuclear reactions, 90

obesity, 44
oil, 74
optic fibre, 62
organic, 24, 35
oxygen, 48, 66, 81, 82
ozone, 82, 83

pesticides, 32
pests, 5
petrol, 72
pH, 12
phosphorus, 34
photosynthesis, 14, 28, 30, 33, 81
phytoplankton, 14
plankton, 16
poisons, 24, 53
pollen, 38, 56
pollution, 35
population, 8, 10, 11
potash, 39
potassium iodide, 29
predation, 9
preservatives, 40, 43
pressure, 80
Pressurised Water Reactor (PWR), 78
producers, 4
productivity, 5
proteases, 24, 26
proteins, 22, 24, 44

radio, 86, 88
radio telescope, 89
register office, 10
respiration, 49
resuscitation, 47
retina, 54
rockets, 84
rock salt, 68
rodent, 18
roughage, 23

salinity, 66
salt, 45, 68
sampling, 12
satellites, 86, 87
sea, 66, 78
seed, 37
short sight, 55
skin, 59
Skylab, 84
sodium chloride, 68
space shuttle, 84
squirrel, 18, 19
starches, 24, 28
stars, 90
sucrase, 24
sugar beet, 38
sugar cane, 38
sugars, 49
sun, 90
sunbeds, 58
sunburn, 58
supernova, 91
surrogate, 63
sweeteners, 40
synthesiser, 28

TB, 20
territories, 9
TT, 20
tuberculosis, 20
turbines, 78

ultraviolet, 58, 59, 82, 86
Universe, 88
uranium, 78

vegetables, 36
vitamins, 23, 43, 44, 53
volcanoes, 81

wavelengths, 88
white blood cells, 57
wildlife, 3
wine, 26
wood, 12

yield, 35

zoos, 3